Winning PHOTO CONTESTS

By Jeanne Stallman

Winning PHOTO CONTESTS

By Jeanne Stallman

images
PRESS INC.

Winning Photo Contests

First Edition. Library of Congress Catalog Card Number: 90-081420
Jeanne Stallman
Winning Photo Contests
(Softcover) ISBN: 0-929667-04-2
(Hardcover) ISBN: 0-929667-06-9

Published by Images Press, 22 East 17th Street, New York, N.Y. 10003.
Printed and bound in the United States of America
Book design and typesetting by Jennifer Lawson
Cover design by Brian Stanlake
Cover photo by Peter L. Gould
1 2 3 4 5 6 7 8 9 10

Special Thanks to

E.S.B. and J.F.L.

CONTENTS

1 WHY ENTER CONTESTS?

Photo contests have been around almost as long as photography itself. One of the earliest prize winners was 19th-century photographer Mathew Brady, who won a silver medal for his portraiture at the American Institute Exhibition in 1844, and in 1851 was awarded first prize at the Great Exhibition of the Works of all Nations in London. Although the prizes awarded and equipment used have changed significantly over the past century, the basic principles of photo contests remain the same. You take a fantastic shot, enter it in a contest, and endure a few weeks alternately biting your nails wondering how your work compares to that of other photographers and fantasizing about how you'll spend your winnings. And all the while you're staking out the mailbox or phone waiting to hear if your work has been recognized for the true masterpiece that it is—or rejected.

For amateurs and pros alike, entering a photo contest provides more than a chance to win prizes. It's a great way to gain exposure and recognition, get some feedback on your work, improve your self-esteem, and yes, if you're lucky, win cash, prizes, or both. As a matter of fact, many professionals have found winning a contest to be a valuable stepping-stone in their careers. In 1942, when he was first getting started, famed photojournalist W. Eugene Smith's shot of a World War II battle scene won first prize in a contest sponsored by *Popular Photography*. It was one of the first times he had a picture published nationally. Smith won again in 1948 with his well-known sentimental shot "A Walk in Paradise Garden." Other prizewinners who have gone on to larger successes are Fritz Henle (*Popular Photography* winner), Dennis Stock (*Life* magazine Young Photographer winner in 1951), and Bruce Davidson. Elliott Erwitt, on the other hand, discovered that winning second prize in a contest sponsored by *Life* in 1951 had a different kind of power. After his army sergeant learned that Erwitt had been recognized by the celebrated newsweekly, he was actually nice to him.

Even if you don't come away a winner, you will have benefited from entering the contest. Not only have you gained experience in completing an assignment and meeting a deadline, you've also risen to a challenge. And you have a better idea of what to expect the next time you respond to the lure of an entry form. Either way you win.

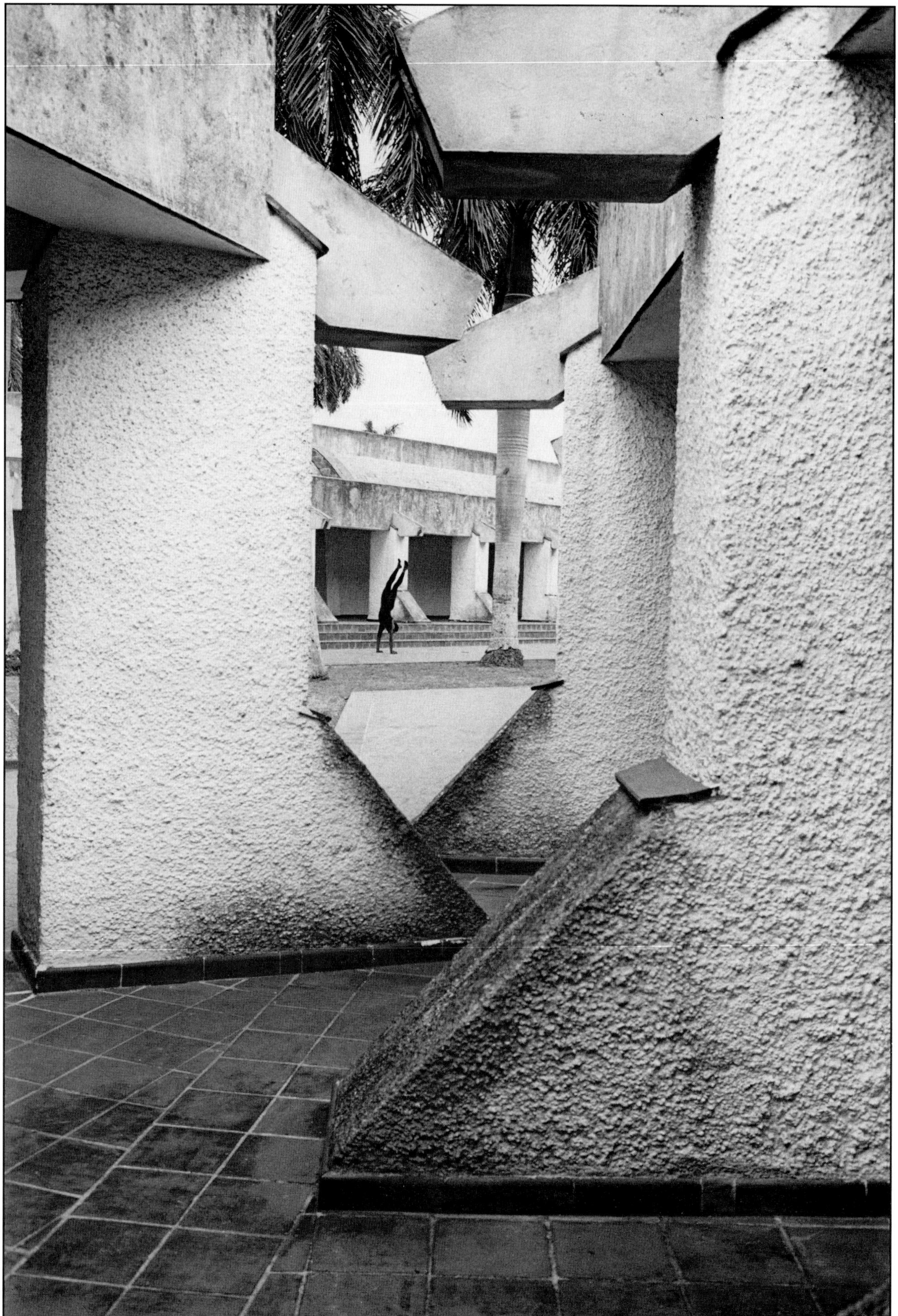

HARVEY FINKLE

2 DIFFERENT TYPES OF CONTESTS

There are as many different types of photo contests as there are pictures. Contests run the gamut from "Mom and Pop" competitions organized by your local camera club or community group, to huge world-wide extravaganzas sponsored by the large camera manufacturers and journalism schools. In between, you'll find competitions held by magazines, newspapers, and chambers of commerce. Some are limited to amateurs; to enter others you must be a working professional photographer, and still others are open to all. Some are pretty straightforward, others tend toward the zany.

Look for a contest that matches your sensibilities. If your photos are best described as traditional and straightforward, you're probably better off avoiding an event like the California Museum of Photography's annual Photographer's Christmas Card Exhibition. "The more offbeat the better" is their operating rule of thumb. After all, one of the keys to winning contests is to find the one that is right for you.

Many contests are annual events. One of the oldest is Pictures of the Year, which has served as a forum for photojournalists for close to 50 years. Magazines such as *Popular Photography* and *Outdoor and Travel Photography* run contest results in each issue, while others like *Sierra* and *Photo/Design* sponsor annual events. You can find entry forms just about anywhere. Look for them at local art fairs, in the magazines and newspapers you read, on your camera-club bulletin board, etc.

One-time contests also abound. Keep your eyes open. You never know where you'll see notice of one. A major dog-food company recently advertised their new photo contest in the coupon section of the Sunday paper!

Although most contests share the common goal of awarding prizes, they do differ in terms of size, sponsors, and entry requirements. Local contests, which tend to be smaller than their regional, national and international counterparts, are generally run by camera clubs, schools, local newspapers, state fairs, and companies for their employees. They are a good place for beginning photographers to test the waters. (If you've got a spectacular shot, however don't rule out the major contests. First-time entrants have been known to enter world-wide competitions and win. Al Borman, the 1988 grand prize

Opposite page
Capture the decisive moment, and you're on your way to winning prizes. Harvey Finkle's shot illustrates the importance of timing. Finkle was a prizewinner in the 1989 *Photo Review* National Photographic Competition.

winner of Olympus' *VisionAge* contest had never entered a competition before.)

The atmosphere at the smaller contests is more likely to be friendly and encouraging than at the huge extravaganzas. Judging is often done in public, which gives you a valuable opportunity to hear the judges critique the entries and give their reasons for acceptance or rejection. If your camera club has such a contest, by all means enter. Not only will you come away with constructive comments and tips to improve your future work, you'll also have the chance to have your work seen and to compare it to others. And if you're a winner, it's always helpful to know what it was about your picture that the judges responded to.

Exhibition Contests

Exhibition contests go one step further than traditional competitions: not only are prizes awarded, but the prize-winning work is put on display and often remains up for a period of time. Here's how they work: After evaluating all of the entries, the judge(s) select a group of

P. Kevin Morley's pint-sized cowboy won third prize of $100 in the March 1990 Your Best Shot contest in *Popular Photography*.

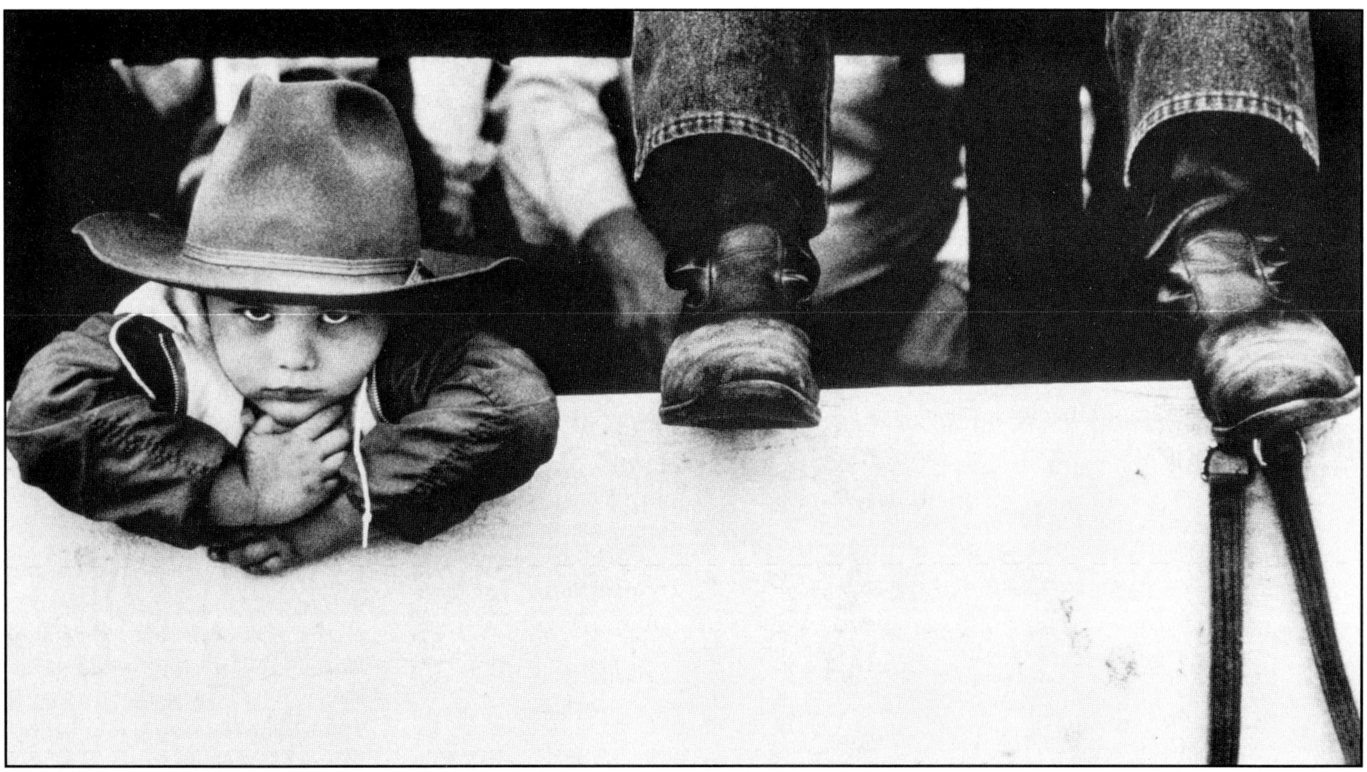

P. KEVIN MORLEY

photos for display. Prizes ranging from first to honorable mentions or certificates of merit are awarded. Exhibition contests are generally small to medium-sized. (In 1988, however, one of the largest group exhibitions of contest winners ever took place at Photokina, the huge biennial photo trade show. Over 160,000 color and black-and-white prints were on display.) They are a good way to have your work seen by a large number of people—and you'll have the added thrill of seeing your photograph displayed on a gallery wall (hopefully with a prize ribbon attached).

Private Organization and Company Sponsored Contests

Private organizations and companies are also enthusiastic sponsors of photo contests. The majority of them are run by companies or businesses for advertising or public-relations purposes. Generally they are centered on a theme. For example, Johnson & Johnson recently announced an "Adorable Babies Photo Contest". Grand prize is a four-year college scholarship for the baby in the winning picture. Often companies will join forces to sponsor a contest. Pictures of the Year is jointly sponsored by The Missouri School of Journalism, Canon, and Kodak. On a smaller scale, Tanqueray Gin and *American Photographer* magazine paired up a few years ago and announced a theme contest in the magazine. The first-prize winner received Leica camera equipment valued at $7,000 (a Leica R5 camera with a 70 - 210mm f/4 Vario lens and leather carrying case) and the pleasure of seeing their work published in a Tanqueray ad which appeared in the magazine. Unlike their smaller local or regional counterparts, the judging in these types of contests is private and only prize winners (and sometimes honorable mentions) are announced.

Because PR and goodwill play such a large part in these competitions, entry forms are widely distributed. You can find them in magazines, supermarkets, newspapers, and on posters and flyers. Another added attraction is the prizes. Because the contests are sponsored by private companies with large budgets, the prizes tend to be more valuable: cash, merchandise, and trips are standard. Winners can also benefit by having their work published either in a magazine, or in a calendar or poster as a promotion for the contest or sponsor company.

Magazine and Newspaper Contests

The number of entries to magazine and newspaper contests depends on the circulation of the publication. A contest sponsored by *Life* magazine, which reaches over one million people each month is going to attract many more entries than one sponsored by *Sierra,* which has a significantly smaller circulation. Most special-interest magazine contests center around a theme that is natural to the magazine, while photography magazines and general-interest magazines tend to have a broader scope. Consequently *Sierra* looks for pictures with an environmental slant for its annual contest, while *Life* magazine has sponsored contests touching on everything from work by young photographers to the Bicentennial.

Camera and Film Companies

Most of the major camera manufacturers sponsor contests. Olympus has the *VisionAge* contest which is open to both amateurs and professionals; Nikon sponsors the International Small World Competition, the Nikon Photo Contest International, and the NPPA/ Nikon Documentary Sabbatical Award; Canon is one of the sponsors (along with Kodak and the Missouri School of Journalism) of the Pictures of the Year contest. Pentax, Minolta and Leica are also awarding cash and prizes on a regular basis. Major film companies also get in the act. Kodak, for example, works with a variety of groups to sponsor everything from the Naval and Maritime Photo Contest to KINSA (Kodak International Newspaper Snapshot Awards).

Grant and Awards Programs

Grant and awards programs are a natural for serious professional photographers (and would-be pros) who are in need of a leg up. The cash stakes are higher in these programs and often reach up into the tens of thousands of dollars. San Francisco-based *Mother Jones* magazine, for example, has just started a new grant program called the Mother Jones International Fund for Documentary Photography. Each year two prizes of at least $10,000 will be awarded to photographers who are documenting pressing social issues. The winning work will be published in the magazine and actively promoted worldwide. Not

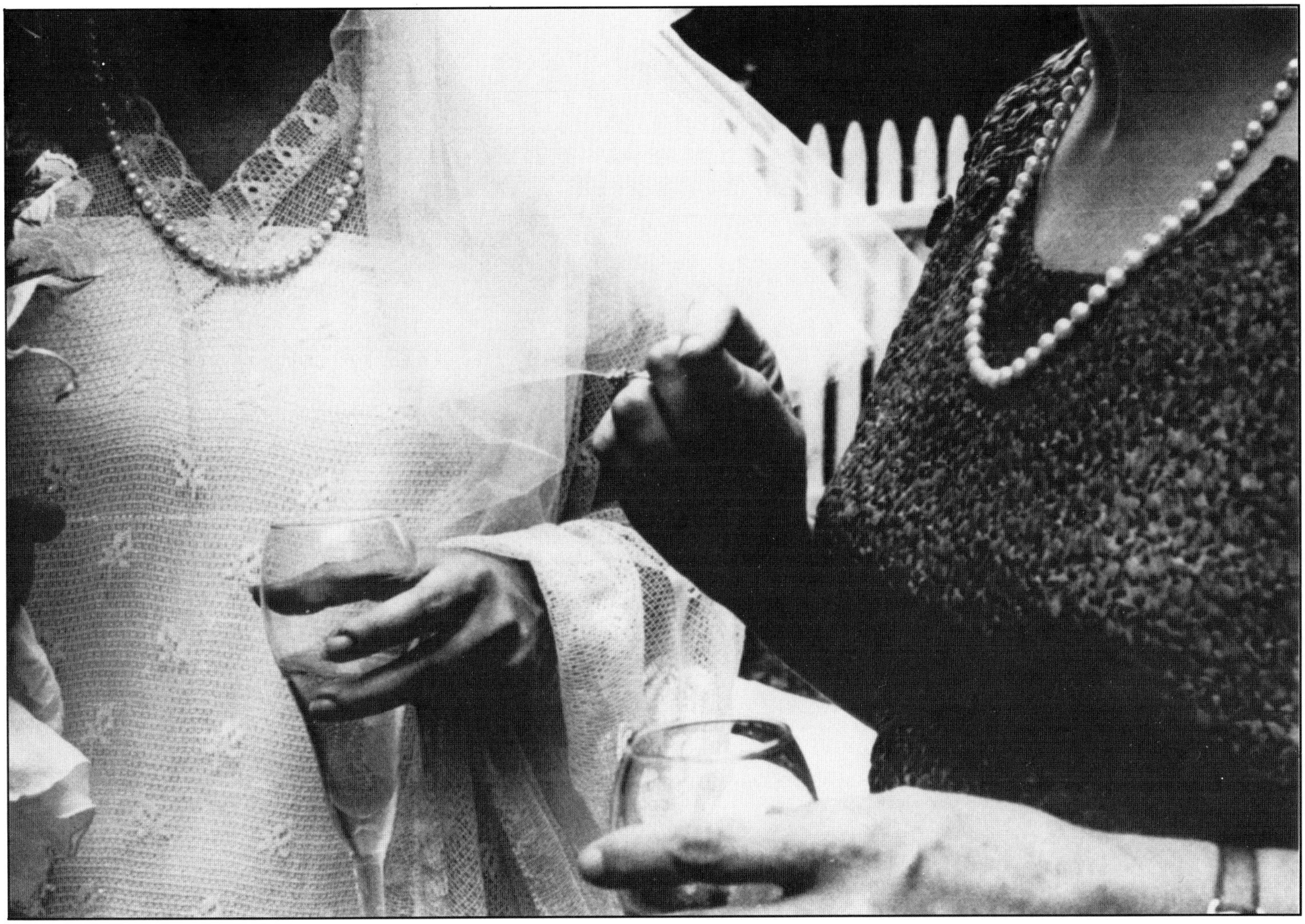

LILA KERNS/COURTESY OF SCHOLASTIC ART AWARDS

Lila Kerns won a $2,000 grant from Kodak in the 1988 Scholastic Art Awards. This untraditional wedding shot was part of her prize-winning portfolio.

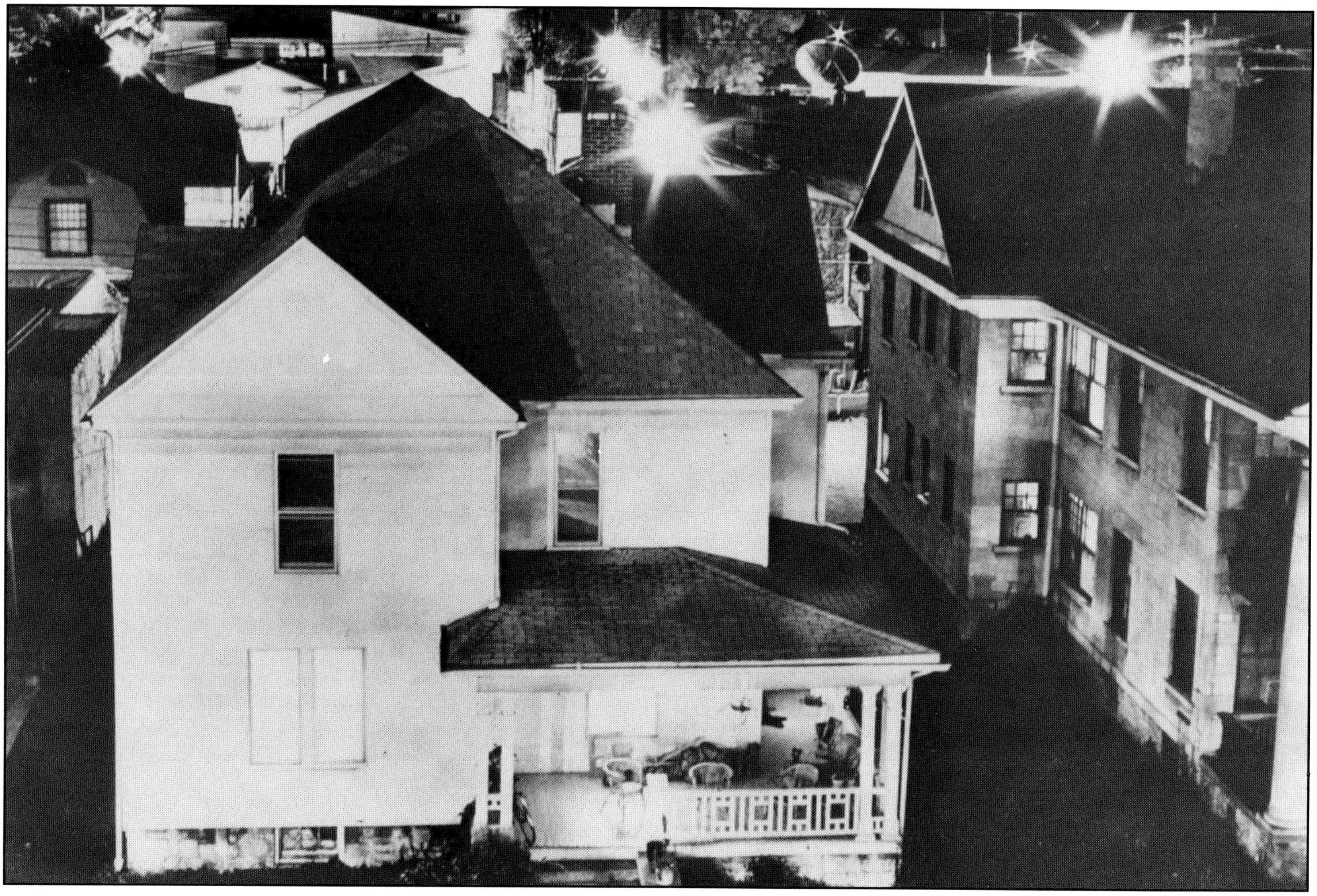

STEVE EVANS/COURTESY OF SCHOLASTIC ART AWARDS

The 1989 Scholastic Art Awards recognized Steve Evans' nocturnal neighborhood with a medal.

only do such grants and awards programs recognize outstanding work, they also give a photographer enough financial freedom to concentrate solely on his or her work. Applicants generally are required to submit a portfolio of photos as well as a written statement discussing their project. Work is carefully reviewed by a panel of jurors before a grant is awarded. Some grant programs require that a photographer be nominated before his or her work will be considered; others are open to all.

3 SPONSORS

Sponsors of a contest do more than provide the money and prizes. When they lend their name to a competition or actively promote it, they also have a sometimes not-so-subtle influence on the types of pictures chosen as winners. Therefore, it's a good idea to find out who is sponsoring a contest before sending in an entry. Judges for a contest run by *Outdoor & Travel Photography* magazine for its readers are probably looking for something quite different than the judges of a contest like the annual World Press Photo Contest which is limited to working professional journalists.

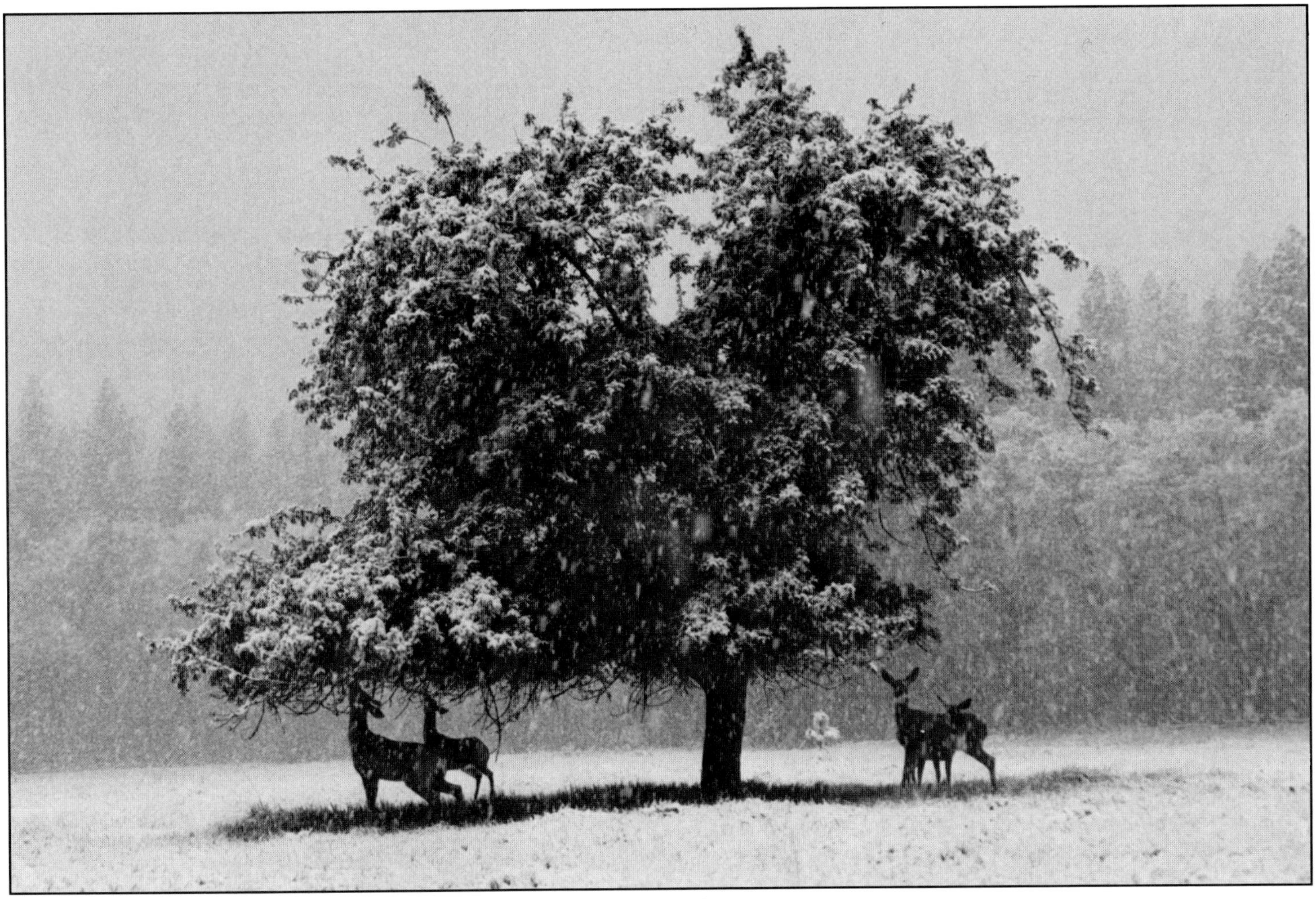

JEFF WAHL

As second place winner in the black-and-white category of the 10th Annual *Sierra* Photo Contest, Jeff Wahl won a special-edition folding knife from Buck Knives and had his shot of foraging deer in Yosemite published in the magazine.

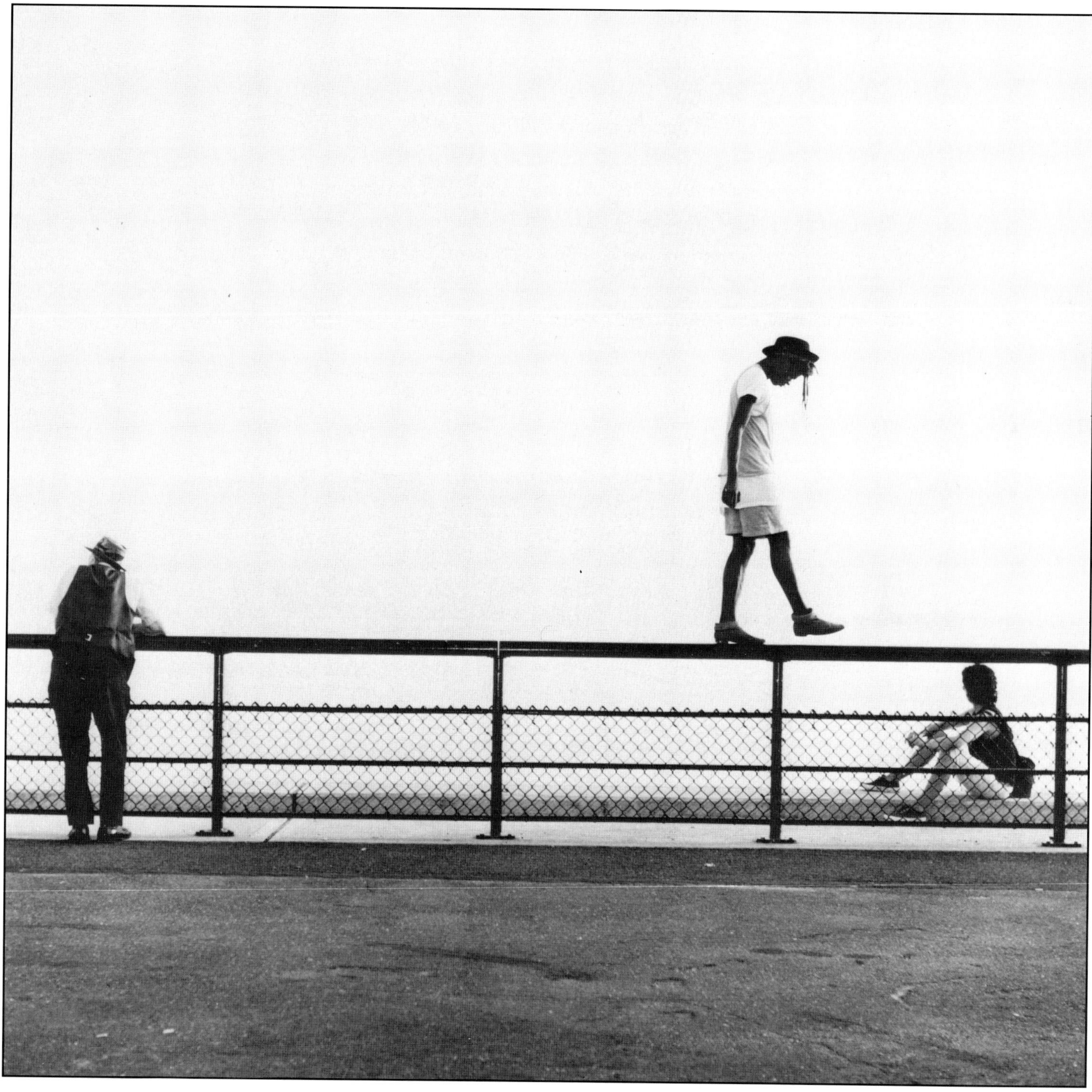

SARA BARCHUS-FERRARI

Timing plays a large part in the success of Sara Barchus-Ferrari's shot. "The Battery" was one of the photos chosen in the 1989 ***Photo Review*** National Competition.

4 PRIZES

When it comes to prizes, the stakes are significantly higher today than they were back when Mathew Brady was collecting awards. Companies today are awarding tens of thousands of dollars and valuable merchandise to lucky winners.

Olympus gave each of the grand prize winners of its 1989 contest $4,000, an OM-4T camera, a 100mm f/2 lens, and a 28mm f/2 lens. *Photographer's Forum* magazine doesn't offer quite as much money—the grand prize for color work in their annual contest is $1,000. However each entrant receives a free six-month subscription to the magazine.

Other prizes have more than a monetary value. They can open up doors that might otherwise have remained closed. The New York State Youth Media Arts Contests offers its winners the opportunity to attend a six-week summer-school program and work with a professional photographer. On a much grander scale, *Reader's Digest's* Artists at Giverny Program awards three six-month residencies to live and work in Giverny, home of celebrated French Impressionist Claude Monet. The 1990 winners received round-trip transportation to Giverny, a furnished apartment and studio space at Giverny, and use of a car. They were also given $2,000 before departure, a $1,600 stipend each month, and $1,000 upon return to the U.S. *Reader's Digest* also arranges for an exhibition in Paris and/or New York of the work inspired by the winner's stay.

As you can see, there is often a connection between the sponsor and the prizes they award. A contest that is sponsored by a camera manufacturer is more than likely to hand out cameras or accessories as prizes. *Sierra* (which as the publication of the Sierra Club attracts a readership of outdoor enthusiasts) gave bicycles and binoculars to some of the winners of its 1989 contest. Other standard prizes include cash, trips, books, scholarships, medals, ribbons, and certificates.

It's often easy to get swept away by the lure of expensive prizes. So it's a good idea to make sure that the awards offered actually interest you. If first prize is a lifetime supply of dog food and you don't have a dog (or any intention of getting one), you can find out if the sponsor will give you the cash equivalent of the merchandise. If the answer is "no", you might wish to pass this particular competition by. Also keep in mind that the IRS is interested in what you win, too. Cash, trips, and merchandise are all taxable.

If you're interested in the prestige of a prize, put it in perspective by checking out how many prize categories there are and how many awards are given out in each category. If everybody who enters a contest receives some sort of prize, then a certificate of mention is not going to have much value as a barometer of the quality of your work.

Jane Alden Stevens was one of the winners in the 1989 *Photo Review* National Photographic Competition.

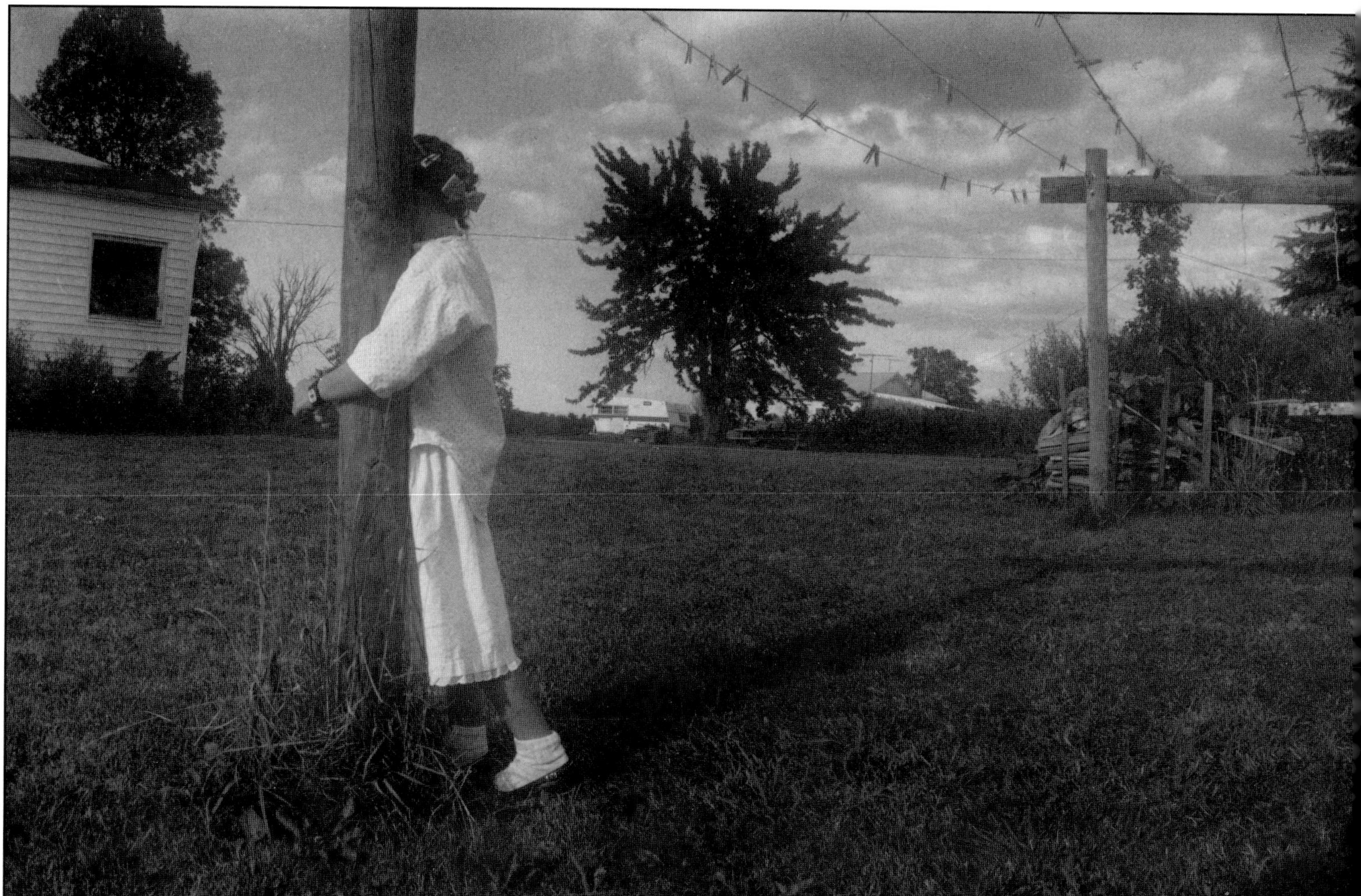

5 ARE YOU RIGHT FOR THE CONTEST?

Once you've found a contest that seems to be right for you, it's time to make sure that you're right for the contest. Using the entry form as a checklist, go through all of the rules and criteria of the contest. Some of them may seem unreasonably nit-picking, but if you don't follow them exactly, you may be disqualified.

First of all, are you qualified to enter the contest? Employees (and their family members) of the company sponsoring the contest are generally ineligible. Age can also be an issue. Is the contest limited to teens, seniors, or first graders? Whatever the rule, make sure you fall into the right category.

If the rules specify that the competition is open only to professionals (a professional photographer is defined as someone who earns

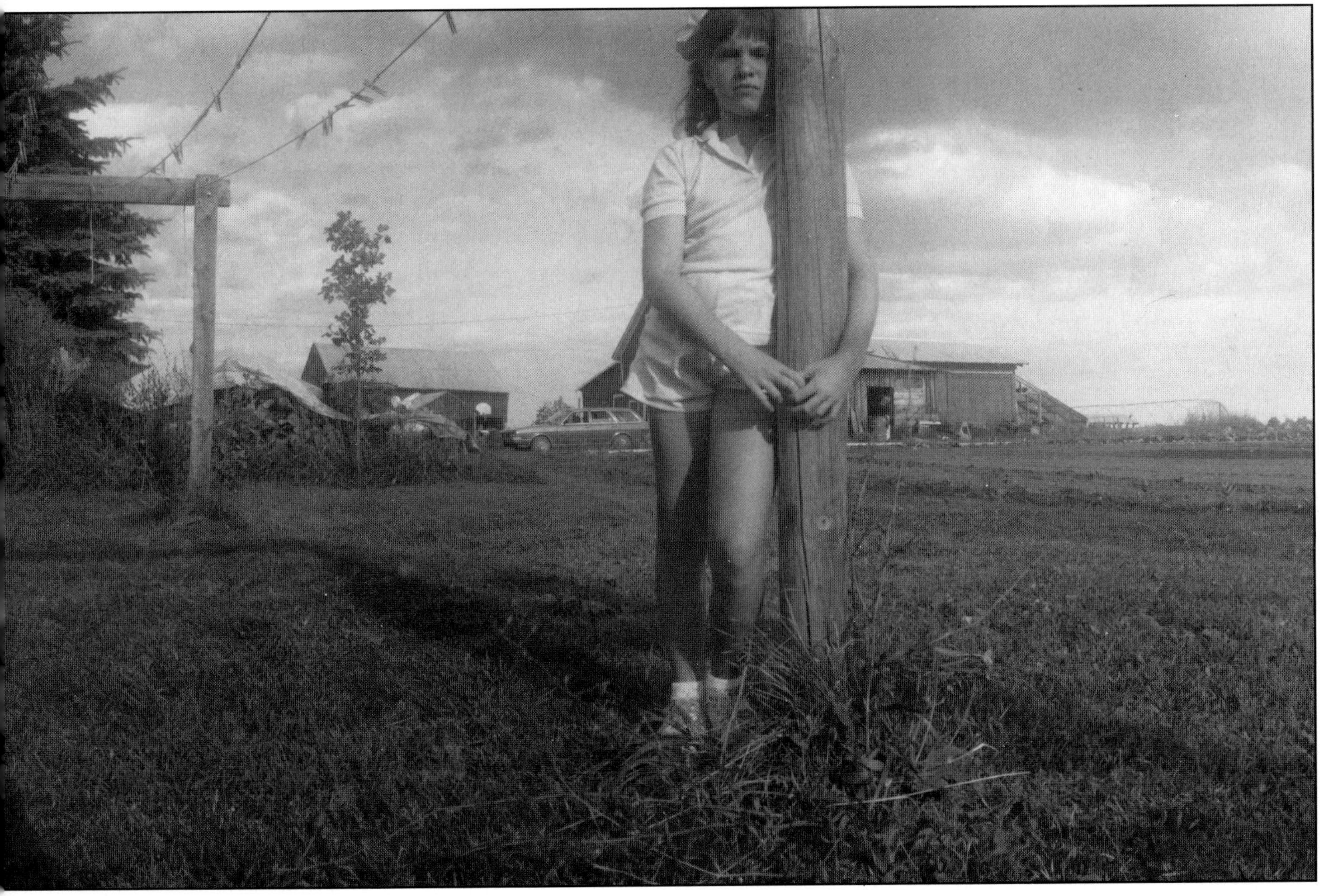

JANE ALDEN STEVENS

his or her living from photography), and you have never sold a picture—look for another contest. Likewise, if you're a pro and the contest is limited to amateurs, step aside and give the less-experienced photographers the chance to compete with their peers.

Next, take a step back, and being as objective as you can, ask yourself if your work is appropriate to this particular contest. If the entry specifies that the image must have been previously published, don't send in something that you think should have been published but wasn't. You may be asked to submit a tearsheet as proof. Contests that require that work was completed within a certain time period, or with certain equipment, also trust that you'll be honest and play by the rules. Once again, it is not a good idea to enter a competition for which you are unqualified. There are plenty of contests out there that are eager for your entries. With a little bit of research you can find one that is right for you.

What sort of subject matter does the contest want to see? Do the entries have to have been taken in a specific place? A contest that is looking for a poster for the city of Chicago isn't going to be interested in pictures of the California coastline, no matter how spectacular they are. Time frame can also be an issue. The popular *Day in the Life* book series has spawned a host of contests that operate on the same theme. Connecticut's Mystic Seaport, for example, sponsors the Mystic Seaport Day Photo Contest.It's an annual all-day event in which costumed members of the Seaport staff pose on the ships and grounds of the Seaport, providing unique photo opportunities. Photographers may submit photos taken only on that day. The 1989 Best in Show prize was a weekend for two in Mystic.

What rights to your submission does the contest want? Most will want to publish the winning photos for contest promotion and publicity. If they request further rights, take a careful look at the fine print and make sure you know what you are getting into. Also check out who retains the copyright to the winning photos. It is never a good idea to give up the rights to your work without understanding the ramifications, and making sure that it's what you want to do.

The entry form will also specify how many photos you can submit. Some want to see only one shot, others are willing to review more. The Nature Images Contest in West Palm Beach, FL, for example, will

Opposite page
Third place for Newspaper Portrait/Personality in the 41st Pictures of the Year went to Jim Gensheimer for his closely cropped emotional portrait of a soon-to-be baptized woman.

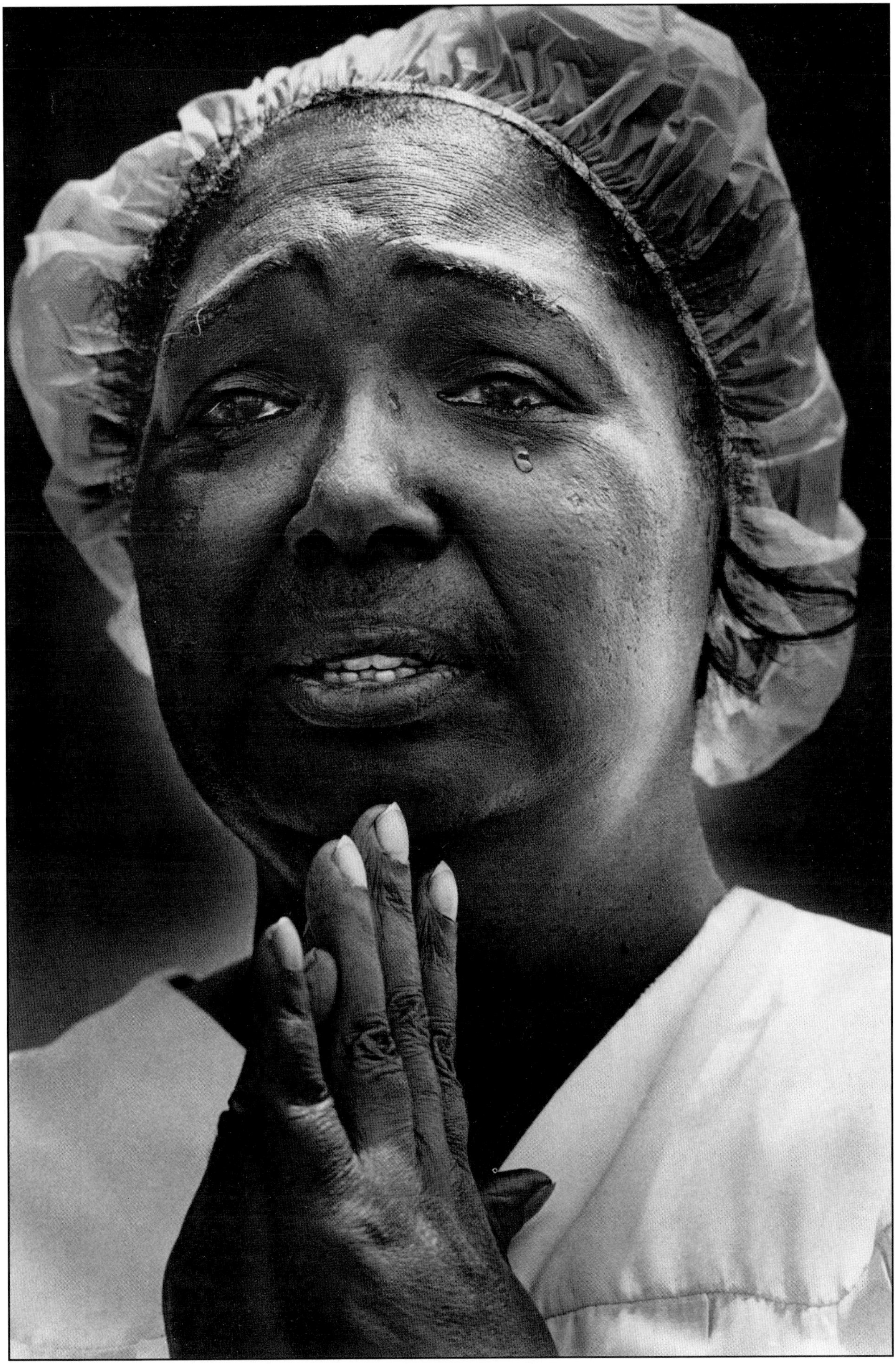

JIM GENSHEIMER

consider as many images as you wish to send in. The Photographic Competition Association of America, on the other hand, has a five-print limit for its quarterly contest.Unless the entry form specifies otherwise, send all your photos together in one package. If, for example, you can send in up to 20 photos, don't send in 20 separate envelopes. Why waste the time and postage?

You should also find out in what format your work should be—prints or slides? To enter some exhibition contests you'll need both: Slides for the initial jurying, and prints for the actual show. If you only have transparencies and the entry calls for prints, take your slide to a local custom lab and have a print made.Never send in negatives.

How about size? Some contests find that large prints are too cumbersome to handle efficiently, so they limit the size of entries.Generally 16x20" is the largest print size accepted. Transparencies vary according to what sort of camera you use. A 35mm SLR or a point-and-shoot camera will give you a 35mm slide.If you're using a square-format 120 camera, such as a Hasselblad, you'll end up with 2-1/4" slides. A 4x5 camera yields, you guessed it, sheets of film that are 4 inches by 5 inches. An 8x10 view camera takes sheets of 8x10" film.

Do the pictures have to have been taken with a certain type of camera or lens? How about film, paper, etc? This can be a crucial factor if the contest is sponsored by a certain manufacturer that only wants to see work done with its product.

Is the contest open to both black-and-white material and color, or is it limited to one or the other? If both color and black-and-white photos are acceptable, determine if they are considered together, or as separate categories. If the contest is for color work, are prints or transparencies (slides) preferred? If prints, should they be mounted or unmounted?Check the entry form carefully for any specifications. If you have a choice between sending in original transparencies or dupes, remember that though most contest directors make every effort to handle photographs carefully, most contests accept no responsibility for safe handling and return of material. If you must send in an original, make a good-quality dupe to keep in your files in the unlikely event that something happens.

6 MODEL RELEASES

If the winning photos will be highly visible, it's best to cover yourself by getting anyone who is recognizable in the picture to sign a model release. (You don't have to send in the releases with the photos, just have them on file in case the subject comes up.) That way, you can avoid any potential problems when your ex-boyfriend opens a magazine and finds a picture of himself staring him in the face. If you don't have any model releases with you when you're shooting, try to get the names and addresses of your subjects so you can track them down if necessary. Remember, a minor's signature on a release is not binding—a parent or guardian must sign on their behalf.

If, after you have carefully read the entry form, you still have questions, don't be afraid to call (or write, if there's time) the contest sponsor. It's better to have a clear understanding of the entry rules than to risk disqualification over a minor misunderstanding or technicality.

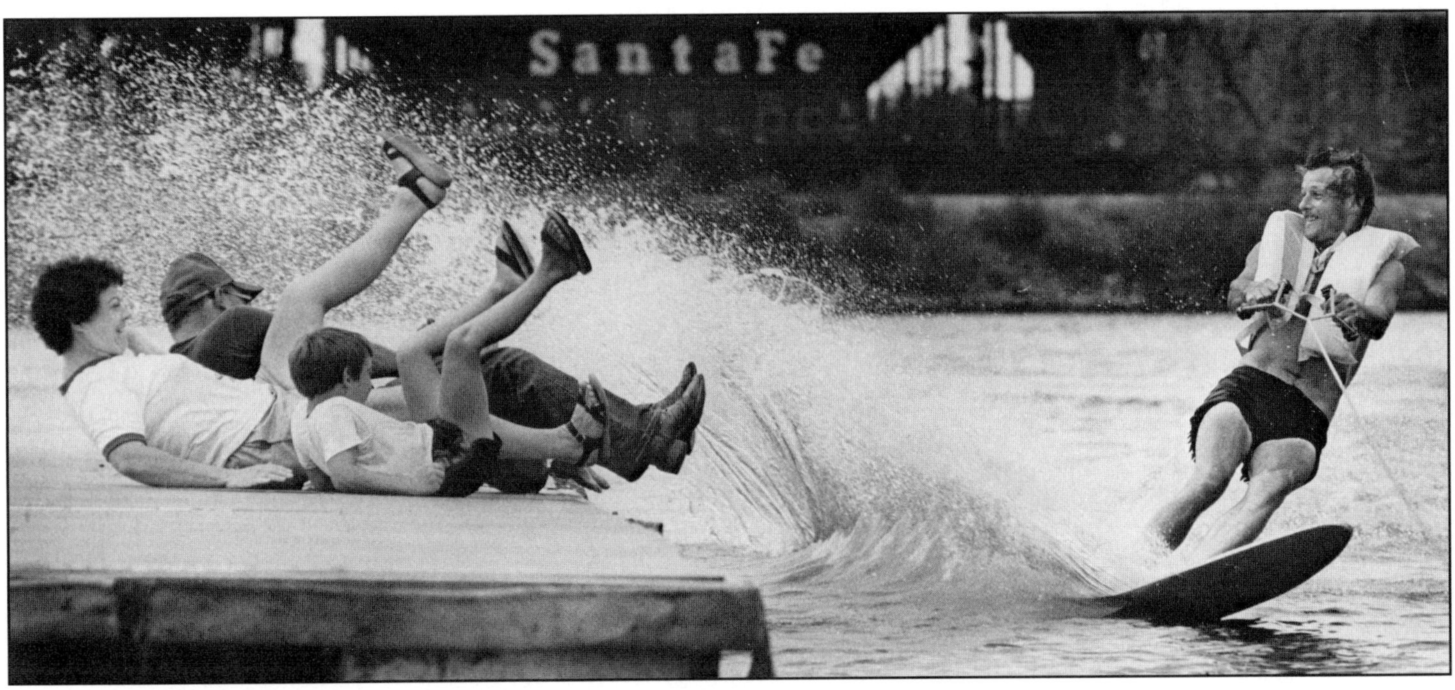

MARSHALL SPURRIER

Marshall Spurrier's humorous shot of a mischievous waterskiier and reacting spectators was an IFPO contest winner.

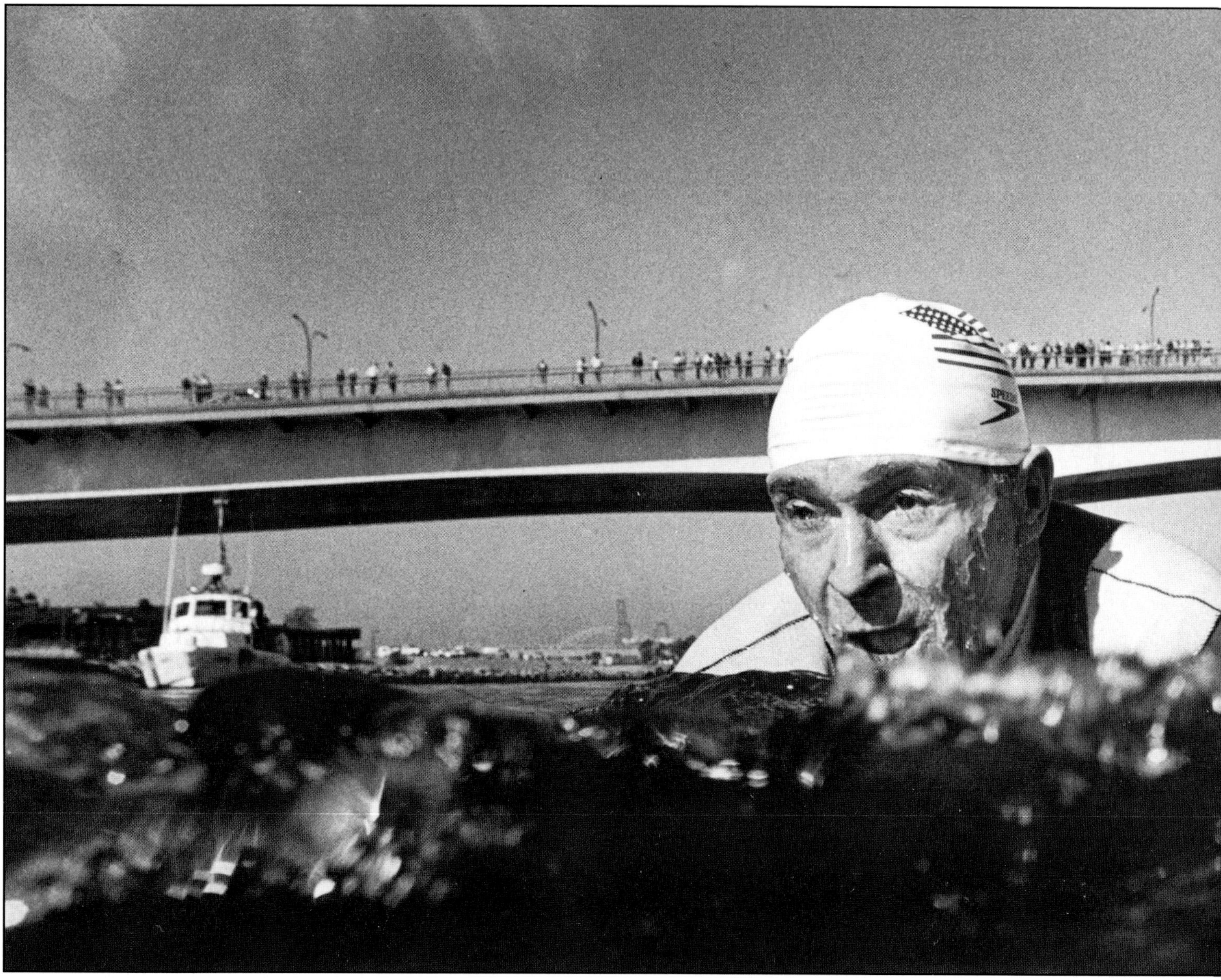

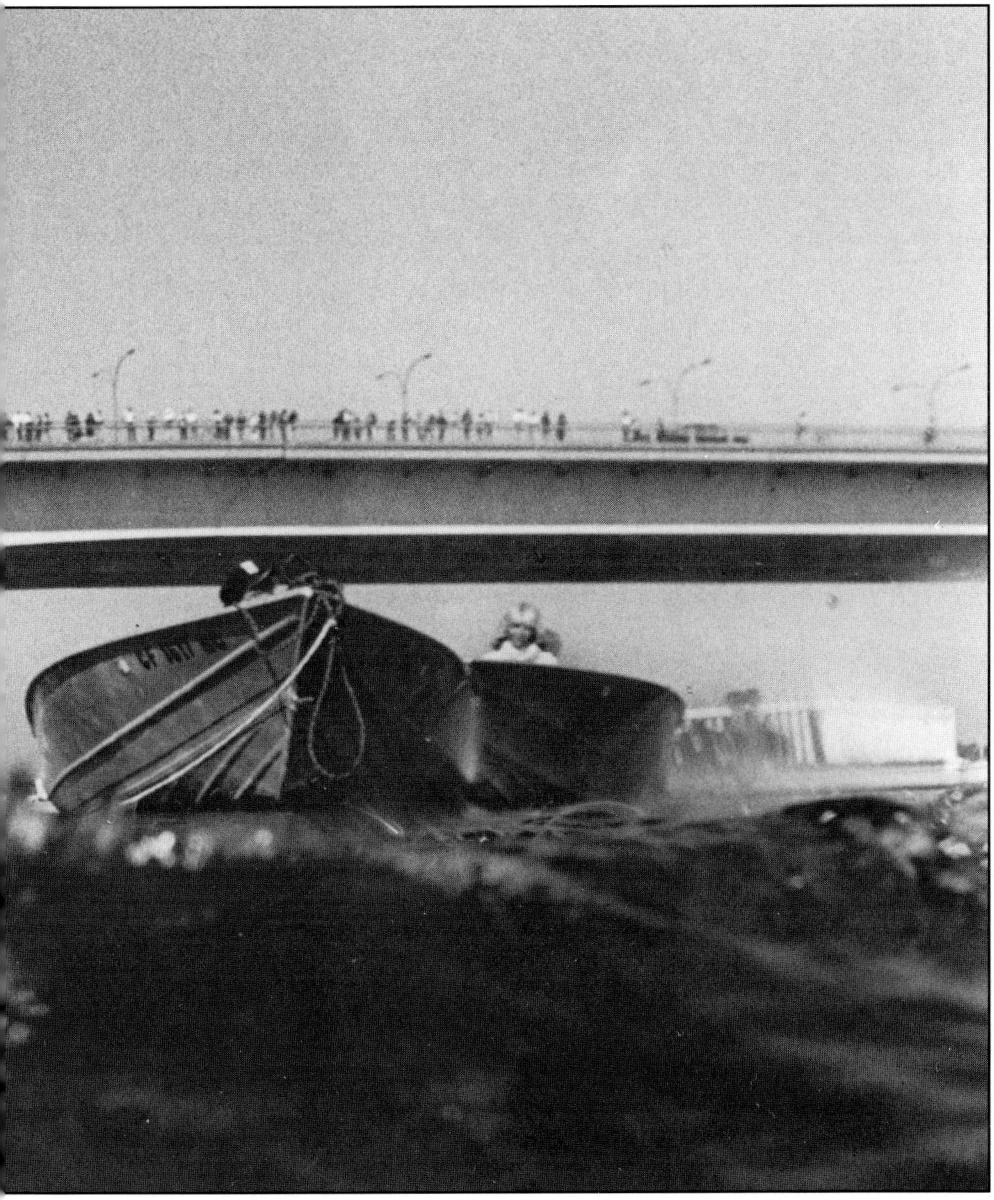

LEO HETZEL

Jack LaLanne celebrated his 70th birthday by towing 70 boats for one mile with his wrists and ankles shackled. Leo Hetzel was there to record the event for the *Long Beach Press-Telegram.* His strong horizontal shot received third place in the Newspaper General News Category of 1984's Pictures of the Year.

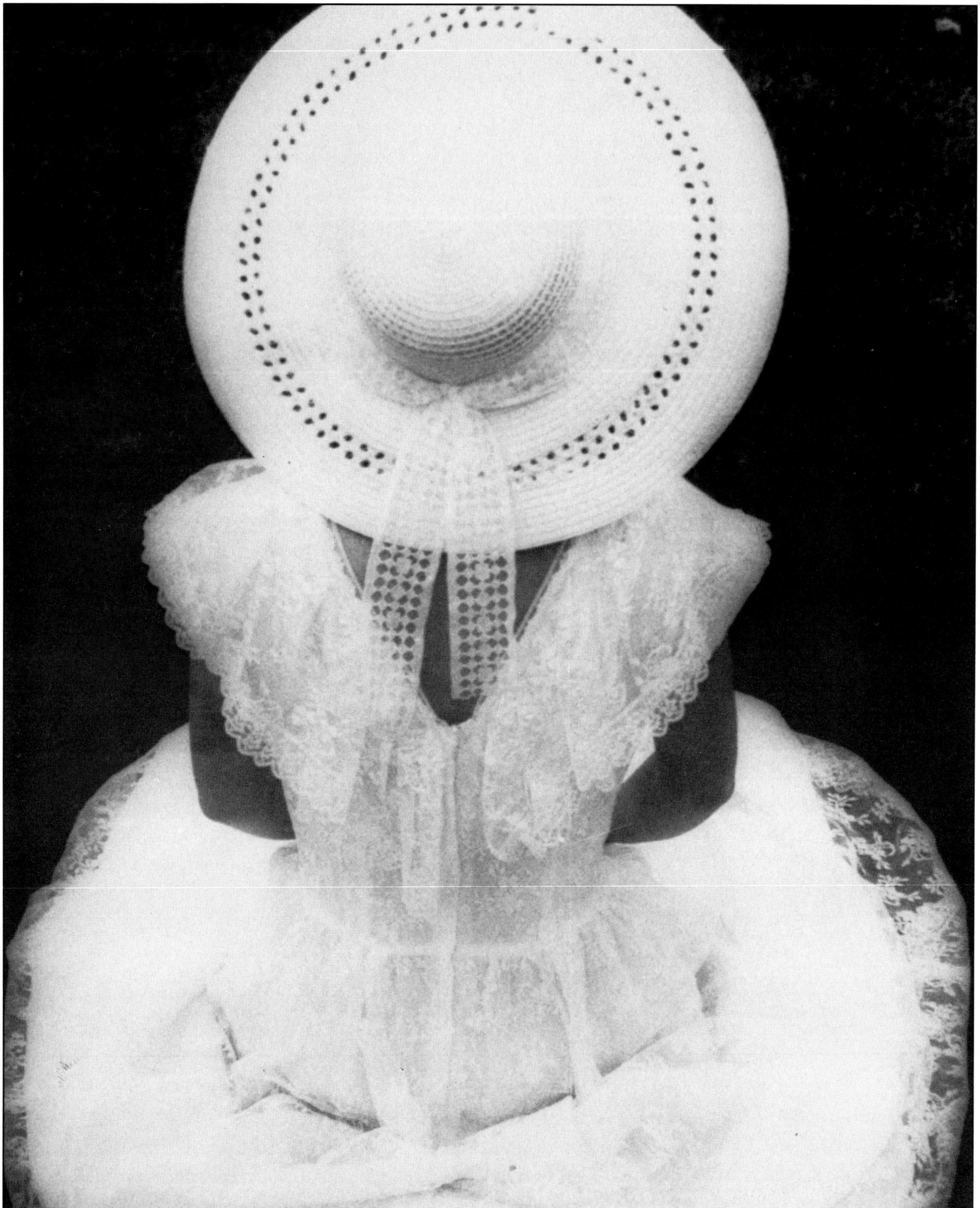

MICHELLE COOK/COURTESY OF SCHOLASTIC ART AWARDS

7

MAILING IN YOUR PHOTOS

OK, you've met all of the requirements stated on the entry form. You've got your prints and/or slides together. Now, it's time to pack them up and mail them in. Here are some general suggestions. If the contest's entry form outlines specific packing instructions, be sure to follow them exactly.

Before you even get out the envelope and stamps, make sure your name, address, and phone number (if there is room) are on each slide mount or print. That way, if one gets separated from the rest, it will stand a better chance of being returned to you. Try to stay away from ball-point pens when you're marking your prints. If you bear down too hard you can raise marks on the face of the prints. If you use a felt-tip marker, make sure the ink is dry before you stack up your prints—otherwise ink from the back of one print might rub off on the front of another. You can avoid this problem entirely by packing your prints image face to image face, or by slipping a sheet of paper between prints. You should avoid writing on RC (plastic-coated) prints at all—use a self-adhesive label with the pertinent information typed or stamped on it.

To prevent bending, sandwich your prints between two pieces of cardboard the same size as or a bit larger than your prints and slip them into an envelope or cardboard mailer. (You might also want to stamp "Photos Do Not Bend" on the outside of the envelope.)

If you're sending in slides, you can pack the transparencies in the cardboard or plastic slide boxes provided by your film processor. Another option is to buy some heavy-duty ones at your local photo-supply store.

To make your slides more easily accessible to the judges, buy some plastic slide sheets at a photo-supply store. Generally they are 8x10" and hold 20 35mm transparencies per sheet. (Slide sheets for 2-1/4" and 4x5 transparencies are also available.) Pack slide sheets as you would prints—simply sandwich them between two pieces of cardboard. Whatever you do, don't wrap individual slides in Kleenex, or tape them to a sheet of paper or cardboard. The lint and adhesive can be very detrimental to the delicate emulsion on the surface of the transparency. It bears repeating that it is not a good idea to send in negatives— have a print made instead. And avoid glass slide mounts

Opposite page
You don't have to show your subject's face to make a successful photograph. Michelle Cook won a gold medal in the 1988 Scholastic Art Awards for her nostalgic faceless portrait.

at all costs. No matter how well-protected your package is, the glass is sure to break.

Of course you want your submission to make it through the mail undamaged, but there is such a thing as overkill when it comes to packing your photos. Make it easy for the judges to get to your photographs. If they have to break open yards of tape and unwrap reams of paper, only to be faced by yet another layer of packaging, odds are they are not going to be very receptive when they finally do get to your images.

Keep track of which photos you have submitted to a contest. Some contests hold winning material for as long as a year. *Outdoor & Travel Photography* magazine is a quarterly publication; therefore its consideration period can be as long as four months. It's always a good idea to know exactly where your work is. That way, if someone calls in a photo request, you'll know where the image is without having to ransack your files.

I would hesitate before submitting the same shot to different contests at the same time. Wait until you've heard from one before sending the shot to another contest. No judge likes to find out that she might not be able to give an award to her first choice because it's being considered for another contest.

If at all possible, try to send duplicate transparencies or prints. If the worst happens and your submission is lost or damaged, the image won't be gone forever. If the contest requires that you send in originals, have a high-quality dupe made beforehand for your files. Then in the unlikely event that something happens to the original, you'll still have a copy of the image.

If you want to be absolutely sure that your photos have arrived safely, be sure to submit your entry by a method that will ensure you proof of delivery, and give you a way of tracing the package if it gets lost between the mailbox and the contest director's desk. Registered mail, messenger service (if you're in the same city), UPS, or any of the overnight delivery services are all good choices. Not all contests log in entries as they come in, so a call to the contest director to see if your photos arrived is probably going to be useless.

The best way to ensure that your entry will be returned is to include a self-addressed stamped envelope (SASE) with your submis-

Opposite page
Lawrence Siskind's straightforward shot of smiling boy and his feline friend was published in the *Photo Review's* awards issue.

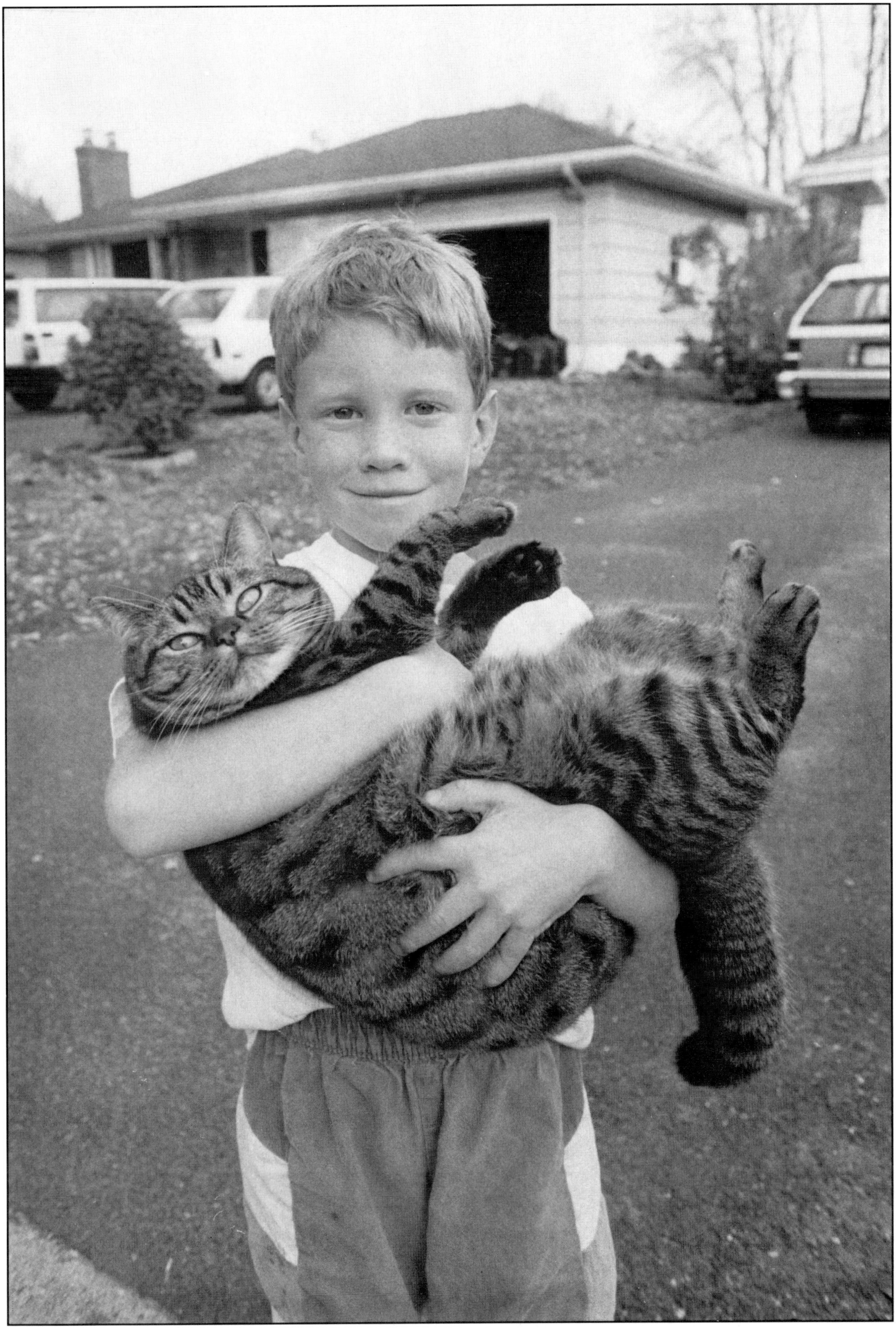

LAWRENCE SISKIND

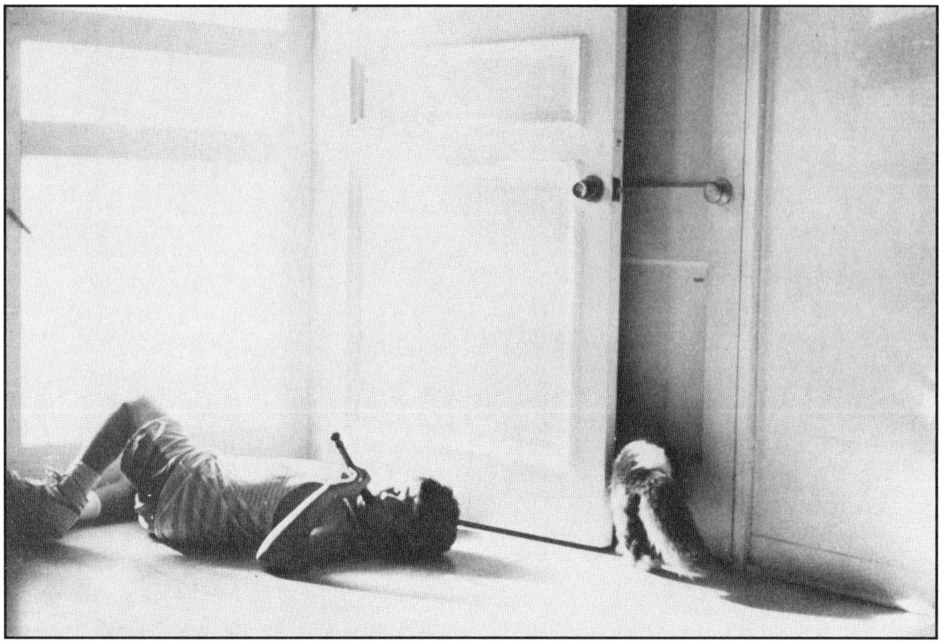

ROBERT REEP/COURTESY OF SCHOLASTIC ART AWARDS

13-year old Robert Reep won a medal in the 1989 Scholastic Art Awards for his impromptu portrait.

sion. It sounds painfully obvious, but make sure that the envelope is large enough to hold your prints and slides. I've seen people send in 8x10" prints and include a #10 letter-sized envelope for their return. Make sure that there is adequate postage on your SASE. Don't include cash (or check or money orders) for postage unless your submission is going to a foreign country and you have no way of getting one of its stamps or an international reply coupon. If you want your photos to be returned to you by registered mail or overnight delivery, make it as easy as possible for the contest director by filling out all the paperwork beforehand. Make sure the overnight delivery is prepaid or include your account number.

Some contests state flat out in the entry form that photos will not be returned. There are variety of reasons why, but usually it's simply that the sheer volume of expected entries makes it impossible for contests to return everything—they just don't have the time or manpower. If this is the case, whatever you do don't send in an original slide or negative. Limit your submission to dupes.

Other contests, however, retain not only the winning photos, but all of the entries—and the rights to them as well. These are the contests to watch out for, and ultimately avoid. Sometimes they are not legitimate contests but instead shady photo agencies looking for an easy and free way to augment their files. If you read the fine print on the entry form carefully, you'll have a better idea of what exactly is involved. If you do enter one of these contests and later see your photos used in a national ad, you may have no claim to any earnings because you have already signed all the rights to the photo away. Be careful, don't get burned.

8 WHAT KIND OF MATERIAL TO SEND IN

Perhaps the most important question when it comes to contests (and rightly so) is "what kind of material should I submit?" The obvious answer is "just send in your best material." While this is certainly true, it is only the tip of the iceberg. There are plenty of other considerations that come into play.

If the contest has a theme, make sure that your entry fits the bill. For example, if you're entering a nature contest, odds are that a shot of a factory interior—no matter how interesting and well-lit—is not going to make it past the first cut. The same shot, however, might do very well in an open contest, or a contest with an industrial theme. Likewise, if an entry form specifies only color images, don't send in black-and-white material.

To get a better idea of the level of quality and the sort of material that has won a particular competition in the past, take a look at past contest results. Many major competitions, such as Nikon Photo Contest International and the World Press Photo Contest, publish books of winning shots for each year's contests. Such magazines as *Sierra* and *Photo/Design* publish their contest winners each year in one issue of the magazine. Magazines that sponsor monthly competitions show their winners' work on a regular basis. See what caliber of work has won in the past, and try to spot any trends. Do the judges consistently favor people pictures or are they more partial to landscapes? Do they seem willing to sacrifice image quality for subject matter or the right moment? While there is no sure-fire way to determine what the judges are looking for (indeed, most judging panels change from year to year) it will give you some idea of what sort of work is expected.

In any case, send in the best work you have. A muddy print with a note explaining that the processor goofed is not going to win you any prizes. Judges make their decisions based on the work that is in front of them. They can't award a prize on the basis of what a picture should look like. So send only your best, and make sure it is properly exposed, in focus (if it's that sort of picture) and of good quality.

Some people greet a notice of an open contest that has no theme with a sigh of relief; others emit a moan of despair. The bright side of open contests is that when it comes to subject matter, anything goes.

All you have to do is send in the strongest examples of the work you like the best.

Don't take an open contest as a license to lower your standards, however—the judges haven't. Even though all subject matter is welcome, it's a good idea to give more than a passing thought to the contest sponsors. A family magazine is going to be more receptive to a G-rated photo of a toddler frolicking with a frisky puppy than they are to a cheesecake shot. And a contest sponsored by Coca-Cola is not going to award first prize to a shot of someone enthusiastically gulping down a Pepsi.

On the other hand, those who don't like theme-less contests also have a legitimate gripe. Open contests can be frustrating. Because you have no clear idea of what the judges are looking for, and you don't know what sort of standards or criteria they are using, it can be difficult to decide what sort of work to send in. If you don't have any idea of what to shoot, take pictures of what you know. If you're a nature lover, go for a hike with your camera; if your interest lies in sports, check out the local Little League game. Try to bring something of yourself to your picture taking. An open contest can provide an opportunity for you to discover something new about yourself and your photography.

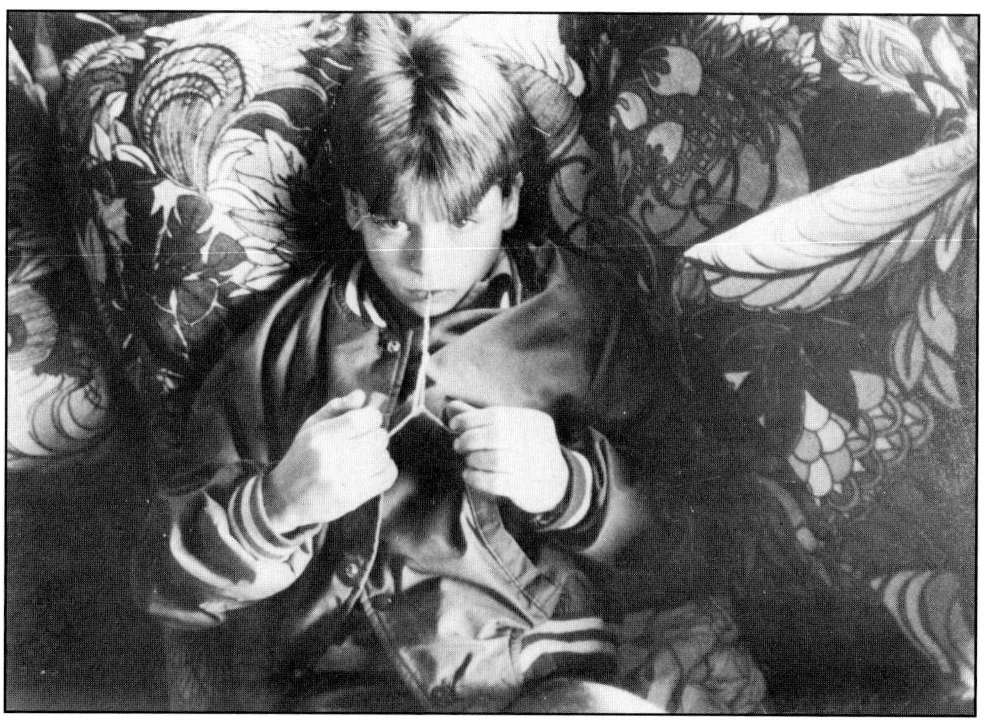

JANIE WRIGHT/COURTESY OF SCHOLASTIC ART AWARDS

Janie Wright's candid character study was a medal winner in the 1989 Scholastic Art Awards.

9

EDITING YOUR WORK

No matter what kind of contest you're entering, one of the most important parts of the process is editing your work. Don't expect the judges to decide which of 20 versions of your favorite shot is the best. That's your job. If you inundate the judges with umpteen takes of the same shot with only minor variations, your picture is going to lose its impact.

Don't be afraid to shoot a lot of film. The more shots you have of a subject, the better chance you have of coming away with one super-successful image. When you go to a photography show or thumb through a photo book, it's easy to forget that the work you're seeing has gone through a stringent editing process. You're not seeing every frame that the photographer shot. S/he (or an editor) has gone through the slides or contact sheets and picked the ones that work. Some photographers are happy if they can get one usable frame out of a roll of 36 exposures. While you don't have to edit yourself quite that tightly, don't get discouraged if not every one of your shots is worth saving.

One good way to edit your work is to go through a batch of film and separate it into three categories. Into the first pile will go the disasters—the shots that are out-of-focus, under- and overexposed, and the horribly composed. The ones where your subject has her eyes closed, or even worse, wide open and devilishly red. Even though your first impulse may be to get the photos out of your sight as quickly as possible, wait a minute. Look at these pictures carefully and try to figure out where you went wrong. With a little bit of sleuthing, you'll be able to determine how you can do better the next time you find yourself in a similar situation. Make notes if it helps. OK, now you can throw them away.

Next, take the remaining pictures and divide them into two groups. Put the pictures you really like into one group. The other pile is for those images that are technically competent, but have something about them you don't like. The third step is an easy one: put both of the piles away. Come back to them in a few days and see if your feelings about the pictures and the choices you've made have changed. Perhaps some of the images you liked at first now seem tame or boring. Conversely, maybe some of the shots you initially hated will have

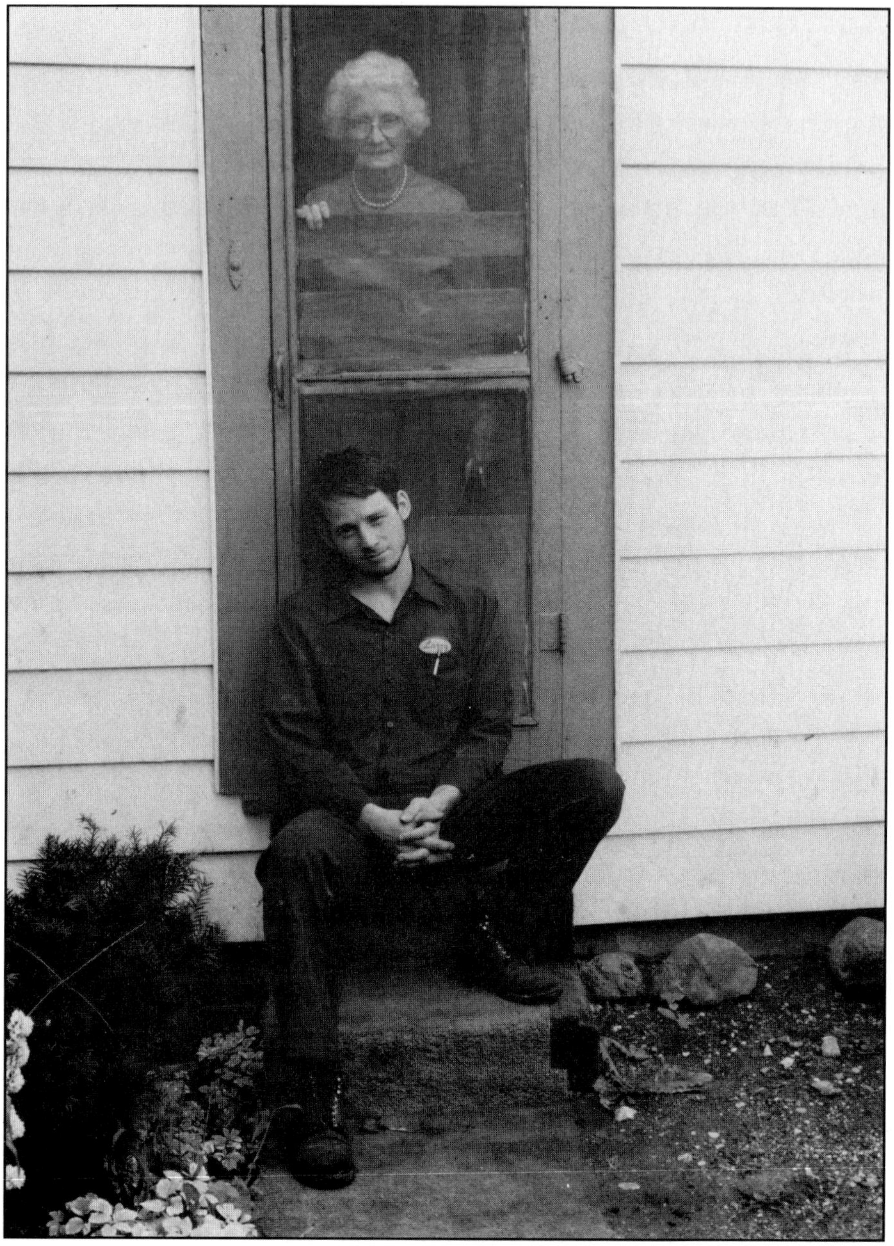

MARY BOL VINCENT

Color and black-and-white entries are judged together in *Popular Photography's* Your Best Shot contest. Mary Bol Vincent of Cedar Lake, IN was the first entrant to win first prize for a black-and-white shot.

begun to grow on you. Remember, if a photograph elicits a response, it has power. You may never feel 100 percent positively or negatively about any picture. But if it provokes a response, it's worth saving.

A final editing note: Don't send in anything you'd be ashamed or embarrassed to see in print. If your shot features a friend or family member prominently, you might want to get their permission before making the submission.

10 CONTESTS TO WATCH OUT FOR

Most contests are aboveboard and legitimate. Unfortunately, however, there are a few unscrupulous outfits with less than honorable intentions that masquerade as competitions. These are the ones to watch out for. The more carefully you read the entry form, the better chance you have of spotting (and avoiding) this type of pseudo-contest. Here are some of the warning signals that a contest might be best avoided.

One way to determine if a contest is one you want to enter is to check out who retains the rights to the photo — you or the sponsor. Legitimate contests will want rights to use the winning images as promotion or publicity for the contest or company for a limited period of time. The Scholastic Art Awards for example, requests the reproduction rights to the winning photos for two years. If you come across a competition that wants to retain all rights—not only to the winners but to all of the entries they receive — stay away.

Next, check to see if your photos will be returned to you. If they are not, proceed with caution: this can be a tip-off. Some legitimate contests state that they cannot return photos because of the volume of material they receive. This is fine—just read the rest of the entry very carefully to see who retains the rights to the photos. If, however, an entry form states that the sponsor owns the copyright to all entries, again stay away.

Pay close attention to the address on the entry form. If no street address is listed, proceed with caution. A post- office box can be a sign of a potential fly-by-night operation. Contests that ask for a large entry fee also warrant careful scrutiny.

It's not always easy to determine the legitimacy of a contest. But if you pay attention to the above warning signals, you should be able to avoid becoming involved in an unpleasant situation. If the contest is run by a reputable organization, has a good reputation and a proven track record, you should be able to send in your work with no qualms.

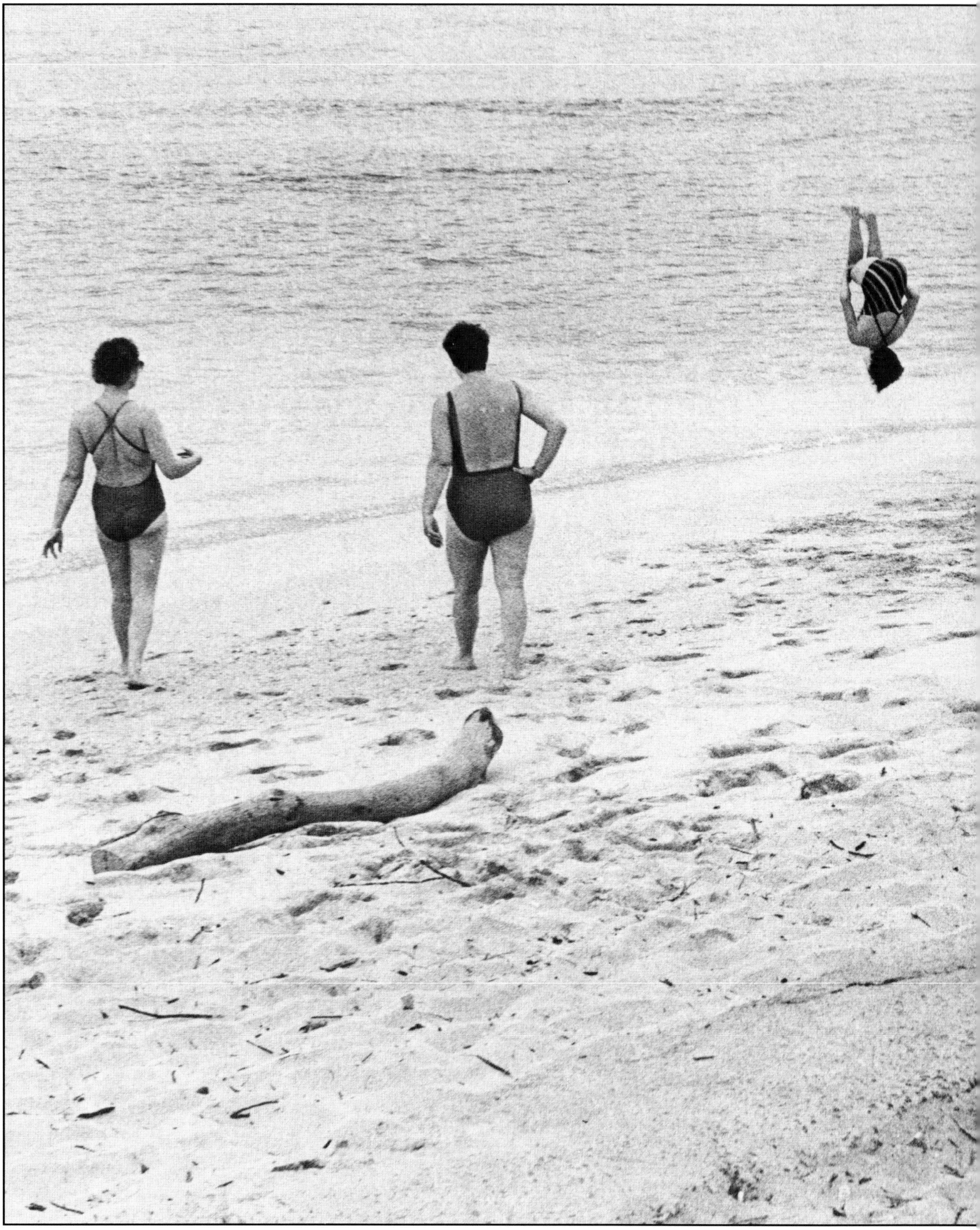

"Levitation", Glen Fukunaga's beach scene with a twist, won an Honorable Mention in the 1987-1988 Nikon Photo Contest International (NPCI).

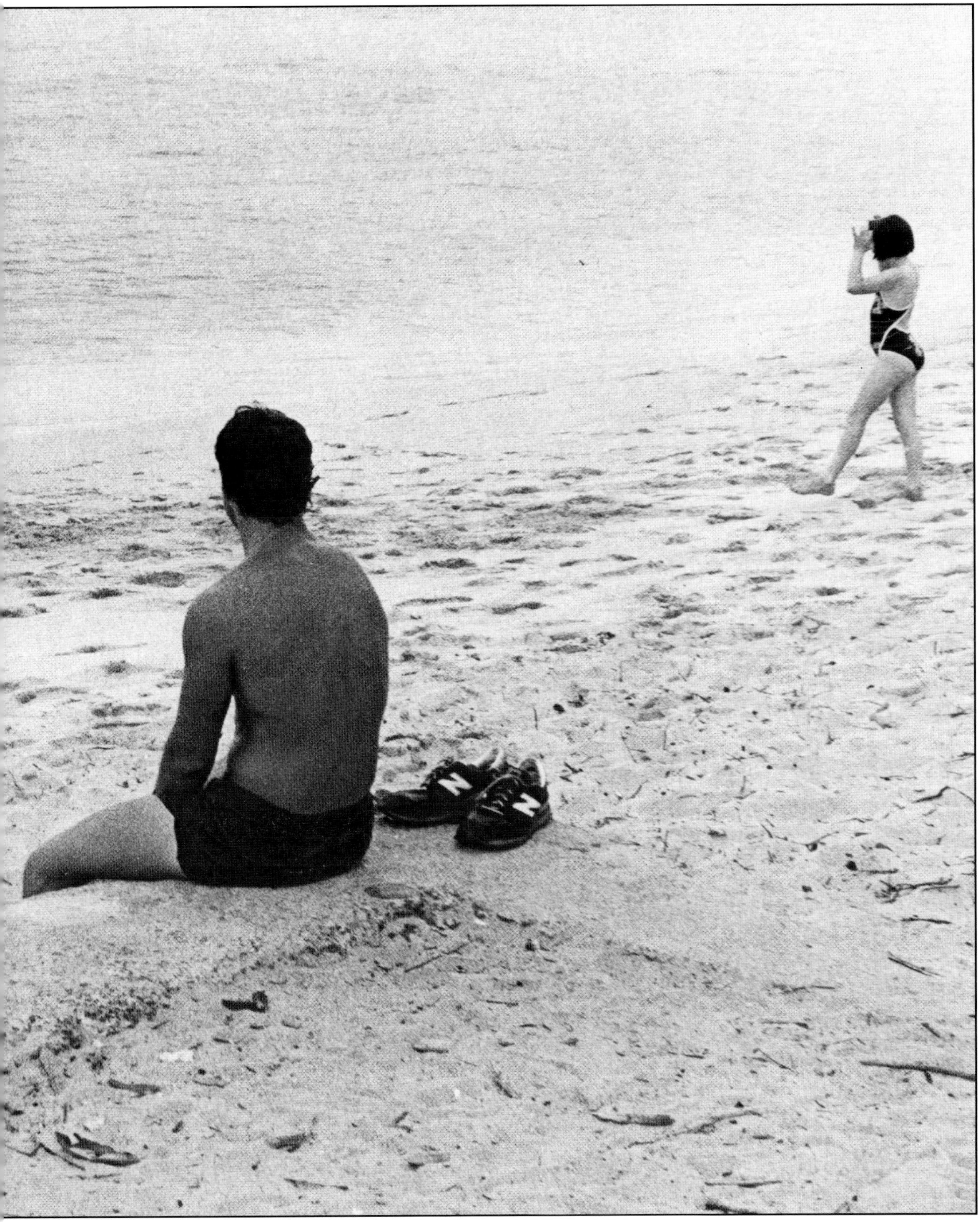

GLEN FUKUNAGA

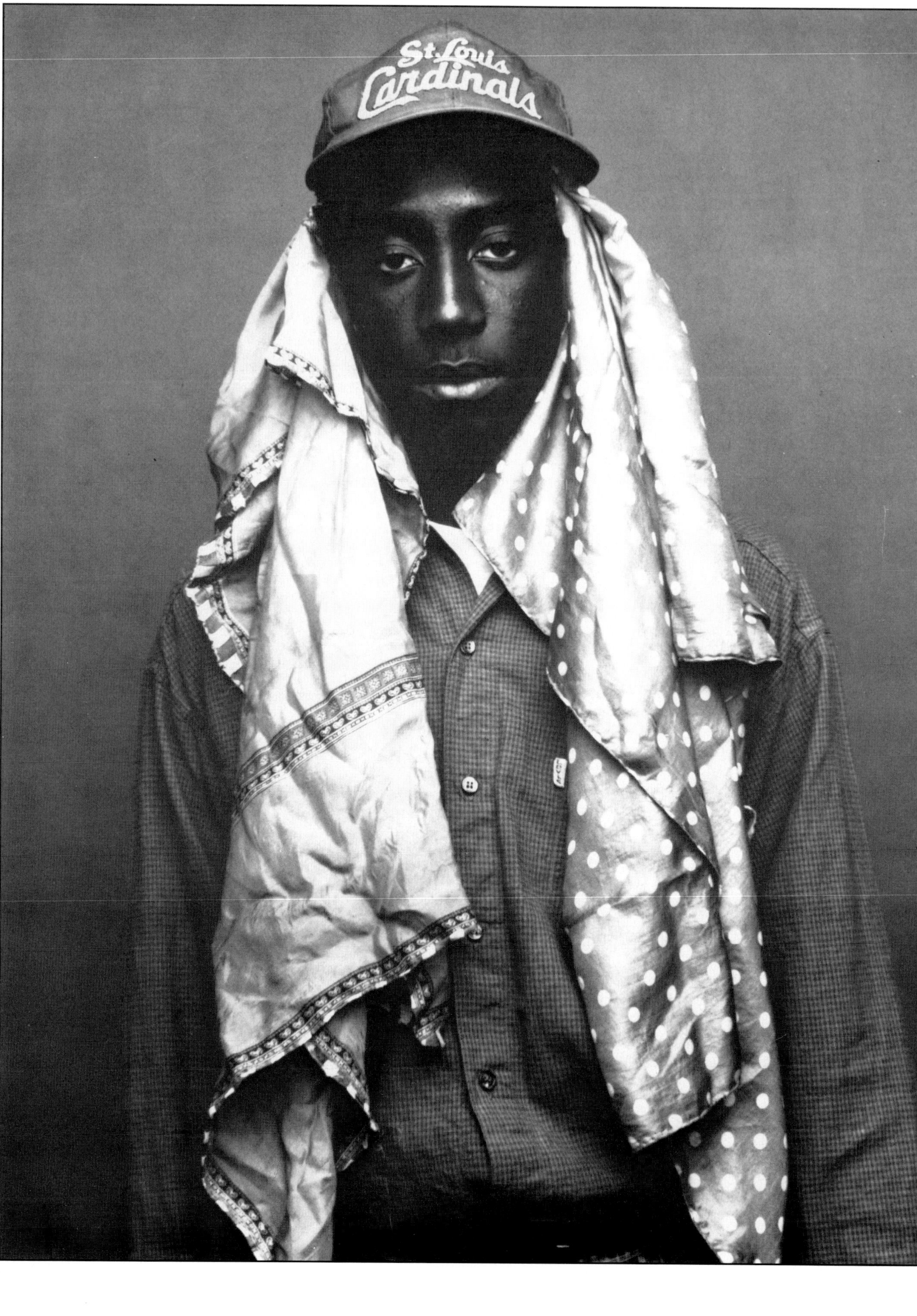

GAVIN A. BENJAMIN/COURTESY OF SCHOLASTIC ART AWARDS

11 IMPROVE YOUR CHANCES OF WINNING

Entering any photo contest is a gamble. There are, however, some simple ways to improve your odds of winning a prize. One way is to pay attention to the number of prizes that are awarded. The more prizes there are, the better chance you have of winning one. You should also look into how many entries a contest attracts. Don't rule out a contest just because it doesn't receive a lot of publicity. Your photo is much more likely to catch a judge's eye if it is one of 100 than one of 10,000. While the prizes may be more valuable in the larger contests, if you go by the numbers, you'll have a better chance of winning a smaller competition.

Opposite page
A medal in the 1989 Scholastic Art Awards went to Gavin A. Benjamin for his straightforward portrait.

Below
Curt Geber found beauty in an unexpected place and won a $1,000 scholarship from Brooks in the 1988 Scholastic Art Awards for his efforts.

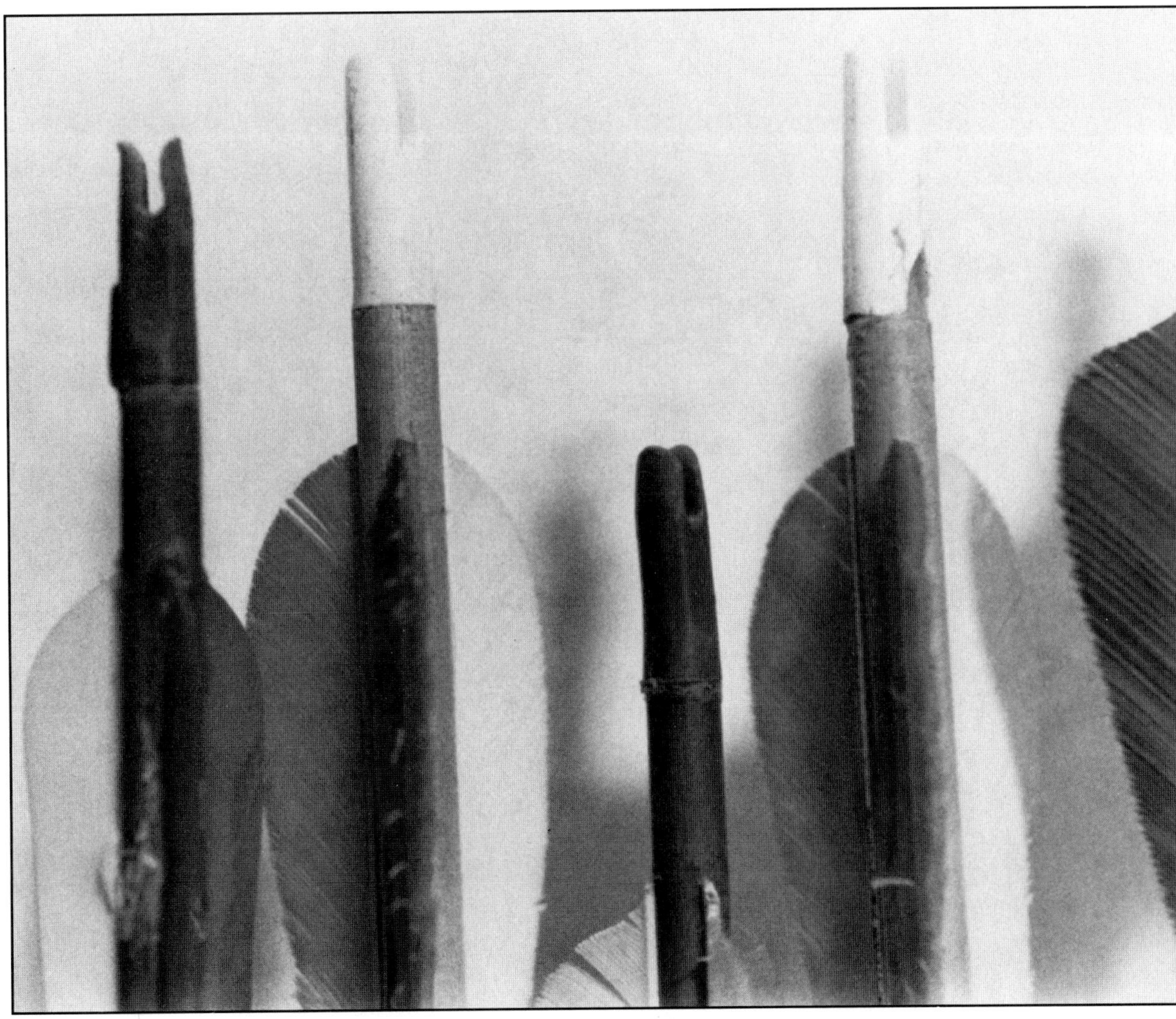

CURT GEBER/COURTESY OF SCHOLASTIC ART AWARDS

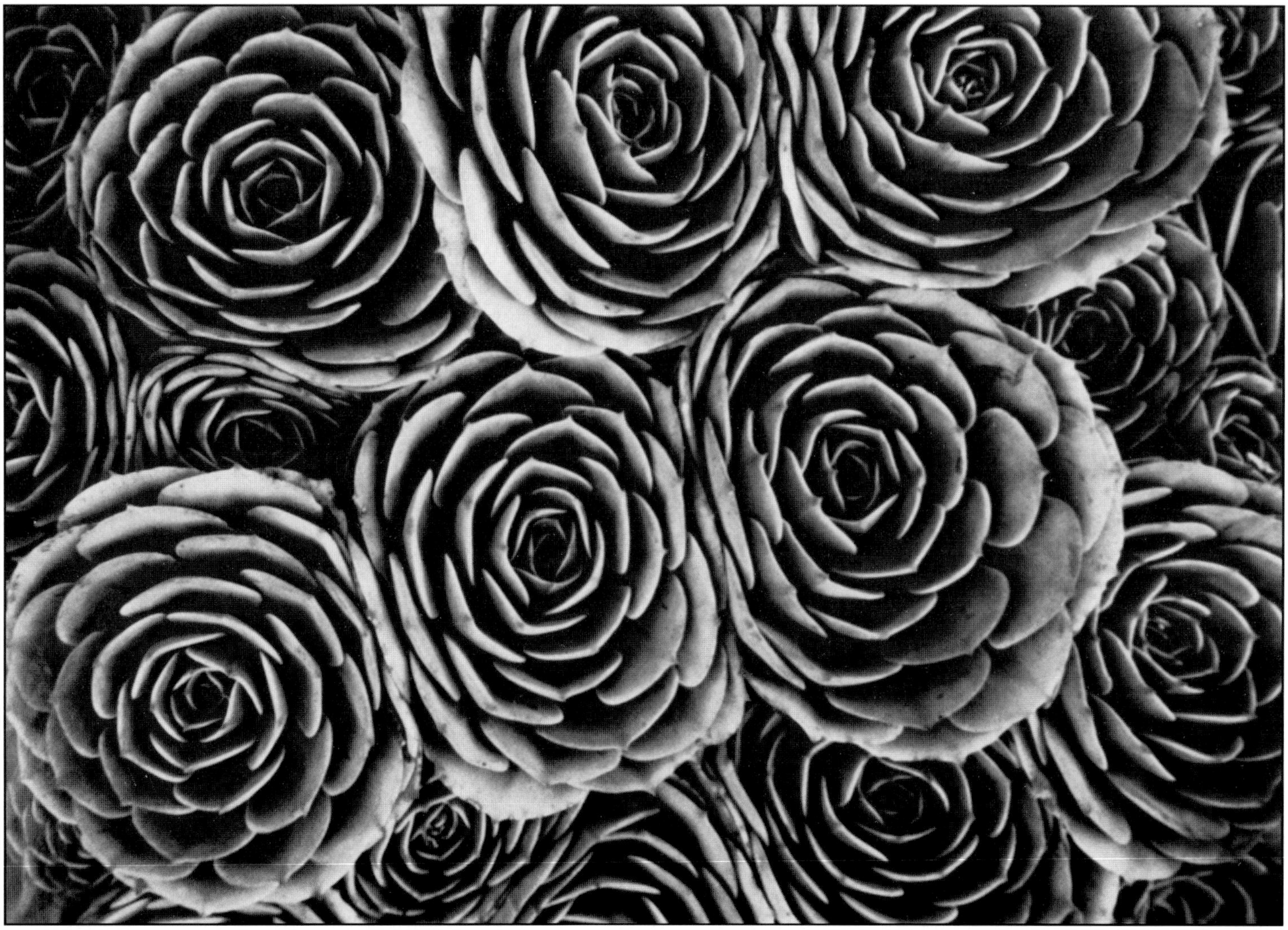

BRIAN KUIPERS/COURTESY OF SCHOLASTIC ART AWARDS

Brian Kuipers graphic organic shot was part of his prize-winning portfolio in the 1988 Scholastic Art Awards.

12 JUDGING

Just how does the judging process work? When you see the results of a contest that rejected your work, it may seem as if the judges just shut their eyes and randomly picked the winners. However tempting it may be to entertain thoughts of such a scenario, it's simply not true. Neither is judging a mystical process. When it comes down to it, it's basically a straightforward procedure.

The number of judges will vary depending on the size of the contest. Jurors are generally drawn from the photography field; they may be photographers, teachers, or picture editors. Most panels will also include someone who is affiliated with the group or company sponsoring the contest.

No matter how large a contest and how large the jury is, all judging follows basically the same format. First the judge or judges quickly go through all of the entries and immediately eliminate the shots that are out-of-focus, under- and overexposed, or not in keeping with the theme. Generally at this preliminary stage a "nay" from any judge is enough to disqualify an entry. Later as the process gets more intense, the judges may move on to a majority vote or a consensus system of eliminating entries. Depending on the amount of entries and the number of prizes that will be given out, the judges will go through several rounds of knocking images out. When they have arrived at a core group of "keepers," the jury will then determine which image gets which prize. In most cases they will start with first prize and work down the scale to the honorable mentions.

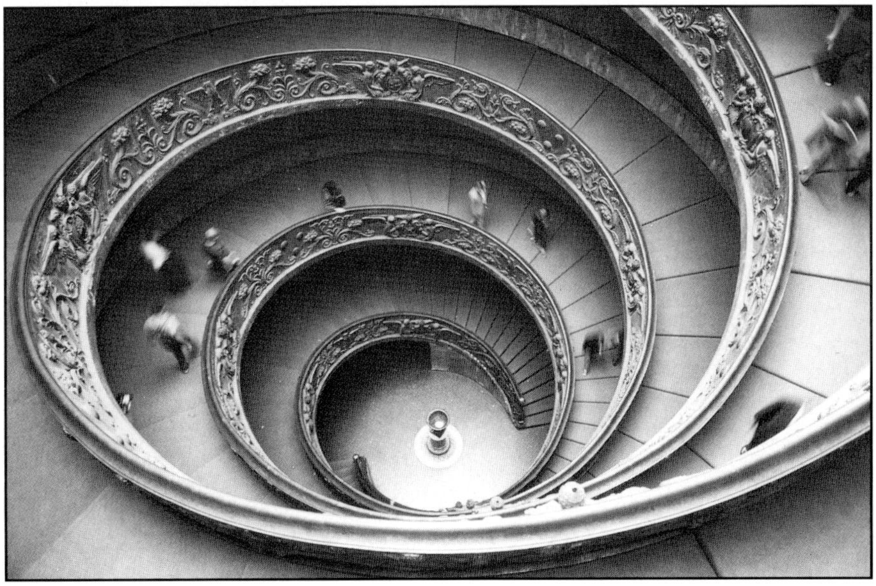

PETER L. GOULD

Our cover shot, by Peter L. Gould was one of the British Photos of the Year in 1973.

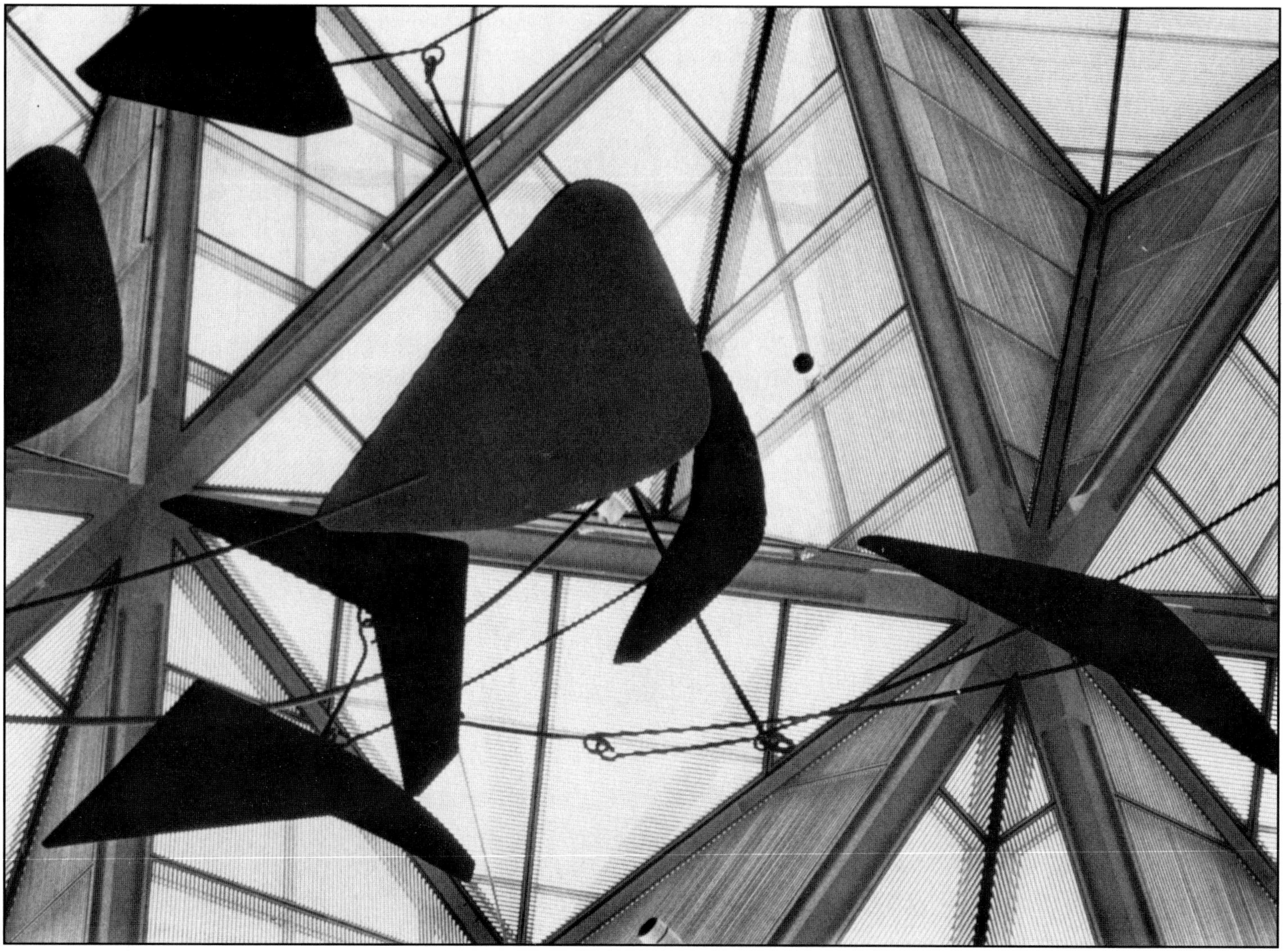

ARIANNA ROSATI/COURTESY OF SCHOLASTIC ART AWARDS

Hanging mobiles take on an abstract quality when viewed from directly below. Arianna Rosati won a $1,000 grant in the 1988 Scholastic Art Awards.

13 PERSISTENCE

If you've gone through the entire submission process only to have your entry rejected, the first thing to do is to try to figure out why. Did you follow all of the entry rules exactly? Was your entry technically competent? Could it have been the subject matter, or composition? Did your shot meet the contest's criteria? Finally, remember that impartiality aside, judging is subjective. Not everyone has the same taste. You could have unwittingly hit on one of the judge's pet peeves.

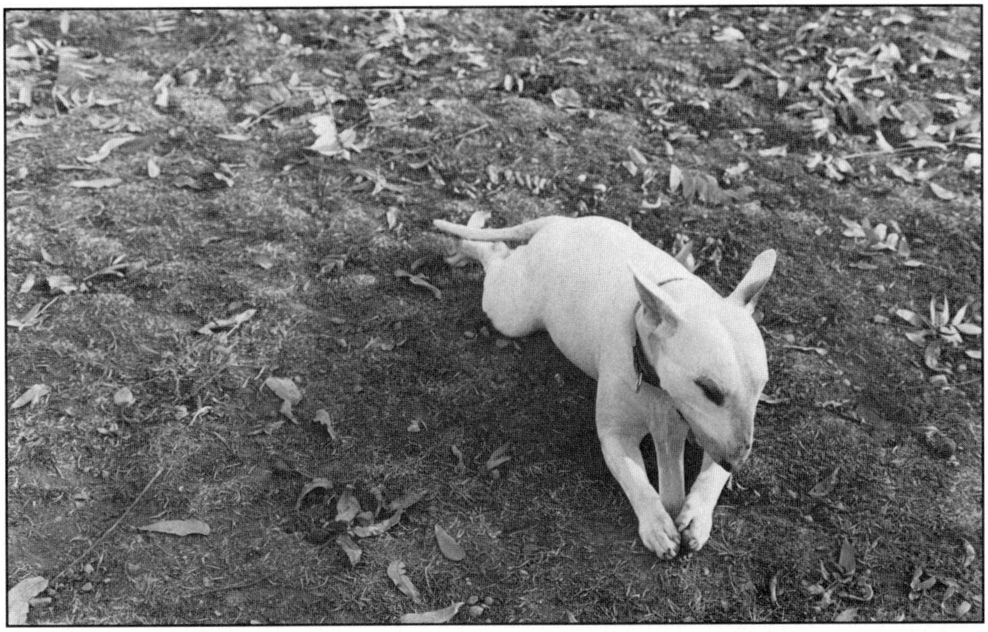

MELISSA LEE HARRIS

Above
As one of the winners in the ***Photo Review*** National Photographic Competition 1989, Melissa Lee Harris of San Francisco, had her photograph published in the awards issue of the magazine.

Whatever you do, don't get discouraged. Be persistent and enter the same shot in another contest. Just because one judge didn't like your work, it doesn't mean that every contest will reject it. Conversely, if a particular contest rejects one submission, don't give up on that contest entirely. Enter again, this time with different pictures. Rotate your images and keep a constant flow of them circulating among the different contests.

Once a shot does win a prize, don't retire it from the competition circuit. Try your luck with larger, more prestigious contests. After Bahman Farzad's shot of a rim-lit lotus blossom won an award in the Red Mountain Museum national competition, he submitted it to contests sponsored by *Popular Photography* and *Studio* magazine. Farzad came away a winner both times!

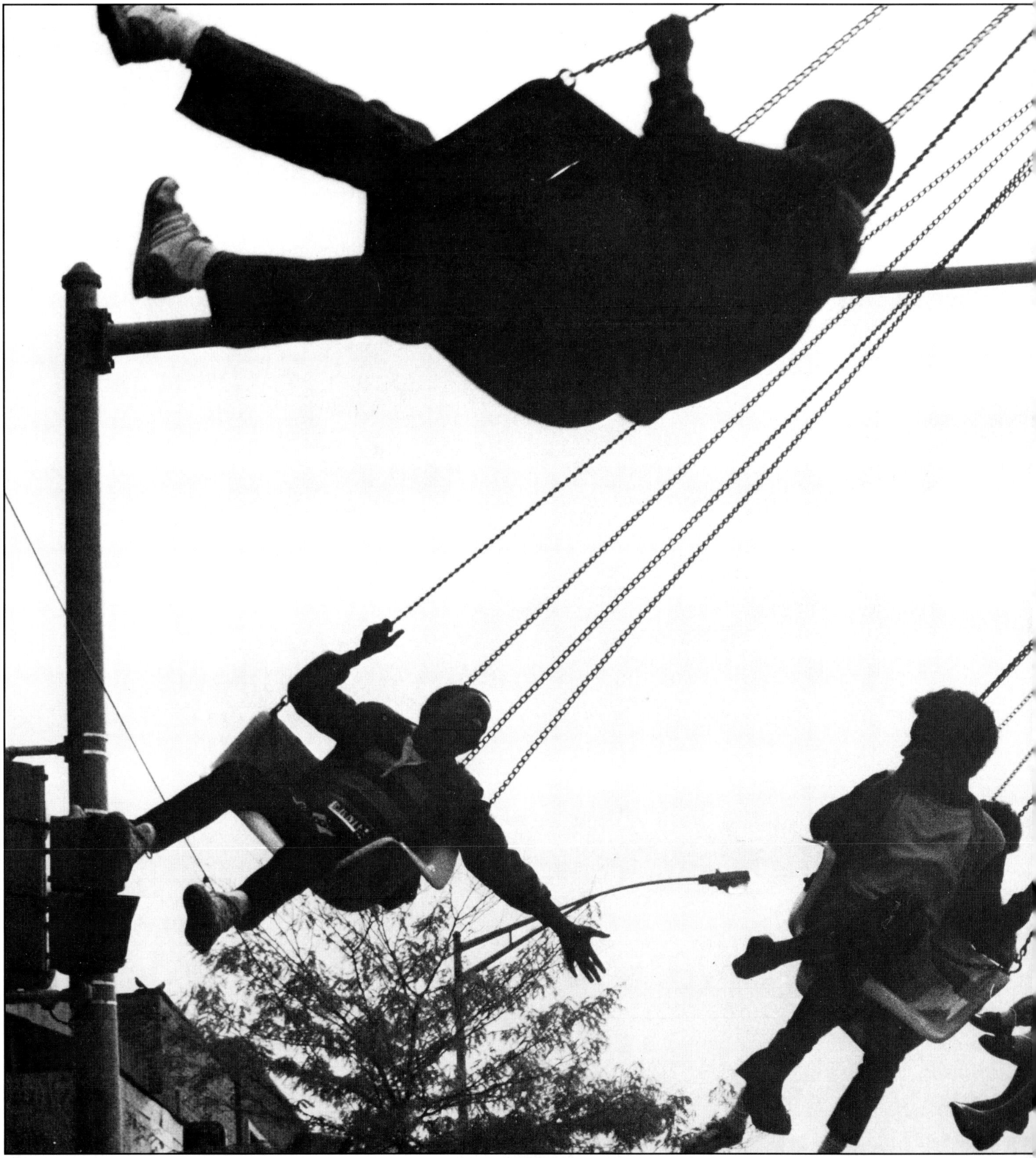

As one of the 1984 Pictures of the Year, Gerald Williams' shot of high-flyers was published in the POY annual, ***The Best of Photojournalism/10.***

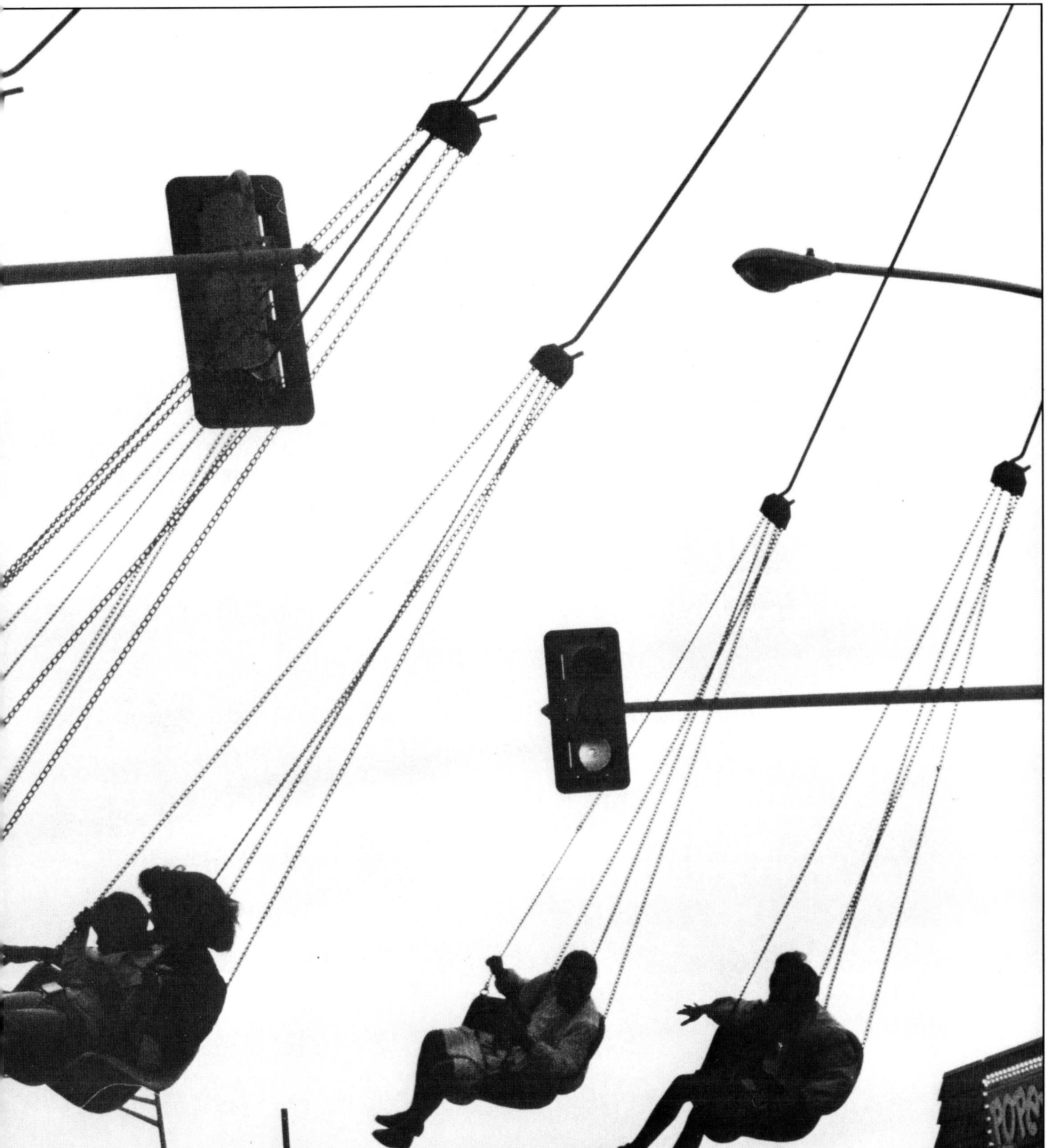

GERALD WILLIAMS

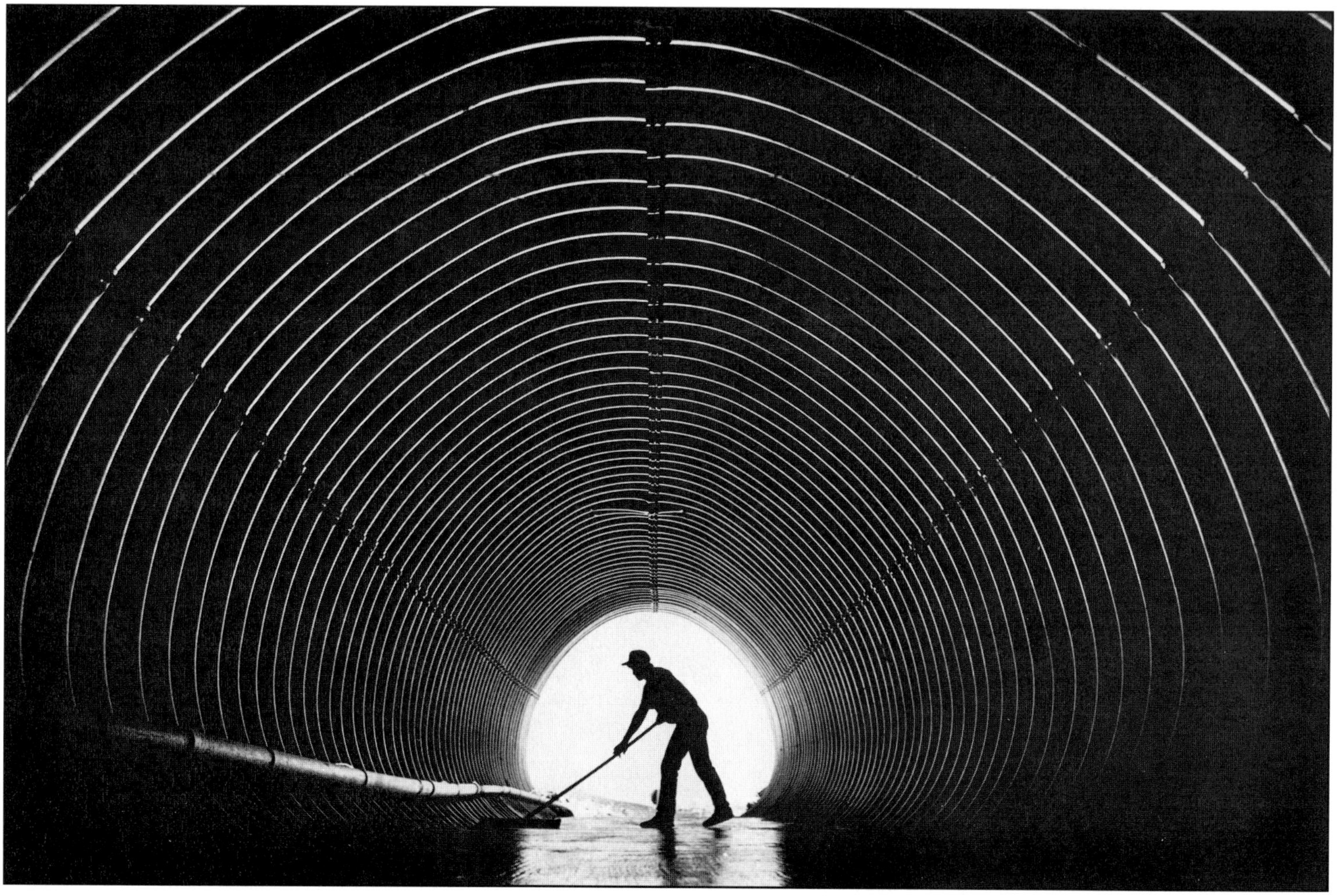

MARK REIS

Mark Reis' graphic shot of a sweeper framed in concentric semi-circles was one of the 1986 Pictures of the Year.

14 HOW TO MAKE YOUR ENTRY STAND OUT

You don't need expensive, sophisticated equipment to take prize-winning pictures (although a top-of-the-line camera certainly will not hold you back). People have won contests with everything from simple point-and-shoot cameras to the latest professional autofocus SLRs. Learning how to use the equipment is the easy part—learning how to recognize a good image is where the challenge comes in. Everyone has a unique viewpoint; the challenge is translating your particular vision to film.

In judging *Popular Photography's* "Your Best Shot" contest one month, we received two shots of the same subject from two different photographers. One version won second prize that month. It was a well-composed, graphic shot, with brilliant eye-catching colors. I had it on my lightbox as I looked over the other entries, and as my co-workers passed by, each had a favorable comment.

A second version of the same scene (sent in by a different photographer) arrived a few weeks later. Although both photographers had shot virtually the same location, the second entry wasn't nearly as successful. Unfortunately, the shot wasn't properly exposed, which made the colors appear drab and muted. As for composition, the prize-winning photographer had filled the frame with a graphic pattern of super-saturated color. The other photographer had shot the scene from farther away and thus had included extraneous detail that detracted from the scene. Both photographers had recognized a potentially dramatic scene. Only one could translate his view of it to film.

If, like the second photographer, you find that the prints or slides you get back from the processor don't look remotely like what you saw through the viewfinder, don't despair. With practice, you can learn to take good pictures. Any photography class, how-to book, or photo magazine can teach you how to take technically correct images. By enrolling in a class, or reading a book or magazine, you can learn how to turn out properly exposed, well-lit, finely focused, well-composed shots. There's no denying that technique is crucial, but there is more to taking prize-winning pictures. Think of technique as a foundation upon which you'll build your shots. Sure you have to know how to operate your camera correctly, but you also need a strong sense of

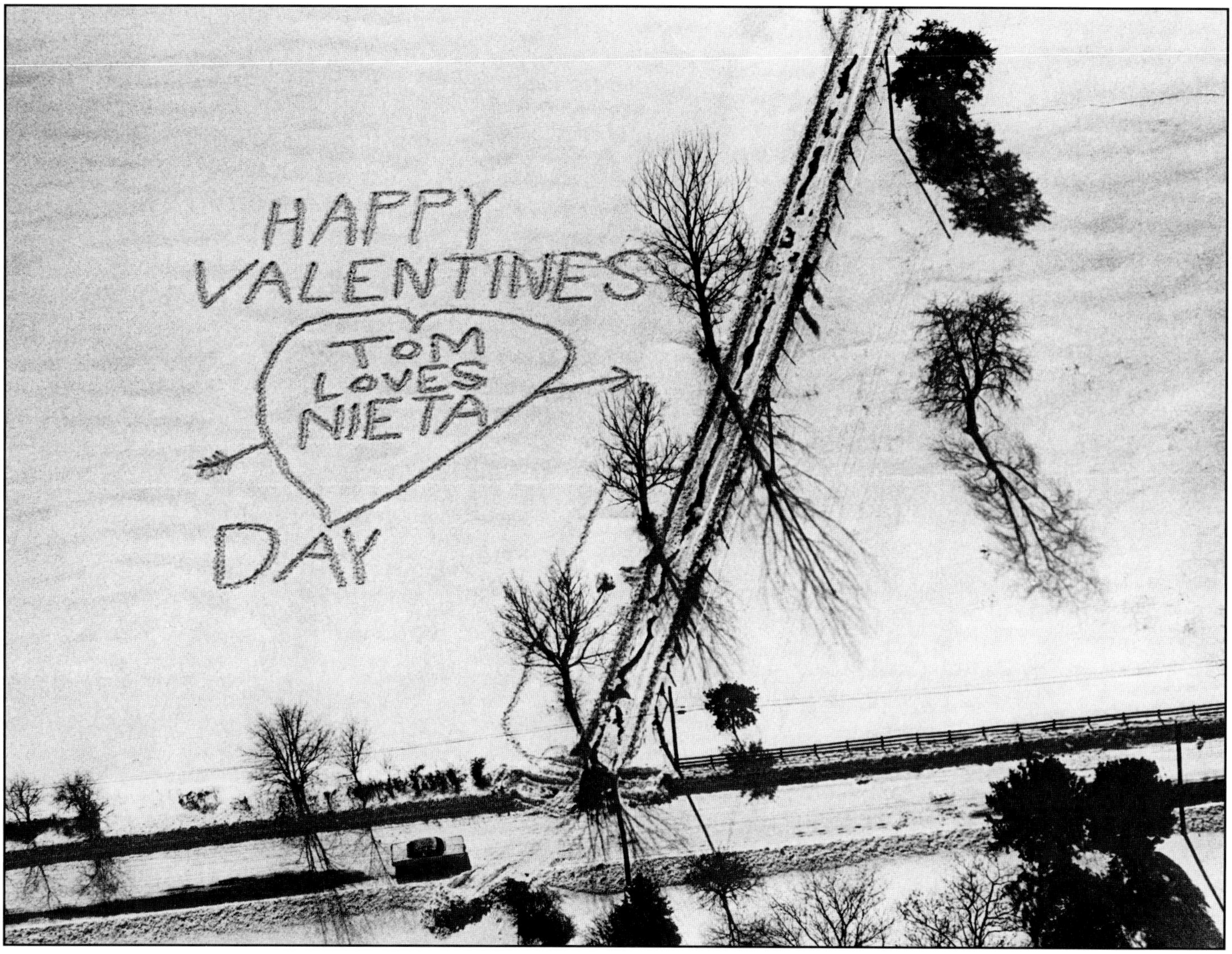

DENNIS MCDONALD

Dennis McDonald's aerial valentine shows that a different point of view helps when it comes to winning contests. McDonald's shot was one of the 1984 Pictures of the Year.

composition and color, and above all an eye for what Henri Cartier-Bresson called "the decisive moment"—the instant when the action peaks, when something happens.

From the basic family portrait or vacation snapshot, to social-documentary photos that expose the injustices of modern life, to photographs that represent the inner vision of a photographer, there are countless inspirations that send people scrambling for their cameras. In most cases, however, it's not the subject matter that makes a photo good or bad. People have won photo contests by taking pictures of everything from babies to Beirut bombings.

What does count is how the subject is presented. Does your picture evoke a mood or feeling? Ideally, a successful photograph is one that elicits some sort of response, be it positive or negative. You can take a technically superb shot, one that is beautifully lit, artfully composed and properly exposed. But unless it has a spark of creativity or feeling, it won't live on the page. It's not as esoteric as it sounds. By paying attention to the mood cast by light, graphic effects, the language of color, and—most important of all—timing, you'll be on your way to taking prize-winning pictures.

Lighting

Let's start with lighting. Late afternoon and early morning provide the most consistently dramatic lighting conditions. Long shadows and the atmospheric haze of twilight or dawn can lend drama to the most mundane of subjects. A good exercise to see how the light changes as the day progresses is to shoot the same object or scene at different times during one day. You'll see how the shadows change and how that change can transform the feeling and mood of a photograph. A vase of flowers in the bright, harsh noontime sun evokes a different mood than the same vase casting elongated shadows in the gathering twilight. Be alert to ordinary subjects in a light that makes you look at them as if for the first time. A picture that makes you look at an object or scene as if you had never seen it before has a good chance of being a prize winner.

Graphic Impact

One of the best ways to get a picture noticed by the judges is to shoot your subject graphically. Separate yourself from the emotion of a scene and concentrate on the forms and patterns rather than the subject itself. For example, a shot of an empty stadium that reduces the rows of empty seats to a pattern of light and shadow is going to grab your attention more than an overall shot of the same site that includes the aisles and field. By eliminating extraneous detail and thinking in terms of light and shadow, color, and pattern, you'll give your subject maximum impact.

Color

Color has a language all of its own. Its vocabulary is varied enough to demand a response by screaming "look at me," or to subtly elicit an emotion by setting a soft, tranquil mood. Strong saturated hues will give an image a different feeling than muted pastel shades.

You can use different proportions of complementary colors (blue-orange, purple-yellow, red-green) in your compositions to come up with different effects. When you place large blocks of them side by side, you'll create contrasts that cry out for attention. Or you can give a subtle lift to a monochromatic scene by using a complementary color as an accent. Perk up a green pastoral landscape by including a spot of red. A seascape in shades of blue will come to life if you add an orange beachball. If you'd rather give your image a more harmonious aura, work with colors from the same family (green-blue-purple, red-orange-yellow).

To emphasize bright colors, shoot at midday, when the sun is strongest. A polarizing filter will help eliminate glare and deepen blue skies. Underexposing slide film by one-half to one full stop will make colors appear more saturated and rich.

Judicious use of color will strengthen your pictures, but color alone will not guarantee you any prizes. Once you've caught a judge's eye, you have to give him or her a reason to linger on your image.

Timing

Timing is crucial in photography. How many pictures have you seen that would have been fantastic if only Junior hadn't blinked, or a passerby hadn't wandered into the dramatic landscape you were preparing to shoot? How about the time you pressed the shutter release button a fraction of a second too late, or too early to capture the moment that would have made the picture? You have to learn to be patient (if the situation will allow). Try to anticipate the moment when the action will peak, or the subject will reveal its quintessential self.

This is what Henri Cartier-Bresson meant when he coined the phrase "the decisive moment." It's the instant when all the pieces of a picture come together. Take a look at Glen Fukunaga's shot of a seaside somersault on pages 40-41. He's captured the precise moment of peak action. If he'd released the shutter before or after the gymnast had performed his aerial somersault, the shot would have been just another beach scene. Yes, it would have been pleasing to the eye, but it would have lost its capacity to surprise and delight the viewer.

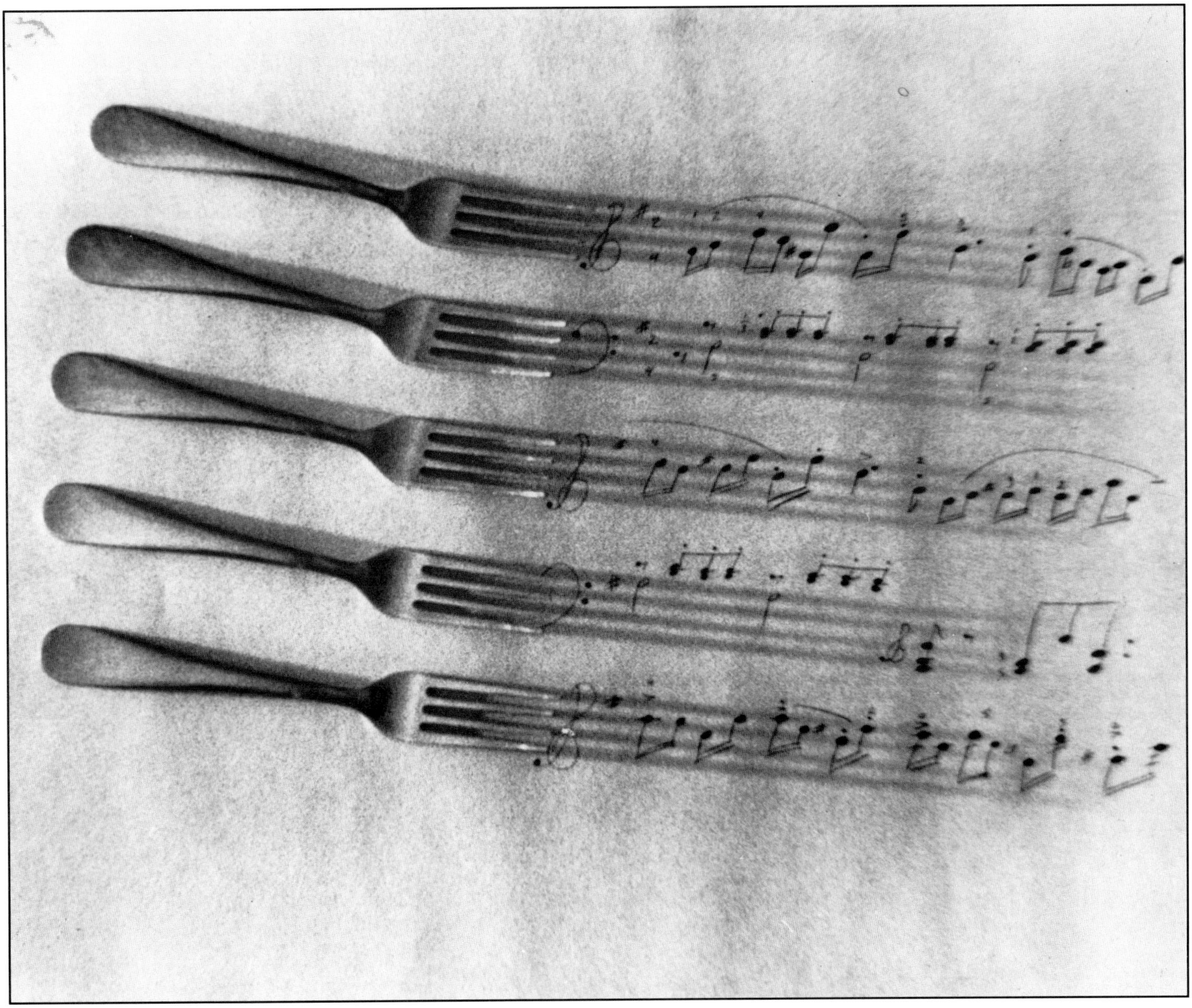

ALLEN TADEO/COURTESY OF SCHOLASTIC ART AWARDS

Allen Tadeo's humorously titled "Tuning Forks" was a medal-winner in the 1989 Scholastic Art Awards.

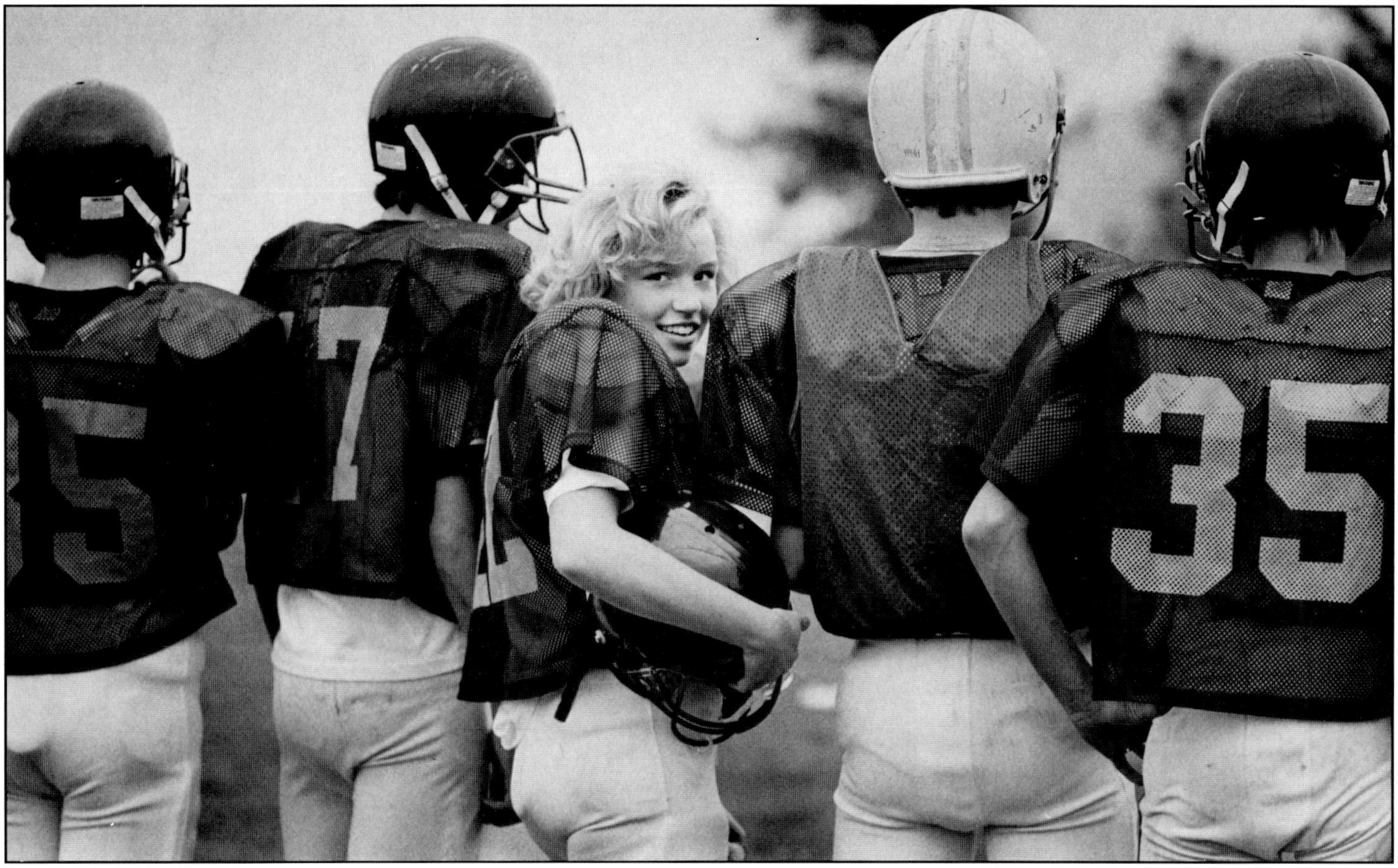

KEITH ANDERSON

Aim for the unexpected. Keith Anderson's double-take provoking photo was one of the 1986 Pictures of the Year.

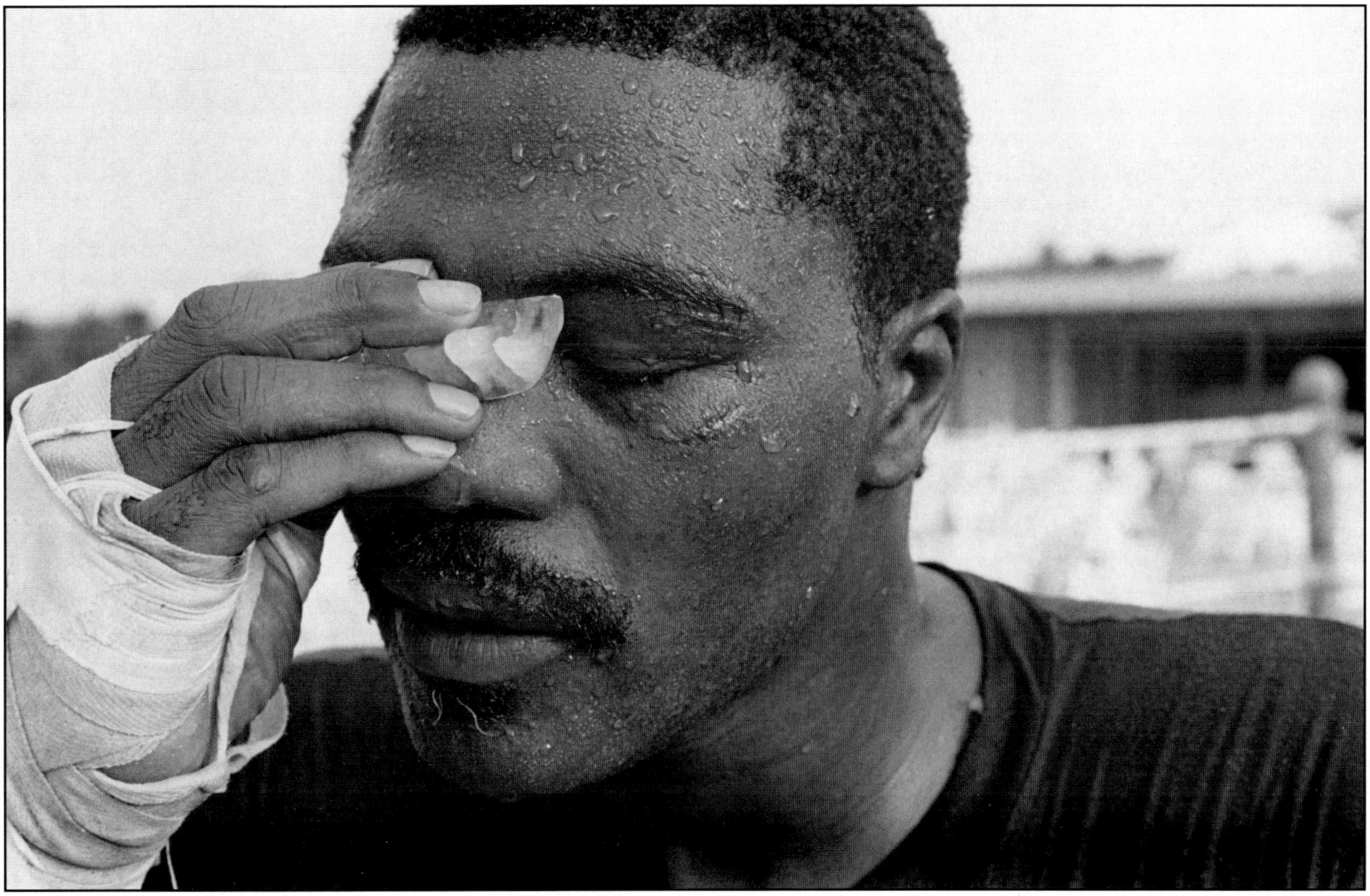

SCOTT LA POINT

Scott La Point, of East Elmhurst, NY, eliminated all extraneous detail by coming in close on a boxer enjoying a well-deserved rest break. La Point won $200 in *Popular Photography's* February 1990 Your Best Shot contest.

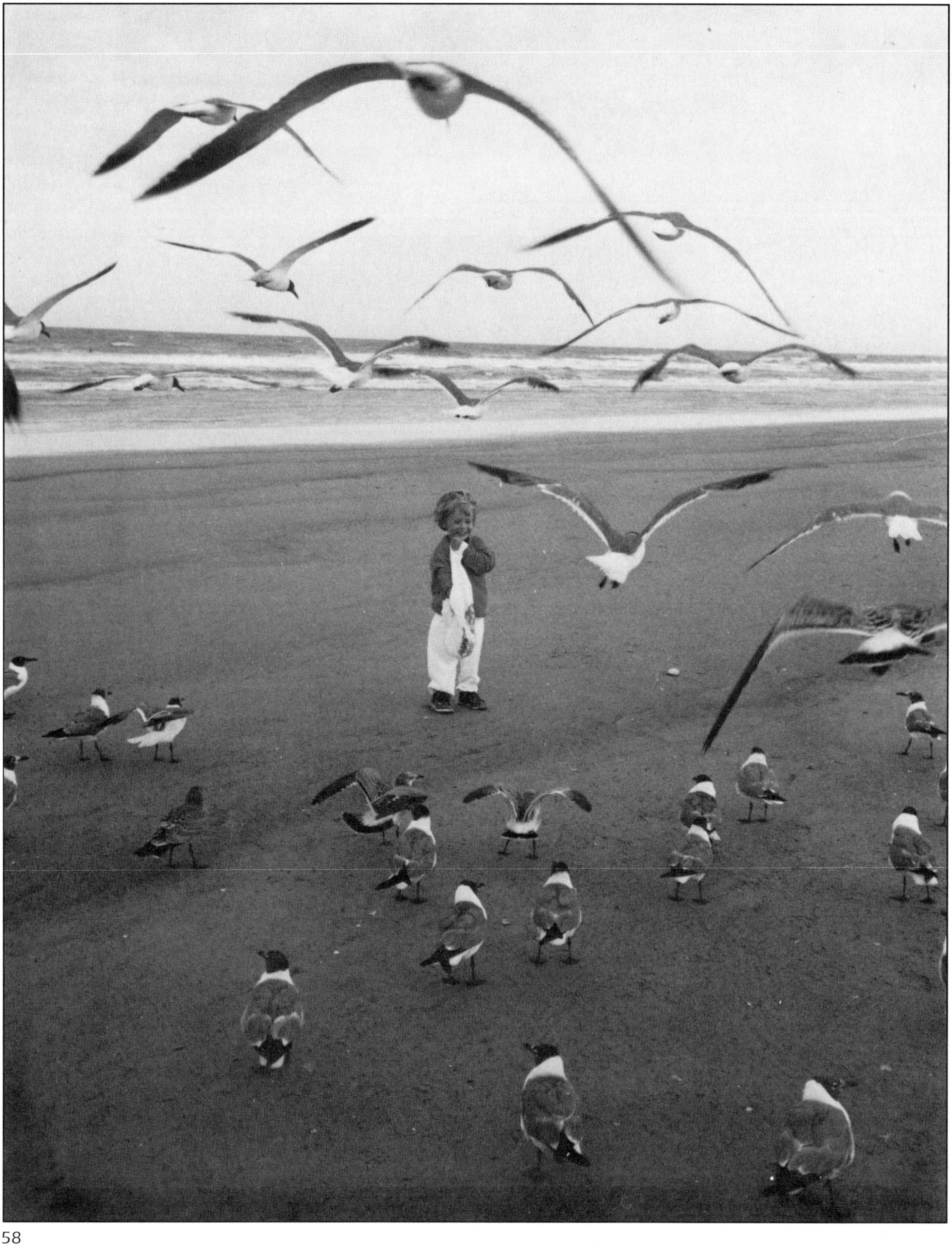

KAREN LALLY MECK

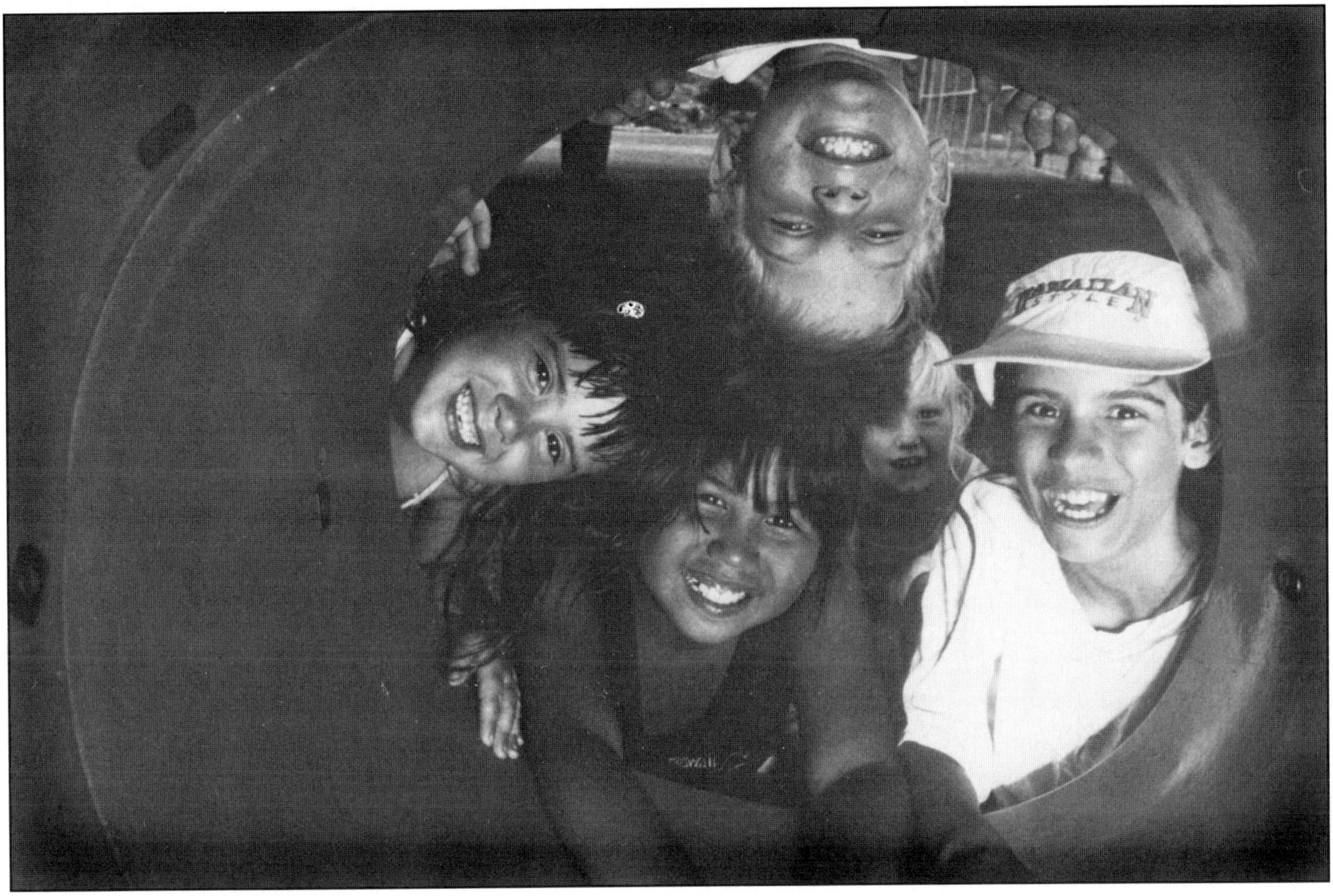

CHRIS DYBALL

People Pictures

The allure of successfully capturing people on film has drawn many a photographer to his hobby or profession. Some photographers dream of shooting high-fashion magazine covers, others would be satisfied with recognizable shots of their loved ones. Everybody at one time or another has been faced with a batch of prints or slides that turned a picture-review session into a nightmare instead of a dream.

Whether you're shooting a formal portrait or aiming for a candid shot, the biggest challenge is getting your subject to relax. Give people the chance to get accustomed to seeing you with a camera. Shoot a lot of film (or pretend to). After a while people will forget you're taking pictures. Then they'll relax and stop mugging for the camera. That's when you'll be able to get natural looking, unposed shots.

Photographing strangers is a different story. Sometimes, as a courtesy, it helps to ask permission to take someone's picture. If you're not certain how your photographic activity will be received, it's a good idea to be as unobtrusive as possible when you're out on the street with your camera. Try pre-focusing and holding the camera at chest level,

Above
Many open contests are on the lookout for people pictures. Chris Dyball, of Honolulu, won the $200 second prize in *Popular Photography's* November 1989 Your Best Shot contest for his colorful and cheerful shot of children in a playground.

Opposite page
Karen Lally Meck's shot of her son feeding gulls was one of 100 images chosen out of 130,000 entries in the "We the People" photo contest sponsored by *Parade* magazine and Fuji films.

or down by your side. If people don't know they're being photographed, they can't react badly.

Composition and Framing

Pay attention to how your image appears when you look through the viewfinder. Extraneous detail can detract from the power of a shot, and retouching is time-consuming and prohibitively expensive. So, take the time to make sure that your image is pleasing before you release the shutter. Look beyond the central portion of the image and consider the entire frame carefully. What appears in the corners or along the perimeter is just as important to the overall image as the main subject.

Do you really want that lamp post growing out of Aunt Cele's head? Would your pastoral landscape look better without that piece of litter in the foreground? Ask Aunt Cele to move, pick up the litter, or change your viewpoint and shoot from a different angle. If, even though you thought you knew exactly what was in the viewfinder, an unexpected object shows up at the edges of a print, you can as a last resort print it again and crop out the extraneous detail.

If you're shooting with a zoom lens, zoom back and forth between the different focal lengths to determine when the strongest version appears in the viewfinder. Then make your shot. If you have a fixed-focal length lens, move around until you get the best vantage point and the best picture possible.

Bracketing

Shooting with slide film can be more limiting than negative film. When you shoot negs you can often compensate for exposure problems when you print. With slide film, what you see is what you get. One way to protect yourself against being stuck with just one poorly exposed shot of the scene of a lifetime is to bracket your exposures. Shoot the same scene at different exposures on both sides of the exposure reading given by your light meter. For example, if your light meter (TTL or handheld) gives you an exposure of f/8 and 1/125 sec, shoot one shot at that reading, one at f/4 and 1/125, and one at f/16 and 1/125. (You can also bracket in half-stop increments.) As an

Opposite page
Christina Faiella's close-up patriotic portrait was a winner in the Scholastic Art Awards.

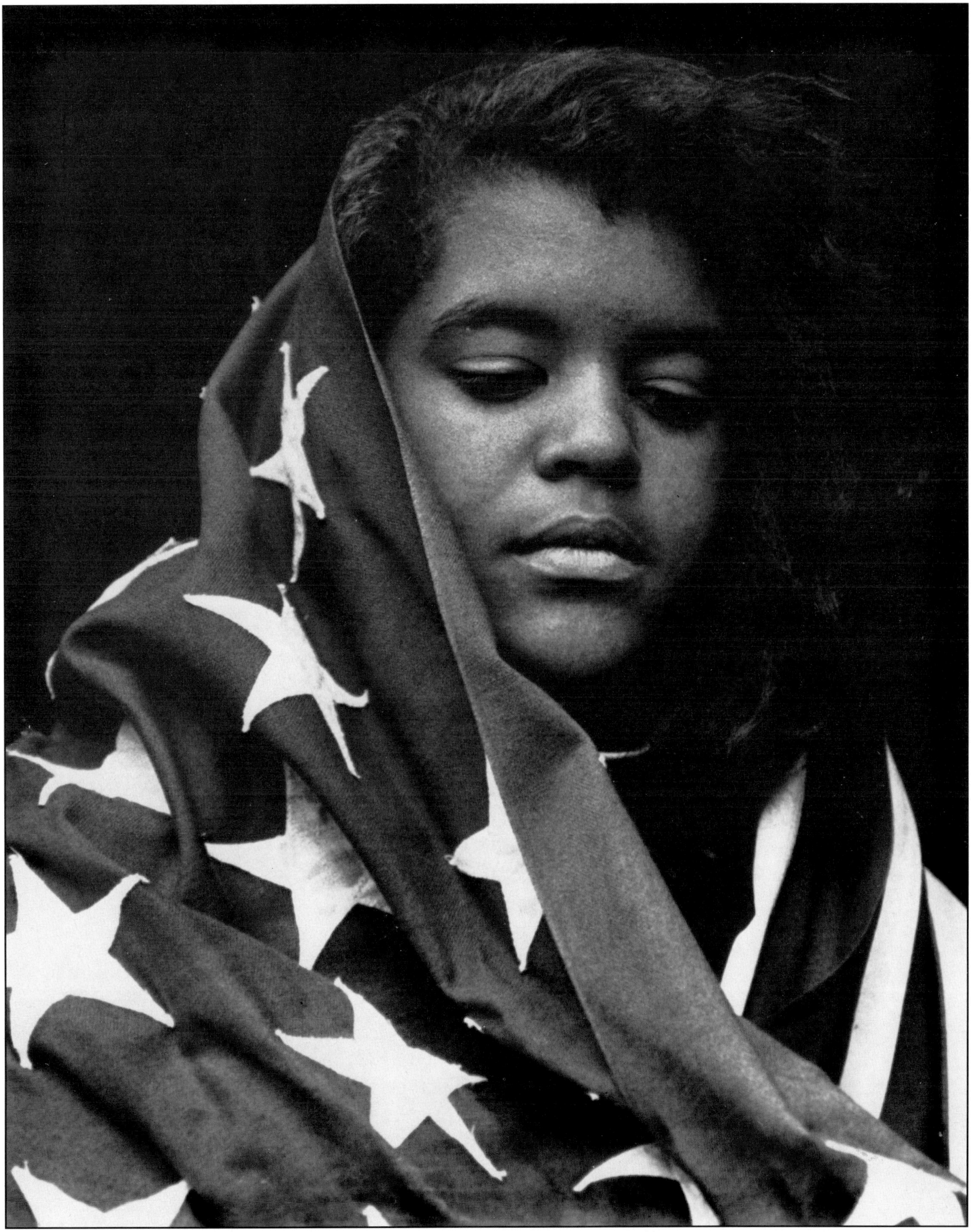

CHRISTINA FAIELLA/COURTESY OF SCHOLASTIC ART AWARDS

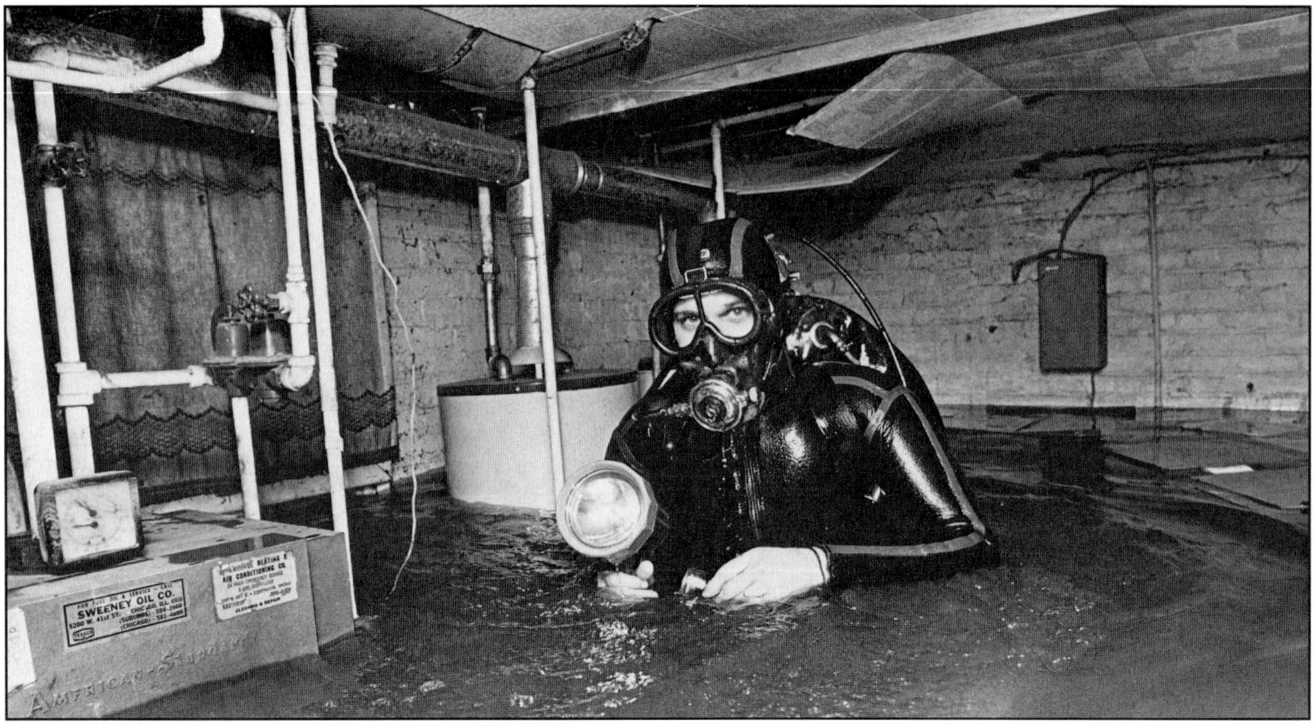

AL PODGORSKI/CHICAGO SUN-TIMES

1986 Chicago Photographer of the Year, Al Podgorski was on assignment for the *Chicago Sun-Times* when he photographed this frog man on flood detail.

alternative, you can keep your aperture fixed at f/8 and adjust the shutter speed by a one-stop increment on either side of the "correct" reading. Bracketing is especially valuable if you're shooting a sunset. Underexposing or overexposing the image slightly can give you dramatic results that may surpass the actual scene.

Don't be afraid to experiment with new equipment, filters, films, or techniques. Sometimes using something new can give you a spark of inspiration or let you look at a familiar subject or scene with fresh eyes. Break out of your routines, and try something new. You just may be surprised and gratified by the results. Some people might tell you to stick to your strong point—the subject or technique that is your specialty. I disagree. A new subject, or technique, could free you to look at things differently.

Remember, photography has the power to record, inform, influence, and entertain. Take advantage of that strength. The strongest picture is probably going to be one that elicits a response—be it positive or negative. A picture that makes people react is one that exemplifies the best of photography.

Whether you come away from the contest experience a happy winner, or a slightly discouraged also-ran, keep on shooting. Get out your camera, load a fresh roll of film, and get out there and start snapping. Maybe there's a prize-winning picture on your next roll of film.

15

INTERVIEWS

Ron Olshwanger/Pulitzer Prize Winner

You might think that only the top news photographers have a chance of winning the prestigious Pulitzer Prize. In reality, at least three amateurs have received the coveted Pulitzer, one of the most well-known and highly regarded of all awards. Endowed by the will of Joseph Pulitzer and administered under the trusteeship of Columbia University, each year the Pulitzer Prize awards two photography prizes of $3,000 each for spot news and feature photography. The competition is open to all photographers; the only requirement is that the photo must have been published in a U.S. daily, weekly, or Sunday newspaper. (Generally the paper in which the photo appeared enters it in the contest.)

The latest lucky amateur was Ron Olshwanger of Creve Coeur, MO, who copped the 1989 spot-news reporting prize for his heart-wrenching shot of a firefighter vainly trying to resuscitate a little girl. Olshwanger, who is a long-time shooter of firefighters and their work, has had a few of his pictures printed in *Firehouse* magazine, but this was his first large-scale success.

On December 30, 1988, Olshwanger, a furniture-company executive was (as usual) at the scene of a fire with his camera in hand. A photographer from the *St. Louis Post-Dispatch,* who had arrived at the scene too late to capture any of the action, noticed him shooting and told him to call if he got any good results. As soon as he saw his film, Olshwanger knew he had a powerful shot, so he called the *Post-Dispatch* photographer and sent in the picture which was subsequently published.

However, Olshwanger had no idea how good his image really was. When the *Post-Dispatch* called and asked for his permission to enter the shot in the Pulitzer competition, "I almost fell on the floor," he says. "And when they called me a few months later to tell me I'd won, I thought someone was playing a joke," he remembers. "It was a total shock. Some guy in the furniture business winning the Pulitzer is ridiculous."

Olshwanger values the publicity his shot has received— but not for what it has meant to him. He's more concerned with the impact it has on others. "It's a tragic picture," he says, "but it's a picture that has saved lives." He has received calls from people all over the country who said that the photo inspired them to buy smoke alarms which later saved their lives.

Olshwanger himself is an inspiration to any amateur who has ever hesitated about entering a contest. "Anybody with a camera can achieve an honor like the Pulitzer," he states. "It's not just for professionals."

Al Borman/Olympus *VisionAge* International Color Slide Photo Contest Winner

Al Borman, of Bothell, Washington had never entered a photo contest when he submitted his shot of the Olympic Choir at the 1988 Winter Games to the Third Olympus *VisionAge* International Color Slide Photo Contest. Luckily he didn't let his lack of contest experience stop him from entering: Borman was the Grand Prix winner.

Borman describes his prize-winning shot as "just a chance thing. As the choir was coming into the stadium, I came down the stairs, looked over the railing at the sea of color and faces and said `wow'", he explains. "I knew I had something really special when I got the slide back," he continues. "My first thought was `I've got to be able to do something with this.'" Borman entered a total of six slides in the competition, but after he entered, he realized that his only chance was with the Olympic choir shot. Like most prizewinners, he was surprised when he found out he'd won: "It was pretty shocking when I got the letter," he recalls.

Considering the odds, it's understandable why Borman was shocked to find himself a winner. His colorful and graphic shot was chosen out of 13,152 entries from 59 countries around the world by a panel of judges that included *Popular Photography* Editor-at-Large Arthur Goldsmith and Magnum Photo member Erich Hartmann. As Grand Prix winner, he received $2,000, an Olympus OM4T, two Zuiko lenses (a 100mm f/2 and a 50mm macro), and a 280 flash unit. More importantly, he retained the copyright to his image. "I wouldn't have entered the contest if I hadn't retained the copyright," he states. As a matter of fact, it was a combination of the copyright factor and the

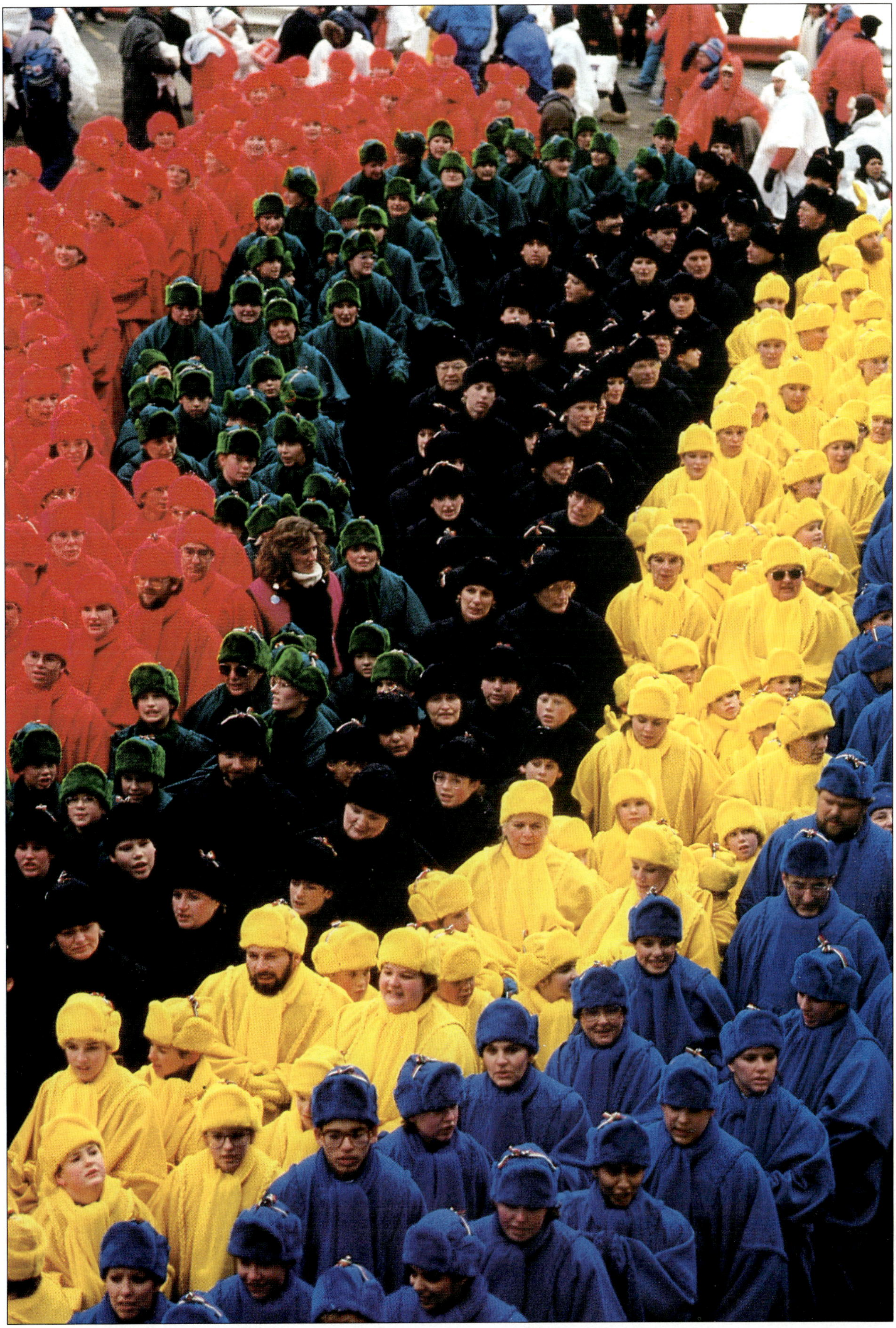

AL BORMAN

Al Borman of Bothell, WA received $2,000, an Olympus OM-4T camera, two lenses, and a flash unit as Grand Prix winner of the 1988 Olympus *VisionAge* International Photo Contest.

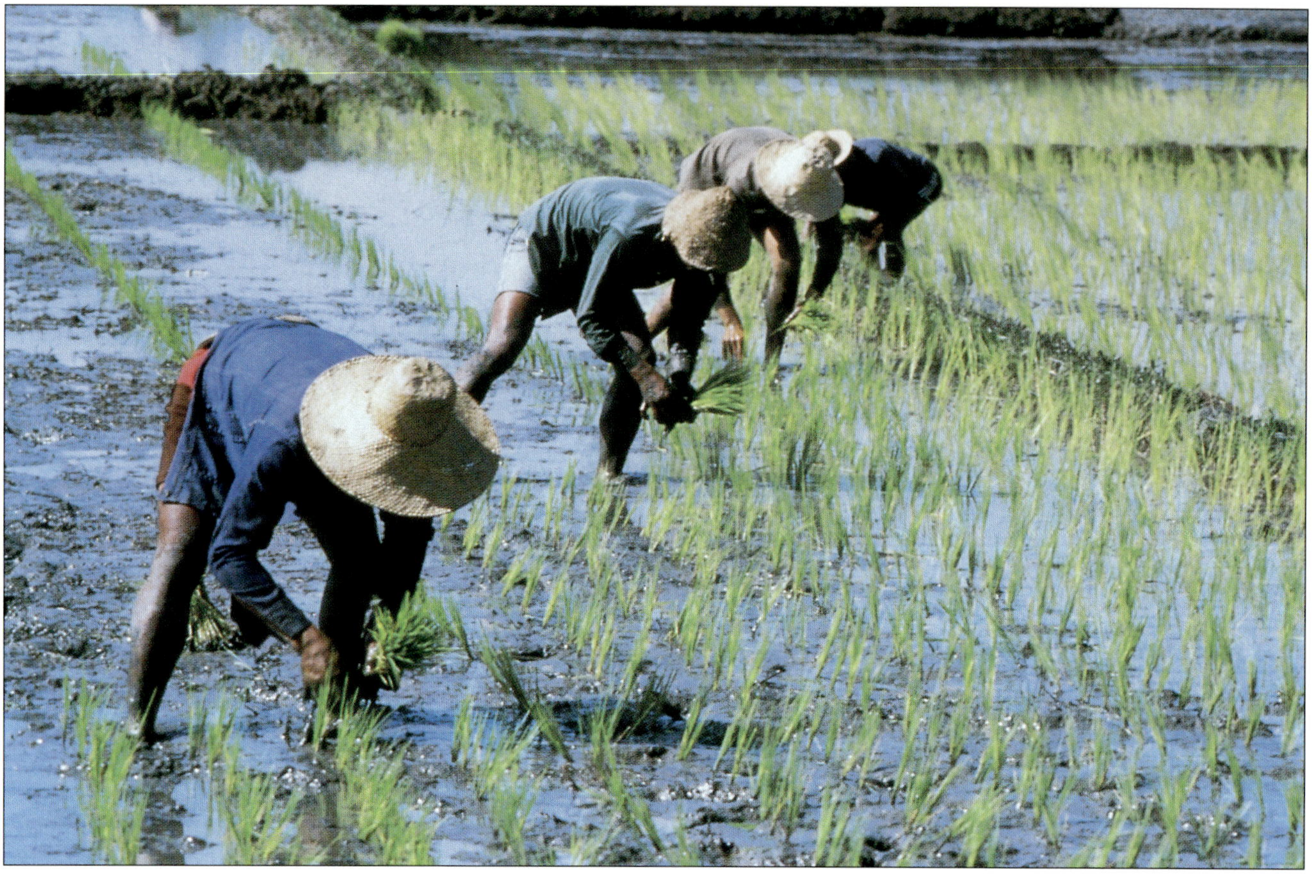
WILLIAM T. ROLEN, JR.

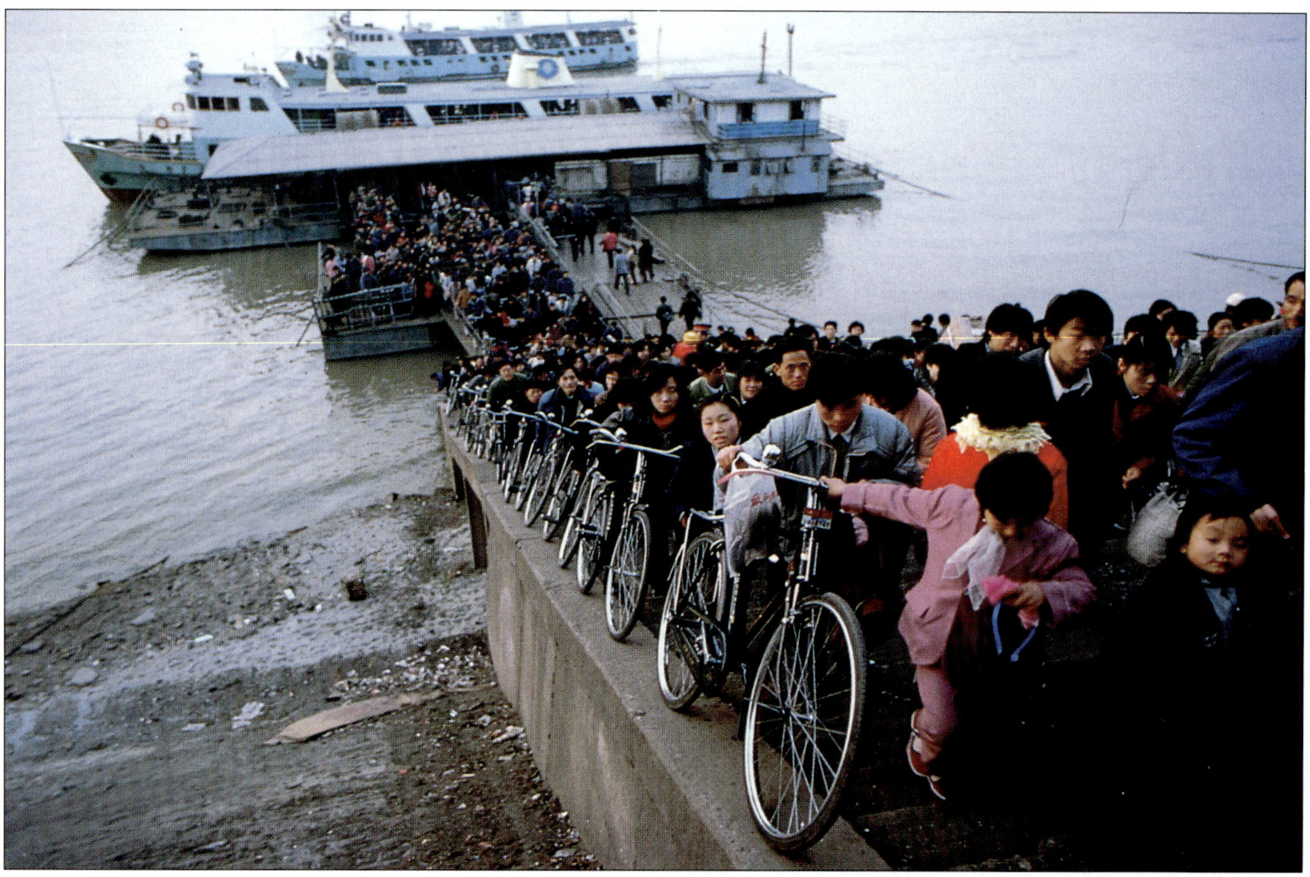
DAVID H. WELLS

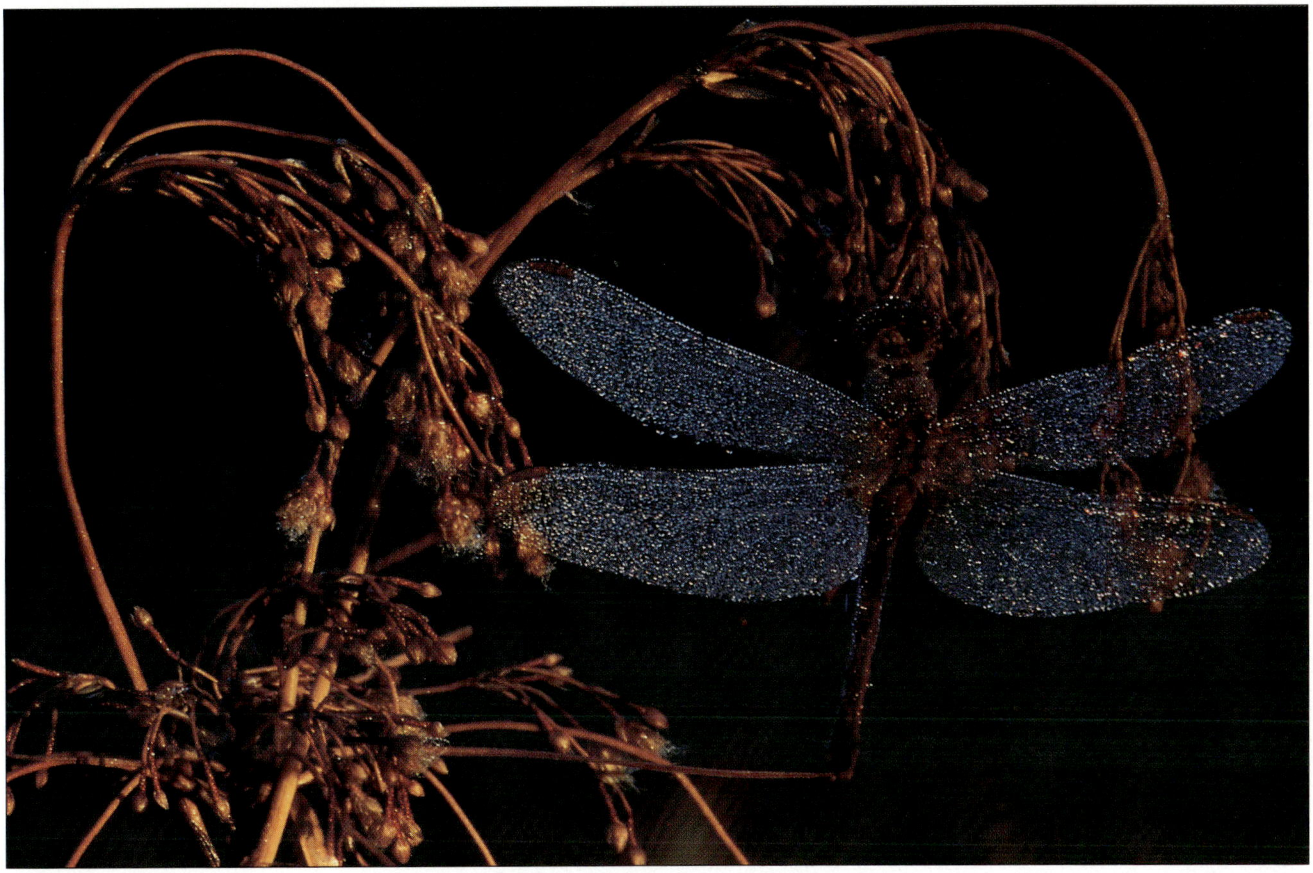

DON JOHNSTON

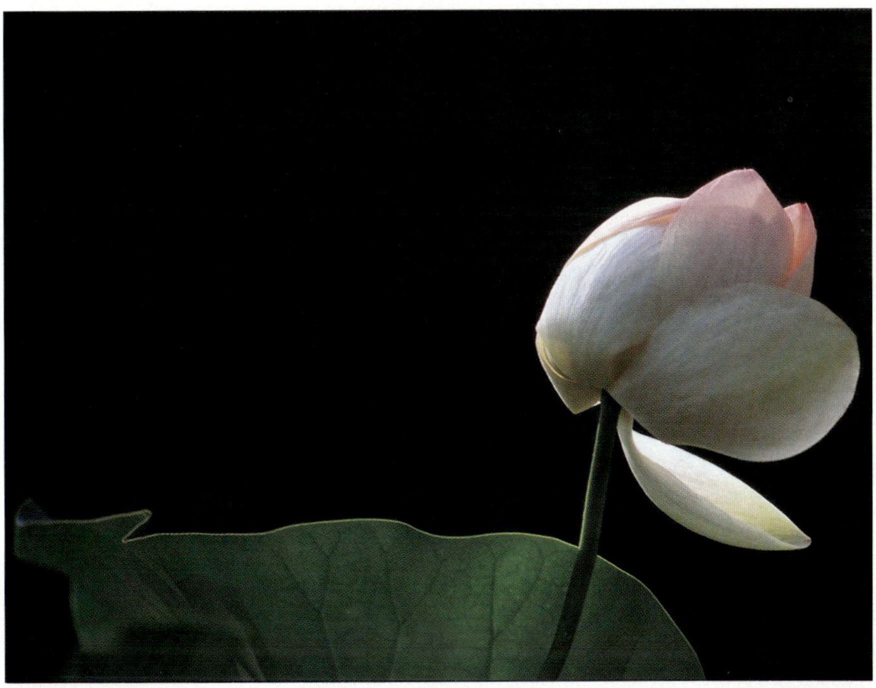

BAHMAN FARZAD

Above
Don Johnston's image of a dragonfly poised in golden light won first place in the Color Wildlife Category in *Sierra's* 10th Annual Photo Contest.

Left
Bahman Farzad's rim-lit lotus blossom won $300 and first place in the first running of ***Popular Photography's*** Your Best Shot contest.

Opposite page, top
As November, 1989 winner in the IFPO International Monthly Photo Contest, William T. Rolen, Jr. is eligible to be a $300 grand-prize winner.

Opposite page, bottom
David H. Wells' shot of ferry traffic in Wuhan, China received an Honorable Mention in the 1987/1988 Nikon Photo Contest International (NPCI).

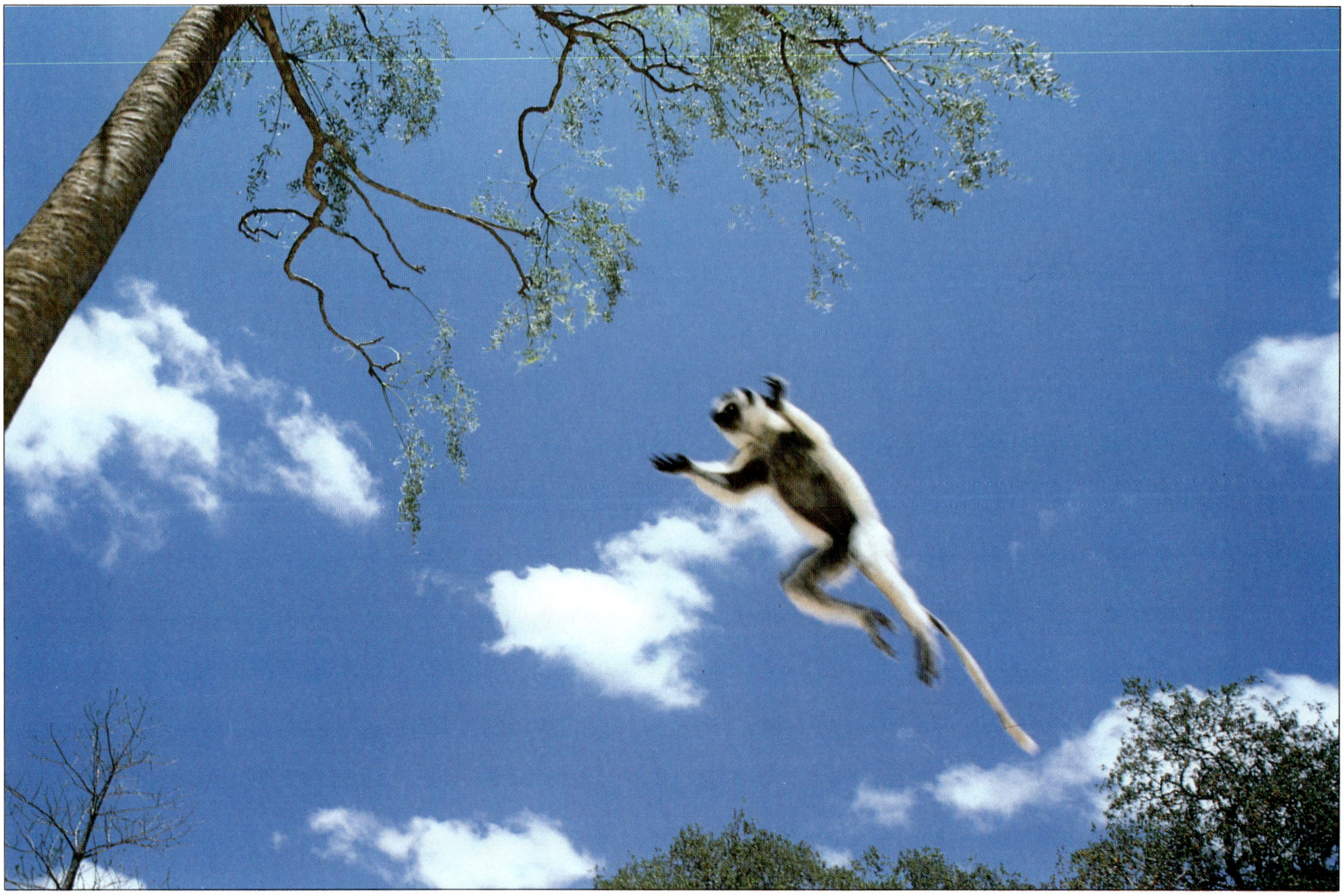

FRANS LANTING/MINDEN PICTURES

Above
A flying lemur in mid-leap won Frans Lanting third prize in the Nature category of the 1989 World Press Photo Contest.

Right
Chuck Zovko's "Sizzling Summer Shades" won third place for Newspaper Fashion Illustration in the 44th Pictures of the Year competition.

Opposite page
First prize ($300) in *Popular Photography's* November, 1988 Your Best Shot contest went to David C. Wendt of Cincinnati, OH for his shot of a solitary swan enjoying an early morning paddle.

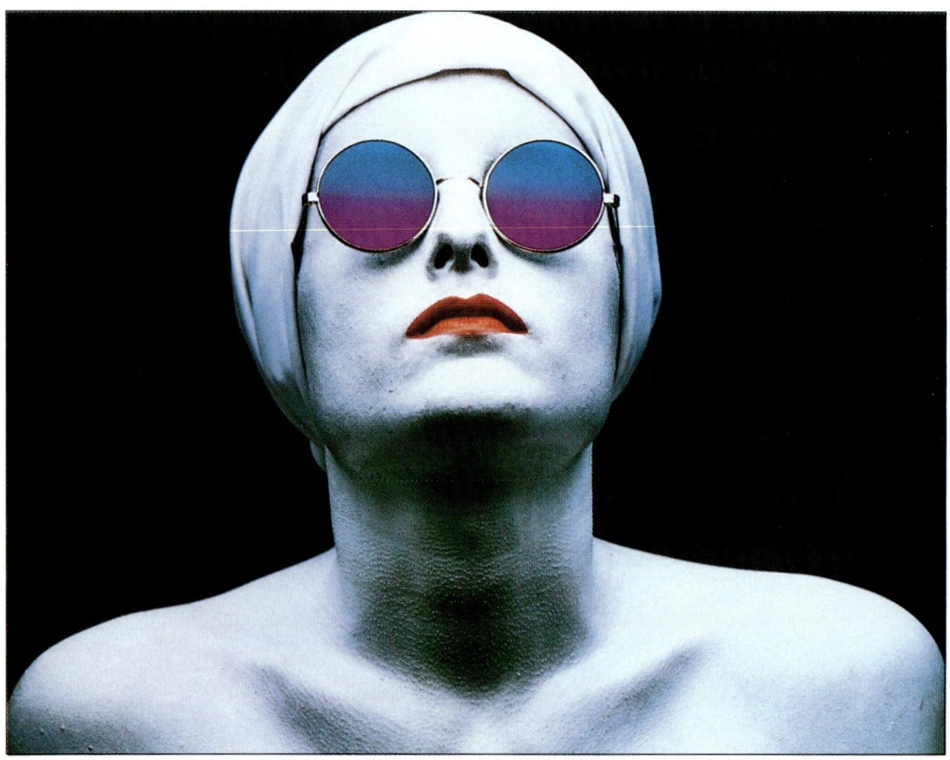

CHUCK ZOVKO

DAVID C. WENDT

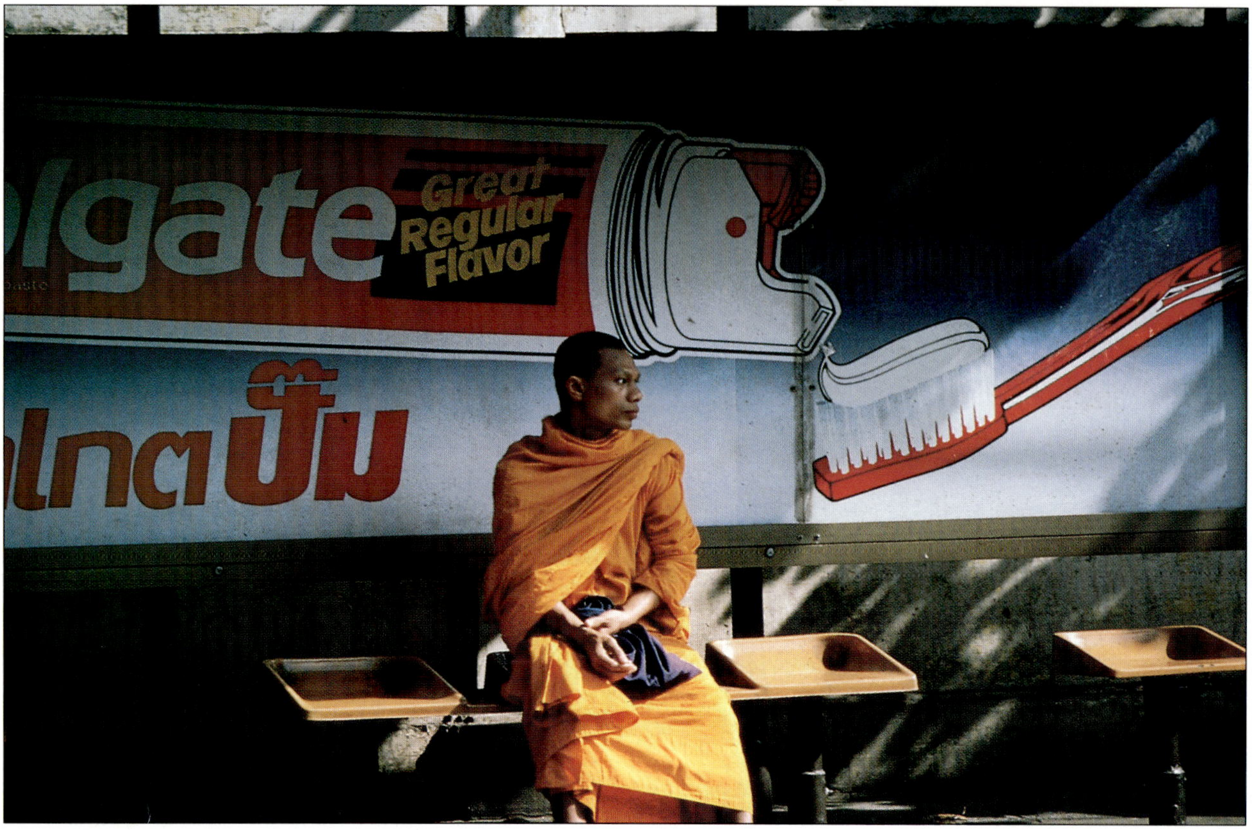

BRUCE STROMBERG

Cultural clash as photographed by Bruce Stromberg of Philadelphia, won first prize in *Popular Photography's* Your Best Shot contest.

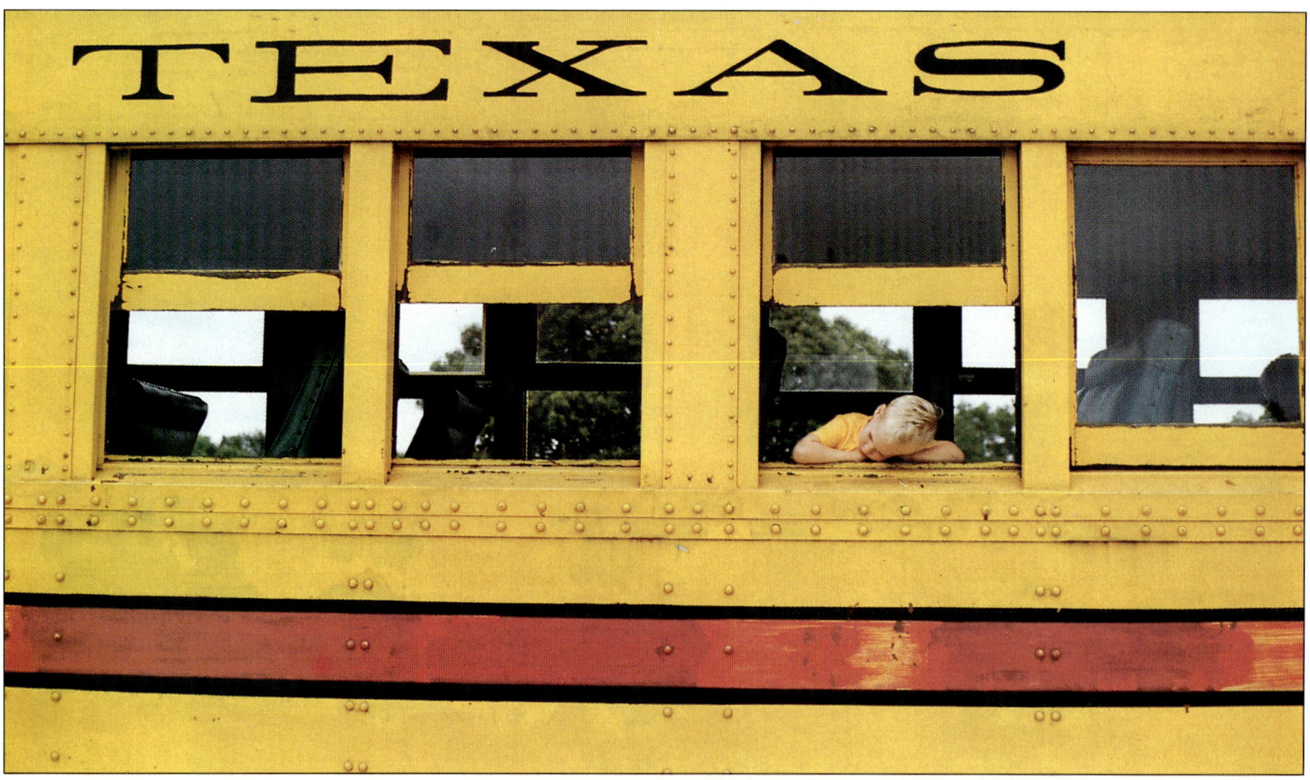

JIM BURKS

As one of the winners of the *Parade* magazine and Fuji Films "We the People" contest, Jim Burks of Granbury, TX had his shot of his son become part of a permanent exhibit honoring the bicentennial of the Constitution.

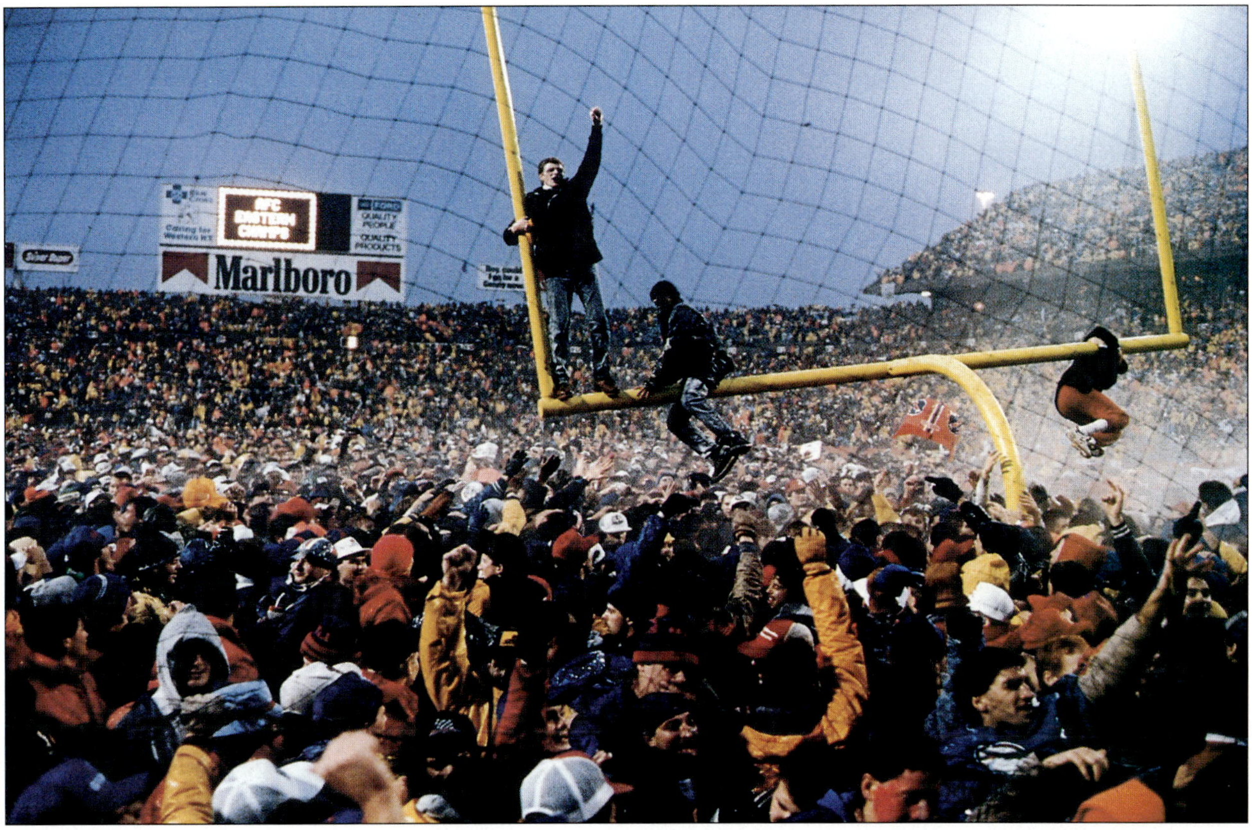

JOE TRAVER

"Fandemonium", Joe Traver's shot of the aftermath of the Buffalo Bills clinching the AFC East title, was the 1988 Pro Football Hall of Fame Contest's photograph of the year. Traver, who was on assignment for the *New York Times,* won $1,000 in the contest.

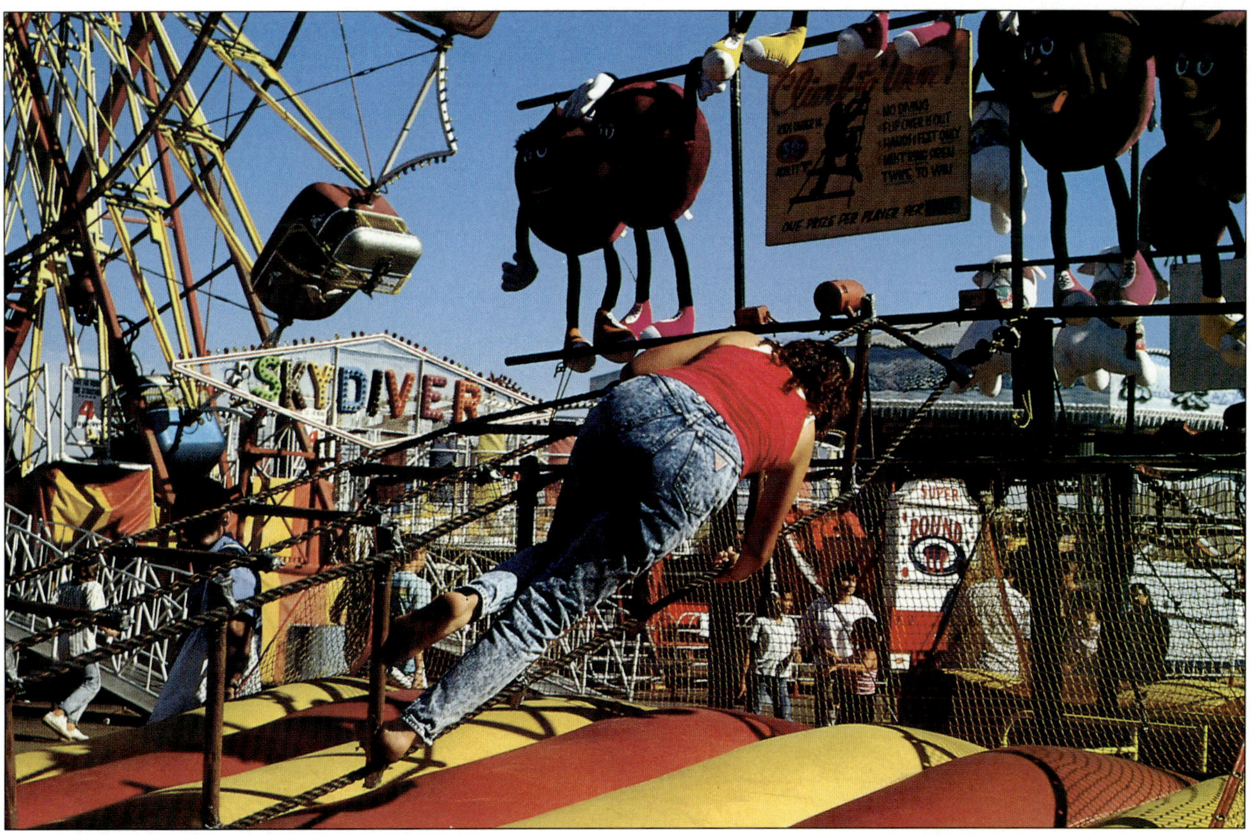

CLIFFORD C.Y. KWONG © 1989

Bright primary colors and a jumbled perspective won Clifford C.Y. Kwong of Sacramento $500 and first place in the September 1989 Your Best Shot contest sponsored by *Popular Photography.*

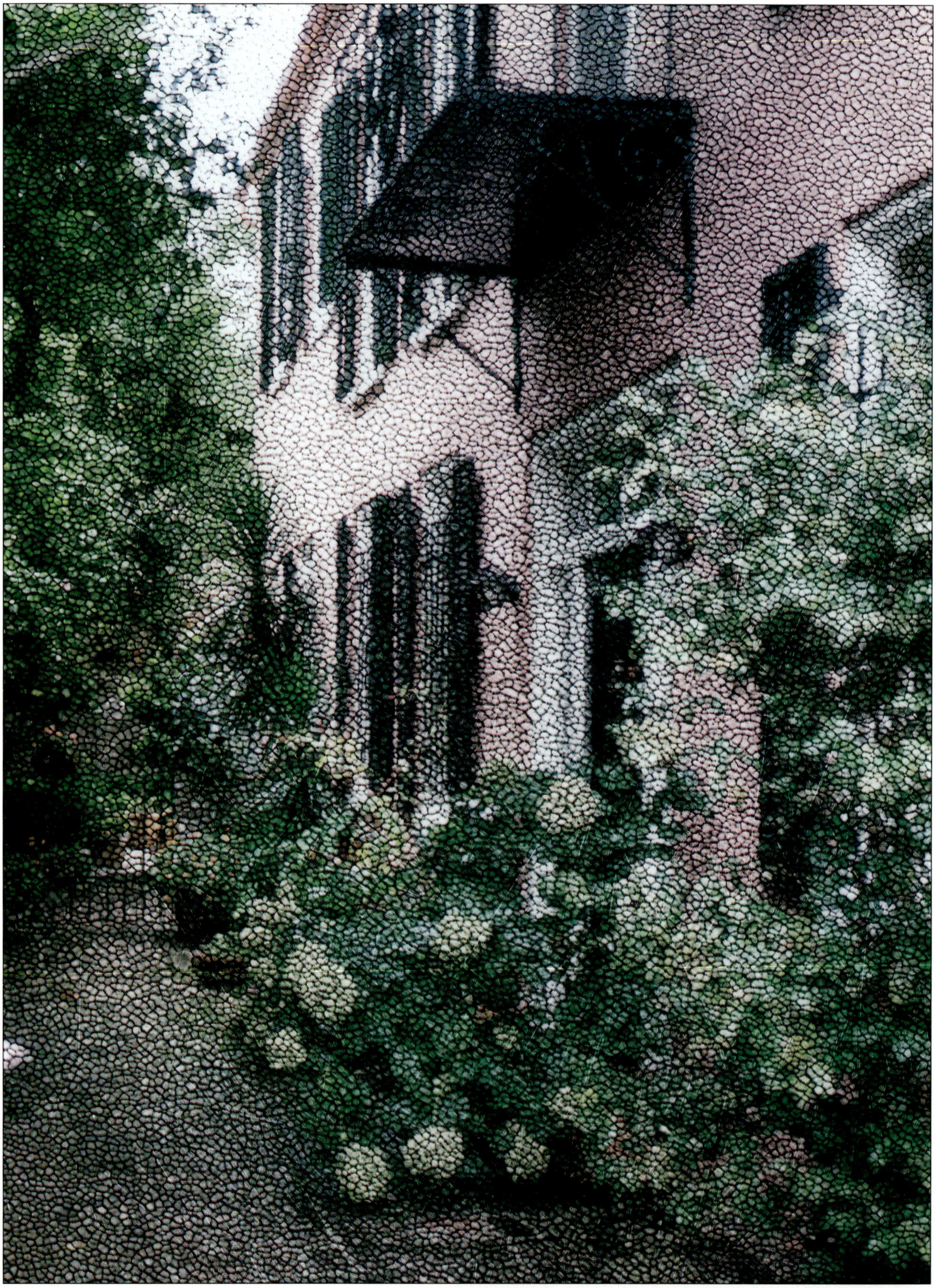

DOUGLAS DEN UYL

Douglas Den Uyl of Louisville, KY used a point-and-shoot camera for his second-prize winning image in *Popular Photography's* February, 1989 Your Best Shot contest.

prizes that led Borman to choose the *VisionAge* competition for his contest debut.

Are there any contest plans in Borman's future? "I'm not actively pursuing it," he says, "But if I think I have a shot that's worthy..."

John Isaac/United Nations Photographer

Winning a photo contest literally changed John Isaac's life. In the mid '70s, Isaac, a clerk at the United Nations, received a 35mm SLR as a Christmas gift from his brother. After spending a year learning how to use the camera, Isaac was confident enough to enter "The Hand of Man," a photo contest the UN sponsors for its employees. Not only did Isaac, a native of India, win first place for his photo of an Indian family, he also won a transfer to the photography department.

While he served an apprenticeship at the UN photo labs, Isaac continued to enter and win contests. (His second-place showing in Minolta's competition in 1975 is the most memorable win for Isaac.) Then in 1978 he was sent to Lebanon on his first overseas photographic assignment. He's been on the road almost constantly ever since, traveling to such far-flung locales as Ethiopia, Chad, China, India (naturally), and Iran to shoot injustice, uprisings, and other difficult situations (and their victims), all with humanity and grace.

For someone who maintains a relatively low profile, Isaac and his photos have received a fair amount of publicity. His work has appeared in *Popular Photography*, he's been profiled in *American Photographer* and he's featured in the 1990 *Minolta Mirror*. Isaac is also no stranger to TV: World Monitor recently devoted a segment to him.

Isaac credits photo contests with a large part of his success. Winning first prize at Photokina in 1978 helped cement his professional relationship with Minolta. He's also made a strong showing in the Nikon Photo Contest International winning six prizes since 1979—with Minolta equipment, no less! (Isaac is living proof that you can do well in a Nikon-sponsored contest with rival equipment.) Isaac feels that his photo contest wins have helped his credibility with magazines as well. "If you can say you have awards, it helps," he says. But for Isaac, perhaps the greatest satisfaction of winning contests is a personal one: "It's great to submit your best work, and win!"

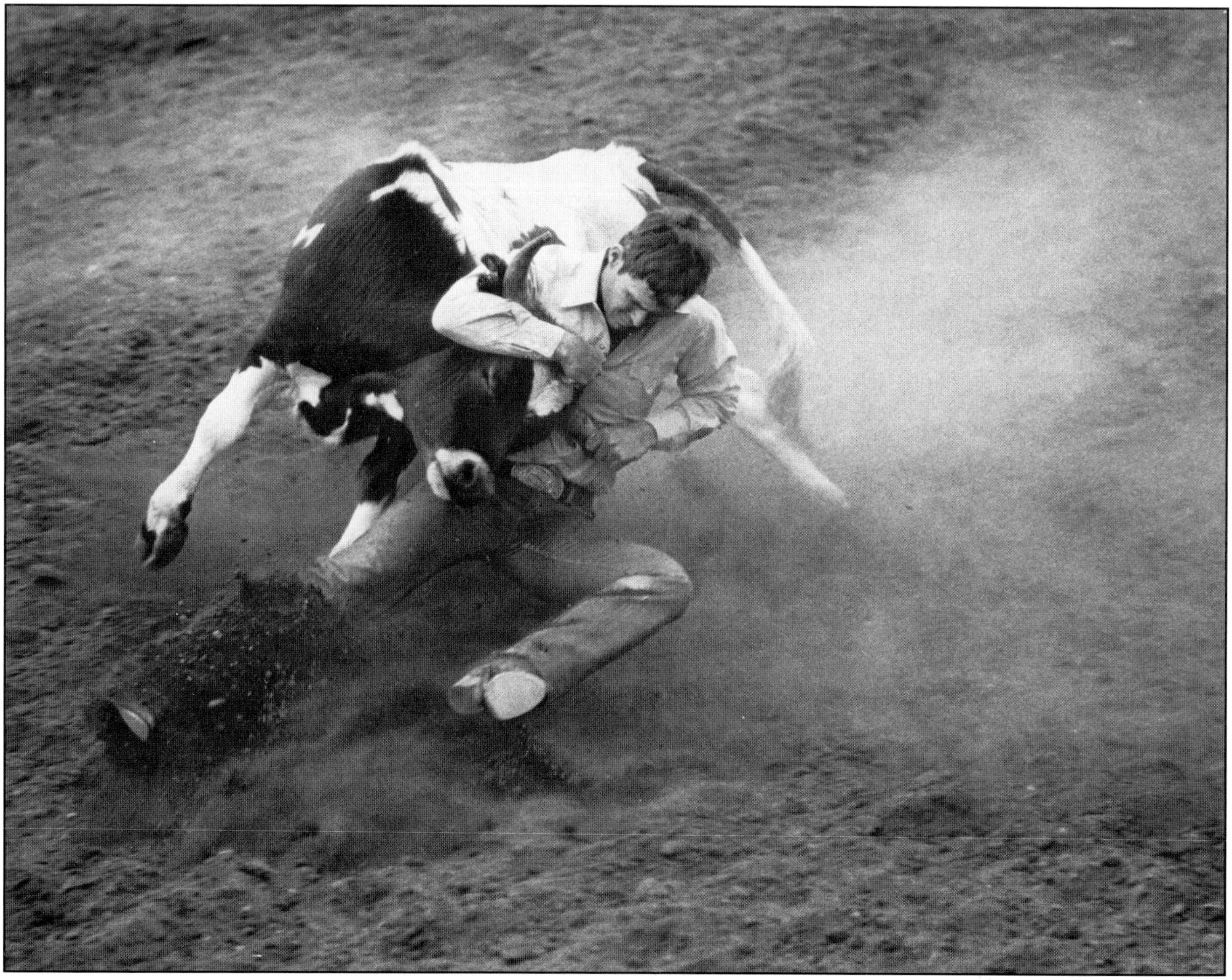

WILLIAM R. SALLAZ

"Power Struggle", William R. Sallaz's shot of rodeo action won an honorable mention in the 1987-1988 Nikon Photo Contest International.

Art Goldsmith/Judge

Art Goldsmith has enjoyed a long and fruitful association with the photo-contest world. As the Executive Editor and later Editorial Director of *Popular Photography* he was actively involved with its prestigious photo contest. He's been a judge for the Olympus Vision-Age photo contest for the past few years, and he recently helped *National Geographic Traveler* magazine launch its new photo contest (which he later judged). Goldsmith has also had a hand in contests sponsored by Maxwell House Coffee, the Famous Photographer's School (he was President and Director from '61 to '72), and various calendar and greeting card companies.

As a judge, Goldsmith looks for originality, freshness, and strong pictures in tune with what the contest is all about. "All contests are different," says Goldsmith. "You have to know the purpose of the contest, because the criteria will vary according to the theme." Sometimes, for example, human interest is the most important factor to the judges, while other contests place more value on the aesthetic quality of the entries.

If you're entering an annual contest, see what won first prize last year, Goldsmith suggests. But by all means, don't then send in your version of last year's prize-winner. "No one wants to see the same thing," he says. Instead, get a feeling for the spirit of the contest and then go out and shoot your take of what you think the judges are looking for. As you work, stick to the theme and shoot as if you were on assignment for a publication. Then send in your best work, once again making sure that it follows the theme.

According to Goldsmith, reading the competition rules is one of the most important things a contestant can do. "Make sure you're doing it right and then send in the very best work you have," he says. Other tips: Pay special attention to the deadline. Never send in work late. And if at all possible, try to get your material in well before the last-minute rush—that's when mistakes are going to happen if they do.

While entering contests can be a delightful experience, Goldsmith cautions entrants to stay away from contests that don't allow the photographers to retain full rights to their pictures. Sponsors have the right to limited usage, he explains, but they shouldn't take over the copyright of an image. "Any reputable contest will spell out carefully

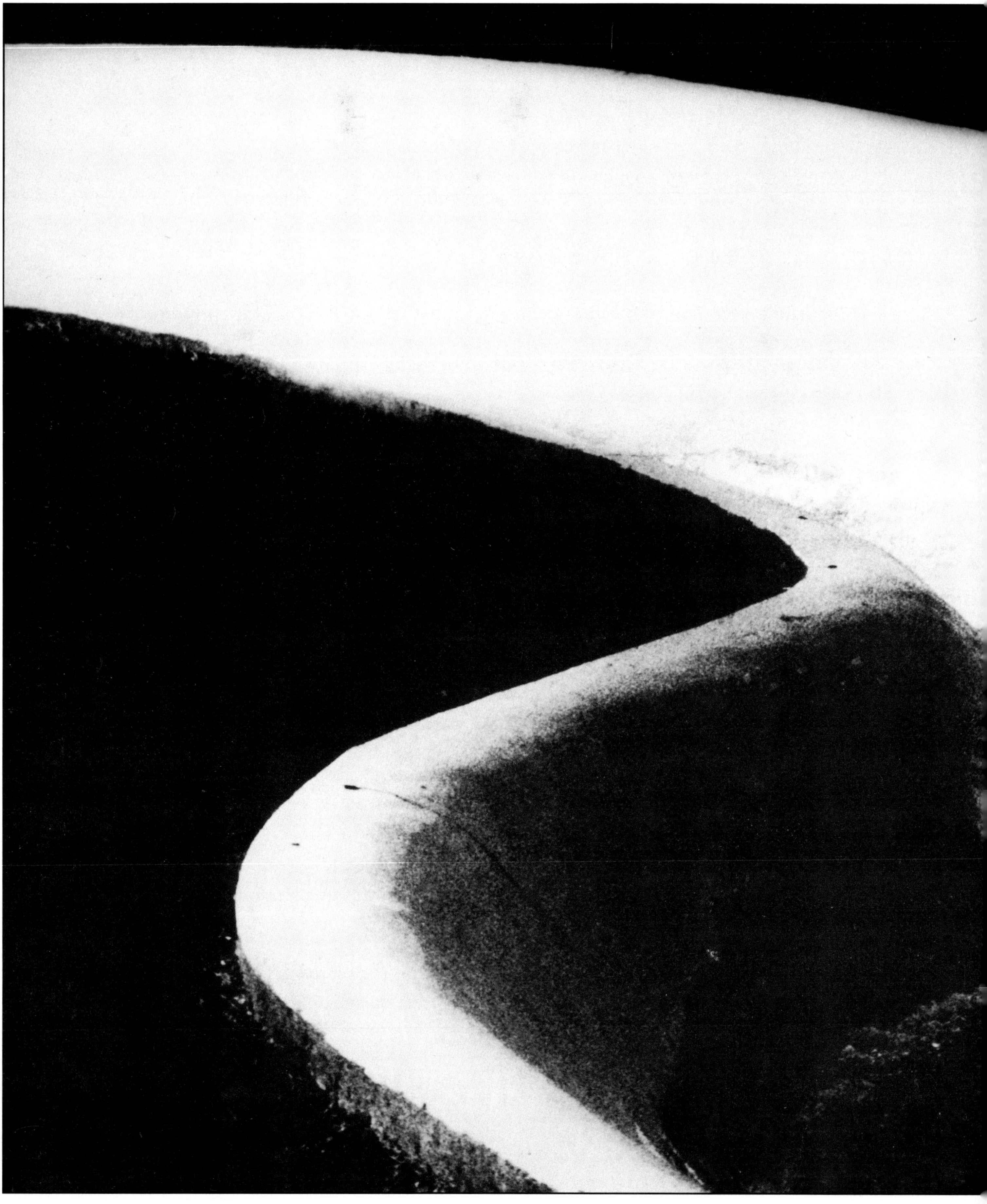

A swooping curve of light and action made Laura Elliott's photo one of the 1984 Pictures of the Year.

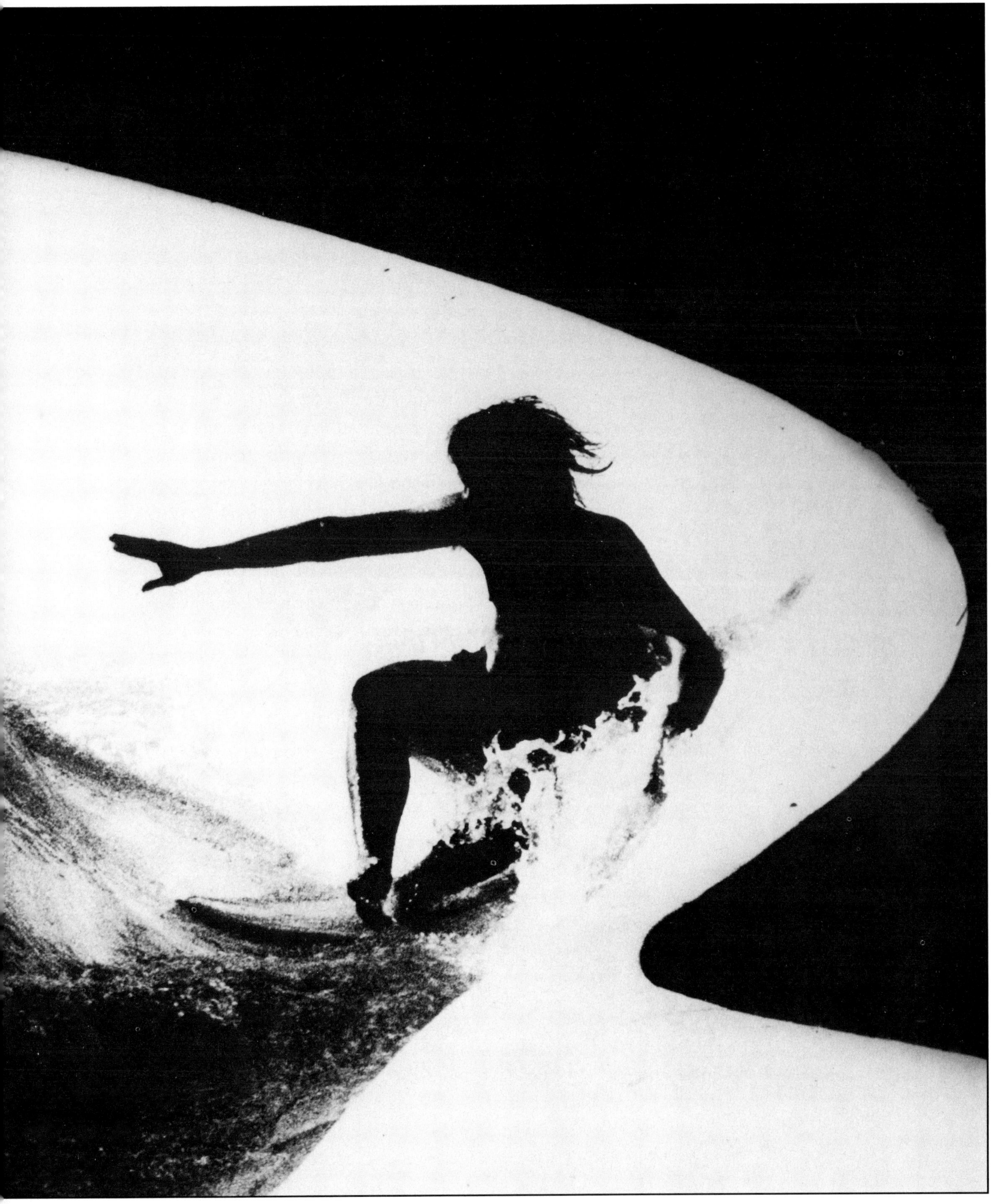

LAURA ELLIOTT

what kinds of rights they want," he says. "Avoid those other competitions like the plague."

Rich Clarkson/Judge

When you ask Rich Clarkson how many photo contests he's judged, he responds, "It seems like a million." Ask him for specific names and he counters with, "you name it, I've judged it."

While there may be some exaggeration to these statements, Clarkson is closer to fact than fiction in his estimates. His stints as President of the National Press Photographers' Association, Director of Photography at the *Topeka Capitol-Journal*, and Director of Photography at the National Geographic Society (not to mention his work as a photographer for *Sports Illustrated* and *Life*) have given Clarkson the chance to be an influential and involved citizen of the photo-competition world.

When Clarkson was at the *Topeka Capitol-Journal*, photographers under his direction had great success in competitions. Chris Johns was named Newspaper Photographer of the Year in the 1978 Pictures of the Year competition; and Brian Lanker won a Pulitzer for his photo essay on natural childbirth.

Clarkson is the first to admit that it's difficult to give blanket advice on how to win photo contests. There are just too many variables and too many different types of competitions to consider. However, he does have some general tips that apply to any contest you might enter.

Be yourself. In Clarkson's opinion, the kinds of pictures that ought to be winning contests are those that show originality. Yes there's been a tendency in the past for annual contests to pick the same kinds of pictures year after year, but he thinks there's a trend away from that. "Originality and uniqueness are being rewarded," he says.

Know yourself – and the competition. Clarkson doesn't think neophyte contestants should make a distinction between large and small contests. "If you have work that you think has a chance of winning, enter it any contest regardless of size," he advises. Skill level is much more important than the size of the field. Clarkson suggests that entrants look at work that has won other contests. If a competition

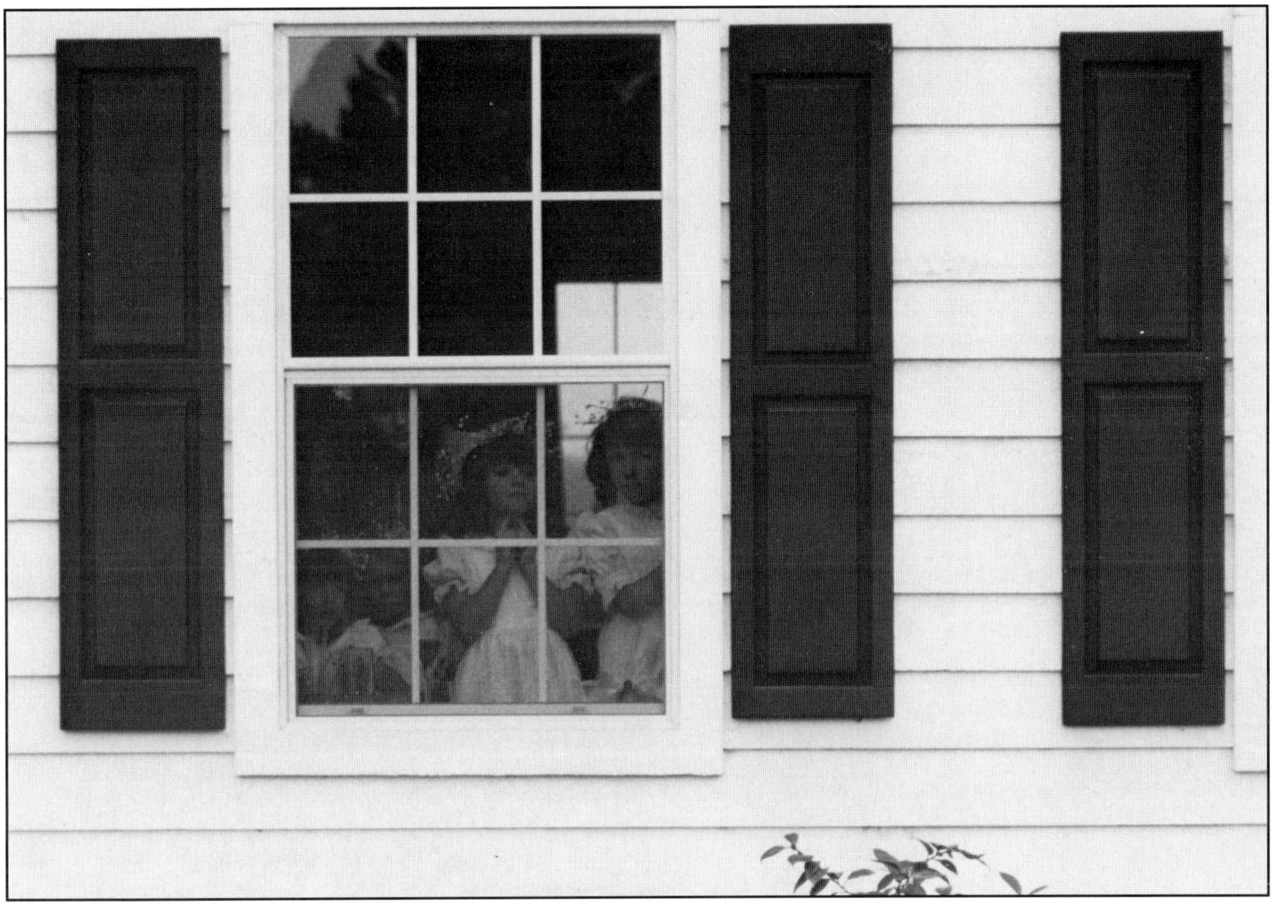

MARYBETH ADKINS/NATURALIGHT PHOTOGRAPHY, SAN RAFAEL, CA

publishes an annual, look at work that has been rewarded and see if you're working at the same level.

Pick your pictures carefully. When Clarkson judges a contest, he starts out by looking for high technical quality. Originality is next on his list, followed by any number of criteria depending on what type of contest it is. "If you're judging a sports competition, you look at the significance of the print in terms of the event," he explains. "If you're judging portraits, you're going to be looking for something different," he continues. "And while uniqueness and style and originality won't play out very well in spot-news pictures, they are important in a picture essay," he concludes.

There you have it. Follow Clarkson's straightforward advice and maybe someday he'll be awarding prizes to your pictures.

Above
The 1989 International Wedding Photography Awards gave Marybeth Adkins of San Rafael, CA first place in the candid category for her pre-wedding shot.

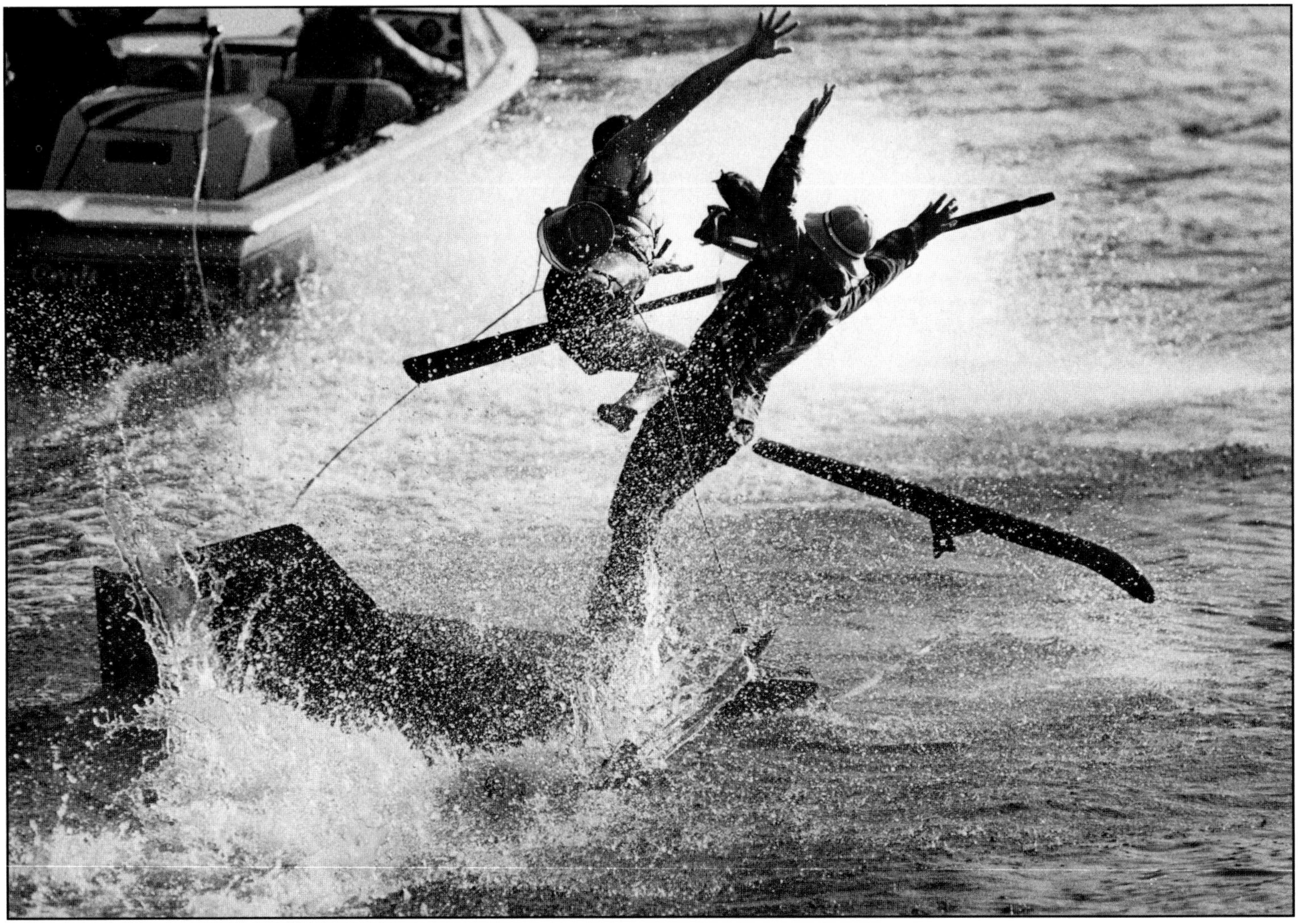

JAMES P. MCCOY

James P. McCoy, freelance photographer from Grand Island, N.Y. captured peak action in the form of a watery collision. His shot was one of the 1986 Pictures of the Year.

16 PHOTO CONTEST **LISTINGS**

ALTERNATIVES
Sponsored by Ohio University School of Art
PO Box 775
Athens, OH 45701
(614) 593-4288
Contact: Arnold Tunstall
An annual national juried show open to all artists. Exhibits the best of experimental photographic imagery. Past jurors have included Duane Michals and Robert Heinecken. Exhibitors have included Joel-Peter Witkin, Arthur Tress, Gloria DeFillips-Brush, and other nationally acclaimed artists.
Eligibility: Open to amateurs and pros.
Subject Matter: All contemporary artwork containing photographic imagery. Emphasis on alternative processes or ideals.
Submission Requirements: Send unlimited number of color and/or B&W transparencies for initial jurying. Exhibitors will then submit prints. Only size limit is gallery size.
Entry Fee: $18 for first 3 slides: $5 for each additional slide.
Awards: Purchase award and jurors awards of merit. Sponsor reserves reproduction and publication rights.
Entries are returned.
Write during October to be placed on mailing list.

THE *AMERICAN PHOTO* PICTURE CONTEST
Sponsored by *American Photo* Magazine
1633 Broadway
New York, NY 10019
(212) 767-6000
"This is your chance to get that great but unseen shot seen by all the right people." *American Photo* is sponsoring what it calls "the biggest reader's photography contest of its kind." The winning work will be published in a special issue of the magazine and hung in an exhibition in New York City.
Eligibility: Open to all readers of *American Photo.*
Subject Matter: Six categories: Still Life; Sports/Adventure; Photojournalism; Humor; Landscape/Nature; Glamour.
Submission Requirements: Enter as many categories as you like, but use a separate envelope for each category. Send color slides, color prints, or B&W prints to Contest (specify category), *American Photo,* 1633 Broadway, NY, NY 10019. Be sure to put your name and address on each slide or print. 1990 deadline is September 30, 1990.
Entry Fee: None.
Awards: Editors of *American Photo* will judge the photos to be published in the magazine and choose a winner in each category, as well as an overall winner. Winning submissions will be published in a special issue of the magazine and will be exhibited in New York City.
Entries will not be returned.
See *American Photo* for information.

AMERICAN PHOTOGRAPHY
Sponsored by American Photography, Inc.
49 East 21st St.
New York, NY 10010
(212) 979-4500
Contact: Bonnie Claeys, Project Director
Ajudication of photographic images submitted by both professional and up-and-coming photographers in nine categories. Winning images are published in the *American Photography Annual.*
Eligibility: Open to amateurs and pros.
Subject Matter: Categories: editorial; advertising; posters; promotional material; books; unpublished work by professionals; unpublished work by students/amateurs; artists' photographs; TV/film/video.
Submission Requirements: Send an unlimited number of color and/or B&W prints/transparencies. Anything larger than 20x30" should be in transparency form.
Entry Fee: Varies according to work submitted.
Awards: Publication of accepted work in *Annual.*
All entries (except for tear sheets) are returned.
Write for information.

ANNUAL PRINT & SLIDE COMPETITION
Sponsored by the Maine Photographic Workshops
2 Central St.
Rockport, ME 04856
(201) 236-8581
Annual contest recognizes the work of 8 photographers each year with $2,400 in cash purchase awards.
Eligibility: Open to photographers everywhere.
Subject Matter: Personal statement; Social documentation; Portrait; Landscape; Architecture; Still-life.
Submission Requirements: Submit 15-25 unframed prints no larger than 24x30" or 40 duplicate color slides. Both color and B&W are accepted.
Entry Fee: $25 per entry, plus $5 per photograph.
Awards: $2,400 in cash purchase awards to eight photographers. First place winners each receive $300 in cash as purchase awards. Second and third place winners receive scholarships to summer workshops. Honorable mention recipients are awarded certificates. All winning photographs will be exhibited during the International Photography Congress in Rockport in August. Winners will also be honored at the awards presentation in New York City, and published in the Annual Awards Catalog.
Sponsor reserves the right to use winning work for public display, in ceremony announcements, catalogues, and other Workshop publications with regard to the Grant, Competition or Annual Presentation, without further permission or renumeration. Photographs published in other magazines will be by approval of the photographer. Each recipient agrees to credit The Workshops and Kodak for their support in the eventual publication and exhibition of completed projects.
Entries are returned.
Write for information/entry form.
NOTE: The Maine Photographic Workshops also sponsors the Golden Light Awards; The Photographic Book of the Year; The Career Achievement Awards; The Inservice To Photography Award; The Ernst Haas Award; The Photographer's Work Grants; and the Photographers' Support Grants. Write for information.

ART ANNUAL
Sponsored by The Howard County Arts Council/Rockland Arts Center
8510 High Ridge Rd.
Ellicott City, MD 21043
(301) 465-6700
Contact: Carla L. Dunlap
Annual juried competition which features photography every other year. Jurors have included Ned Rifkin of the Hirschorn and Helaine Posner of the National Museum of Women in the Arts.
Eligibility: Open to amateurs and pros.
Subject Matter: Open.
Submission Requirements: Send color and/or B&W prints. Submission limit varies yearly.
Entry Fee: Varies.
Awards: Best of show, juror's choice, honorable mention, etc.
Unaccepted entries are returned with SASE.
Call for prospectus.

ART DIRECTORS' CHOICE
Sponsored by Professional Photographers of America
Advertising/Commercial Group
1090 Executive Way
Des Plaines, IL 60018
The Art Director's Choice Awards recognize photography which makes a superior contribution to the effectiveness of printed communications.
Eligibility: Open to all photographers, graphic designers, art directors, or other creators of printed communications using photography.
Subject Matter: Advertising, printed marketing literature, annual reports, promotional material, self-promotion.
Submission Requirements: Send tear sheets or final printed products mounted to a 16x20" black Salon board. For entries that cannot be mounted (billboards, etc) send an 11x14" color photo of the finished piece mounted to a 16x20" board. An entry form and a description of the communications goal of the entry must be attached to each board. Model releases must be available.
Entry Fee: $40 for the first entry, $30 for the second, and $20 for subsequent entries. No submission limit.
Awards: One "Best of Show" award in each category will be awarded a distinctive trophy honoring the photographer. The contributing art director and client will each receive a certificate. "Awards of Excellence" certificates will also be awarded.
Sponsor reserves publication rights for all submitted entries. Publication rights are limited to this photo contest only.
Entries will not be returned.
Write for information/entry form.

ART ON THE GREEN
Sponsored by Citizens' Council for the Arts
P.O. Box 901
Couer d'Alene, ID 83814
(208) 667-9346
Contact: Kathy Flint, Secretary
Annual outdoor arts and crafts festival including national juried show for both flat and 3-dimensional pieces.
Eligibility: Open to amateurs and pros.
Subject Matter: Open.
Submission Requirements: Send up to two color and/or B&W prints no larger than 4 feet in any direction.
Entry Fee: $5.00 per entry.
Awards: $3,100 total plus purchase prizes.
Entries are returned.
Write for information/entry form.

ART SHOW AT THE DOG SHOW
Sponsored by Sunflower Cluster Kennel Clubs and Hill's Science Diet
11301 W. 37th North
Wichita, KS 67205
(316) 722-6181
Contact: Joe Miller
Annual juried fine arts contest for all media including photography. All entries must be for sale.
Eligibility: Open to amateurs and pros.
Subject Matter: Must include dog(s).
Submission Requirements: Send up to 3 color and/or B&W prints. No size limit.
Entry Fee: $20.
Awards: $6,000 in cash awards.
Sponsor reserves publicity and catalog publication rights.
Entries are returned.
Write or call for information/entry form.

BEST IN THE WEST CREATIVE COMPETITION
Sponsored by American Advertising Federation
251 Post St., Suite 302
San Francisco, CA 94108
(415) 421-6867
Contact: Janet Kennedy
Annual advertising and graphic design competition recognizing work created in the 13 Western states. "This is not a photography competition per se. But, the work of photographers, when in conjunction with advertising and design is eligible."
Eligibility: Amateur and pros from the 13 Western states may submit advertisements, brochures, catalogs, calendars, etc. in which their photographs have been used.
Subject Matter: See eligibility.
Entry Fee: $80-$90.
Awards: Best of Show, Best of Division, First, Second, and Merit Awards winners.
Entries are not returned.
Call or write to be placed on mailing list.

CMP ANNUAL PHOTOGRAPHER'S CHRISTMAS CARD EXHIBITION
Sponsored by the California Museum of Photography
University of California
Riverside, CA 92521
(714) 787-4787
Contact: Roy McJunkin
Submit photographic Christmas cards for December 1 to January 1 annual exhibit. All entries are exhibited.
Eligibility: Open to amateurs and pros.
Subject Matter: Photographic or photographically derived Christmas greetings—"the more offbeat and creative the better."
Submission Requirements: Anything goes: color, B&W, transparencies, prints; no size limits.
Entry Fee: None
Awards: Entrants receive a letter of thanks.
All entries are retained in CMP permanent collections.
CMP reserves the right to reproduce entries.
Write or call for information.

THE CAMERA BUG PHOTO CONTEST
Sponsored by The IPAC/Group
PO Box 843
Philadelphia, PA 19105
(215) 742-5515
Contact: Leonard or Nicholas Friedman
Contest seeks photographs which relate to the four seasons: Spring, Summer, Fall, Winter. "This is a special contest which will award photographers who have imagination and a sense of humor to capture what their eye sees within the camera."
Eligibility: Open to amateurs and pros.
Subject Matter: Open, but must related to month and/or season being entered. Example: pumpkins in the Fall (October).
Submission Requirements: Color and B&W ok; Prints

up to 8x10": all formats of transparencies (mounting is optional).
Entry Fee: $2.50 per photograph.
Awards: Camera Bug Medals and merchandise with a value of $75 for 1st prize; $50 for 2nd; $25 for 3rd; and $10 4th prize.
All rights remain with photographer.
Entries are returned with a SASE.
For entry and information, send SASE to 2106 Hoffnagle St., Philadelphia, PA 19152.

THE CENTER FOR PHOTOGRAPHY AT WOODSTOCK

59 Tinker St.
Woodstock, NY 12498
(914) 679-9957
The Center sponsors juried exhibitions and solo shows during the year.
Eligibility: Open to amateurs and pros.
Subject Matter: Varies.
Submission Requirements: Send transparencies of color and/or B&W prints for jurying. Prints of accepted works will be required.
Entry Fee: Varies.
Awards: Varies.
Entries are returned.
Call or write for information.

CHAUTAUQUA NATIONAL EXHIBITION OF AMERICAN ART

Sponsored by the Chautauqua Art Association Galleries
Wythe Ave.
Box 1365
Chautauqua, NY 14722
(716) 357-2771
Contact: Jeffrey Crist
Annual juried exhibition of different media, including photography.
Eligibility: Open to amateurs and pros.
Subject Matter: Open
Submission Requirements: Artists must submit a minimum of 3 color and/or B&W slides in one media category.
Entry Fee: $6 per slide.
Awards: Over $5,000 in cash and purchase prizes.
Sponsor reserves the right to photograph work for publicity purposes.
Entries are returned.
Write for information/entry form.

COLLEGE PHOTOGRAPHER OF THE YEAR COMPETITION

Sponsored by Kappa Alpha Mu, The National Press Photographers Foundation and the University of Missouri School of Journalism; with educational grants from Canon USA, Inc. and Eastman Kodak Company.
University of Missouri School of Journalism
9th and Elm Streets
Columbia, MO 65201
(314) 882-4442
Contact: Julie Ostrem, CPOY Coordinator
The College Photographer of the Year competition recognizes outstanding work of college and university students currently working toward a degree. The contest embraces diverse approaches to photojournalism and visual communication as well as providing a forum for student photographers to gauge their skills against those of their peers.
Eligibility: Open to enrolled undergraduate or graduate students. If you have worked three years or more as a full-time professional publications photographer (paid internships included) you are not eligible to enter this contest.
Subject Matter: 13 categories: Spot News; General News; Sports; Sports Feature; Feature; Portrait; Pictorial; Food Illustration; Fashion Illustration; Picture Story; Sports Portfolio; Documentary; Personal Vision.
Submission Requirements: Submit only 35mm duplicate slides, even if originals were B&W prints or color negatives. Portfolios must be entered in a Kodak Carousel 80 Transvue slide tray and a duplicate set must be in 8-1/2x11" polyethylene slide files. Individual categories must be submitted in 8-1/2x11" slide files. Write name, category number, picture title on slide mount. Give complete caption information. Identify your college affiliation. Winning entrants (1st, 2nd, and 3rd place) must supply unmounted 11x14" prints for the CPOY permanent collection and traveling exhibit. Failure to do so will lead to forfeiture of prize(s).
Entry Fee: None.
Awards: First Place Portfolio: A summer internship at National Geographic Society, an NPPF $1,000 award, a Canon camera and 100 rolls of Kodak film. The winner will receive an all-expense-paid trip to Columbia, MO to receive his/her award as a guest of Canon USA, Inc. and Eastman Kodak Company. Second Place Portfolio: A $500 award and 60 rolls of film. Third Place Portfolio: A personalized certificate of merit, $250 and 40 rolls of Kodak film. First place

CPOY

THE RULES

Undergraduate or graduate students enrolled in the academic year of Fall 1989-Spring 1990 may enter. **If you have worked three years or more as a full-time professional publications photographer (paid internships included,) you are not eligible to enter this contest.**

Pictures must have been taken or initially published from March 1, 1989 to February 28, 1990. However, photographs need not have been published.

There is no entry fee.

KAM cannot assume responsibility for loss or damage of entries.

For questions regarding eligibility, contact :

David Rees, CPOY Director
(314) 882-3635

For more entry forms write or call:

Julie Ostrem, CPOY Coordinator
University of Missouri
School of Journalism
Ninth and Elm Streets
Columbia, MO 65201
(314) 882-4442

EXHIBIT & SLIDE SHOW

Winning entrants (1st, 2nd & 3rd place) must supply unmounted 11" X 14" prints for the CPOY permanent collection and traveling exhibit. Failures to do so will lead to forfeiture of the prize(s.)

DEADLINE

All entries must be sent prepaid and be received by contest officials in Columbia, MO, no later than March 28, 1990.

PORTFOLIO

A portfolio may contain no more than 20 entries, totaling no more than 80 slides.

Picture stories and sports portfolios and documentary entries each count as a single entry.

A portfolio must include at least one story or sports portfolio or documentary entry and entries in four of the other categories.

THE CATEGORIES

1. **Spot News:** A picture from an unscheduled event that has significant news value.

2. **General News:** A picture from a scheduled event.

3. **Sports:** A peak action photograph that captures the competitive spirit.

4. **Sports Feature:** A sports-related feature picture.

5. **Feature:** An enterprise or "found" picture of strong human interest. Shows an ordinary situation in a fresh way, often with humor or insight.

6. **Portrait:** A picture of a person that, through use of environment, expression and mood, reveals the subject's character.

7. **Pictorial:** A beautiful, graphic image: composition, tonal and color qualities are more important than subject matter. Sometimes of places, but may include people.

8. **Food Illustration:** Often a created picture, showing food in a way that is both inventive and appetizing. Each entry must have a title.

9. **Fashion Illustration:** Often a created picture, emphasizing clothing, jewelry, cosmetics or some other aspect of human adornment.
Each entry must have a title.

10. **Picture Story:** A series of pictures of a subject that, when viewed together, provides an overall understanding of that subject. May be news, feature or sports.
(Eight slides maximum per story.)

11. **Sports Portfolio:** Using pictures from a variety of sporting events or athletic endeavors, demonstrate versatility. (Maximum of six entries, one of which may be a story or series; the story or series may include no more than six slides.)

12. **Documentary:** An issue-oriented series of pictures that may be in essay or story form. Portray broader concerns present in today's society—racism, ecological dangers, loss of personal freedom, hunger in our midst, etc. (Maximum of 15 slides.)

13. **Personal Vision:** A picture that doesn't 'fit' into any of the other categories. May be an abstraction of an interior, personal vision or any other non-traditional photograph.

COURTESY OF COLLEGE PHOTOGRAPHER OF THE YEAR

45th Annual College Photographer of the Year entry form. (next 3 pages)

ENTRY PREPARATION

Submit only 35mm slides, even if originals were black and white prints or color negatives.

Do not send original slides. Do send duplicate slides. Do not use glass mounts.

If you enter a portfolio, include one set in a Kodak Carousel 80 Transvue slide tray ordered by category 1-13, and a duplicate set in 8 1/2" X 11" polyethylene slide files. Portfolios will not be broken down into individual categories.

Submit individual category entries in 8 1/2" X 11" slide files.

Group stories together in one slide file. Number each slide in order of presentation (i.e., 1/8, 2/8...8/8.)

Write your name, category number, title of the picture and a capital letter directly on the slide mount on the side facing the screen (emulsion side.) Leave the bottom half of the mount blank for official use. Print clearly.

Type the same information and the corresponding capital letter on the caption sheet. Use a separate caption sheet for each category. Use a different letter for each entry, using double letters—AA, AB, AC—if needed.

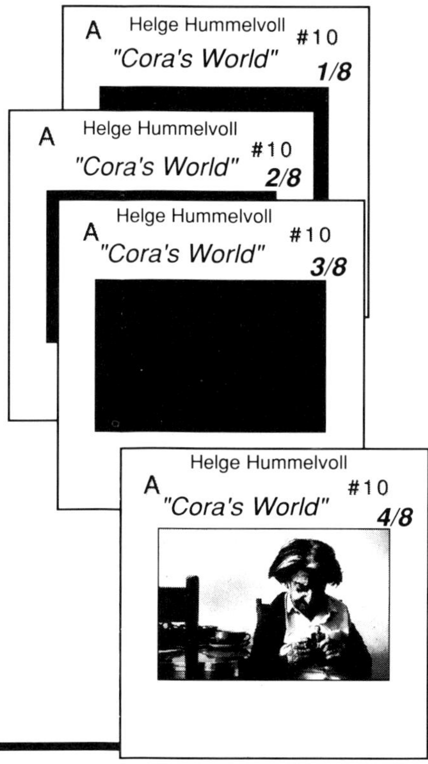

Give complete caption information. Summarize stories in one paragraph on the back of the caption sheet.

Explain any manipulation of the photographic image (other than burning or dodging) on the caption sheet.

No written or printed information may appear on entries, except as required on the slide mount.

A picture entered in the wrong category will not be reclassified; judges have the right to disqualify it.

Do not enter the same picture in two categories. However, if a picture story, sports portfolio or documentary entry contains a photo you wish to enter in another category, submit a separate slide.

Identify your collegiate affiliation and, if pertinent, for whom you were on assignment.

The entry form must be complete and signed. Social Security numbers must be included to receive cash prizes.

SEND ALL ENTRIES TO:

College Photographer of the Year
9th and Elm Streets
School of Journalism
University of Missouri-Columbia
Columbia, MO 65201

Entries must be sent prepaid. C.O.D. packages will not be accepted.
If several photographers' entries are sent in one container, keep each photographer's entry separate. Be sure that each photographer submits an entry form.
Only portfolio carousel tray entries will be returned and then only when a fiber mailing case and a check for return postage are provided. Do not send stamps or cash, but do include a self-addressed return label and check payable to KAM-CPOY for the return postage.

ENTRY FORM

Name____

Address____

Work phone Home phone Year in school

Name of college or university & department & address

Signature of faculty advisor, photojournalism instructor or current internship supervisor and phone number

Number of photographs entered:

CATEGORY	Portfolio	Single entries	
1. Spot News			
2. General News			
3. Sports			
4. Sports Feature			
5. Feature			
6. Portrait			
7. Pictorial			
8. Food Illustration			
9. Fashion Ilustration			
10. Picture Story			
11. Sports Portfolio			
12. Documentary			
13. Personal Vision			
Total # slides			

CPOY

I declare that I meet the eligibility requirements stated in the rules of the competition and that I am authorized by the holder of the copyright (or the right to copyright) to submit photographs to the 45th Annual College Photographer of the Year competition. I grant permission to KAM and the University of Missouri-Columbia to use my submitted photographs in exhibition and for promotional, educational and historical record purposes concerning the competition including, but not limited to, slide/tapes television film/tape, videodisc and any other type of mechanical, electronic or digital recording device. Winning photos become a part of the permanent CPOY collection. **I declare that the photos were taken or initially published from March 1, 1989 to February 28, 1990.**

Signature

Social Security Number

Date

COURTESY OF COLLEGE PHOTOGRAPHER OF THE YEAR

CAPTION SHEET

Portfolio ☐

Single Category ☐

☐ Category Number

Name ______________________________

Letter on slide

Title ______________________________

Caption (25 words or less)

Letter on slide

Title ______________________________

Caption (25 words or less)

Letter on slide

Title ______________________________

Caption (25 words or less)

winners in each individual category will receive $100 and 20 rolls of Kodak film. First, second, and third place winners in each category will receive special recognition from Kappa Alpha Mu and the NPPF.
Only portfolio carousel tray entries will be returned and then only when a fiber mailing case and a check for return postage are provided. Do not send stamps or cash, but do include a self-addressed return label and check payable to KAM-CPOY for return postage.
Write for information/entry form.

COUNTERPOINT
Sponsored by Hill Country Arts Foundation
P.O. Box 176
Ingram, TX 78025
(512) 367- 5121
Contact: Betty Vernon
Annual national juried exhibition of photography, graphics, and fine crafts.
Eligibility: Open to amateurs and pros.
Subject Matter: Open.
Submission Requirements: Send slides for initial jurying and color and/or B&W prints 8 x 10" or larger for show.
Entry Fee: $22 non-members; $15 members.
Awards: $2,200 in awards.
Slides are kept; prints are returned.
Sponsor reserves the right to use images to publicize show.
Write for entry/information.

CREATIVITY
Sponsored by *Art Direction* Magazine
10 East 39th St.
New York, NY 10016
(212) 889-6500
Contact: Mae Wills
Annual international awards show for visual professionals, including photographers.
Eligibility: Open to pros whose photographs have appeared in print in brochures, annual reports, ads, editorially, etc. during the past year (May to May).
Subject Matter: Open. Work must have appeared in print.
Submission Requirements: Submit color and/or B&W transparencies or tear-sheets.
Entry Fee: Single-$14; 3-5 page campaign or story-$28.
Awards: Winning entries are published in the Creativity Annual and exhibited; certificate of distinction is also awarded.
Entries are not returned.
Sponsor reserves exhibition and publication rights.
Write for information/entry form.

CUMBERLAND VALLEY PHOTO SALON
Sponsored by the Washington County Museum of Fine Arts
PO Box 423
Hagerstown, MD 21741
(301) 739-5727
Contact: Erik Nord, Curator
Annual juried photo contest for residents of Cumberland Valley (general territory bounded by Harrisburg, PA; Frederick, MD; Winchester, VA; and Garrett County, MD). 1990 marked the 57th year the Salon was held.
Eligibility: Open to amateurs and pros.
Subject Matter: Prints—Pictorial and Still-life; Portrait and Figure Studies; Abstract Effects. Slides—same categories as above plus Nature.
Submission Requirements: Color and B&W ok. Send up to 4 transparencies and 4 prints (prints no larger than 16x20").
Entry Fee: $2 per entry
Awards: Best of Show-$100; 1st-$25; 2nd-$15; 3rd-$10.
Sponsor reserves reproduction rights for museum publicity and a 25% sales commission.
Write for information/entry form.

DESERT WEST JURIED ART EXHIBITION
Sponsored by City of Lancaster Museum/Art Gallery
44801 North Sierra Highway
Lancaster, CA
(805) 723-6250
Contact: Norma Gurba, Curator or Lindsay Watson, Associate Curator
Biannual juried competition for all media including photography.
Eligibility: Open to amateurs and pros.
Subject Matter: Open; the title "Desert West" refers to geographic location.
Submission Requirements: Preliminary judging by 35mm slides of color and/or B&W prints. Model releases required.
Entry Fee: $10 for one entry; $15 for two entries; $20 for three to five entries.

Awards: 1st best of exhibition - $600; 2nd best of exhibition - $300; People's Choice (public vote at reception) - $200; ribbons and certificates of merit. Sponsor reserves the right to reproduce any and all artwork in the exhibition for records, catalogs, publicity and promotion.
Commision is charged on all sales.
Entries are returned.
Send SASE for a prospectus to City of Lancaster, Lancaster Museum/Art Gallery, 44933 North Fern Avenue, Lancaster, CA 93534.

EASTERN SHORE ANNUAL
Sponsored by Foto-Galerie
115-2 S. Main St.
PO Box 1233
Chincoteague, VA 23336
(804) 336-1152
Contact: Lee Baade, Director
Annual open, juried, fine arts exhibition including hand-printed photo or photo-related images of or related to the life and sites of the Chesapeake Bay Eastern Shore/Delmarva Peninsula.
Eligibility: Open to amateurs and pros. Work must be for sale.
Submission Requirements: Send up to 3 color and/or B&W prints no larger than 20x24" matted.
Entry Fee: $10 (includes return postage).
Awards: $100 cash award for Best of Show; exhibition of top 20; gift certificates from local merchants and restaurants.
Sponsor reserves one-time exhibition and sales rights.
Unaccepted entries are returned.
Send SASE for information/entry form.

ECLIPSE AWARD
Sponsored by the Thoroughbred Racing Associations, Daily Racing Form, National Turf Writers Association.
3000 Marcus Ave.
Lake Success, NY 11042
(516) 328-2660
Contact: Rich Schulhoff
Annual contest of thoroughbred-racing related photography.
Eligibility: Contest open to amateurs and pros. Photo must have been published in commercial publication (but not as an advertisement).
Subject Matter: Thoroughbred-racing related.
Submission Requirements: Send up to 3 color and/or B&W tear-sheets (8x11").
Entry Fee: None
Awards: Eclipse Award Sponsor retains rights to one-time release to *Media and Dinner Journal.*
Entries are not returned.
Write for information/entry form.

ELECTRUM
Sponsored by Helena Arts Council/Hotter Museum of Art
12 East Lawrence St.
Helena, MT
(406) 442-6400
Contact: James D. Poor
Annual national juried exhibition open to photography and other media. "The Hotter Museum is a new museum with excellent space and lighting."
Eligibility: Open to amateurs and pros.
Subject Matter: Open
Submission Requirements: Send up to 3 color and/or B&W transparencies. No size limit.
Entry Fee: $15 for 3 slides.
Awards: $2,000 in cash awards.
If accepted, slides are retained for educational file.
Write for information/entry form.

FEDERATION INTERNATIONALE d'ARTE PHOTOGRAPHIQUE
c/o PAUSA
1864 61st Street
Brooklyn, NY 11204
(718) 259-3373
Contact: Henry Mass
The federation sponsors approximately 90 international salons each year for all phases of photography, A/V, and video.
Eligibility: Open to amateurs and pros.
Subject Matter: Varies.
Submission Requirements: Send color and/or B&W prints and/or transparencies. 4-image limit per category. No size limit.
Awards: Varies.
Entries are returned.
Write for information.

FIVE STATE PHOTOGRAPHY EXHIBITION
Sponsored by the Hays Art Council
112 E. 11th St.
Hays, KS 67601

(913) 625-7522
Contact: Leland W. Powers
An annual juried exhibition for photographers from Kansas, Nebraska, Missouri, Oklahoma, and Colorado.
Eligibility: Open to amateurs and pros from the above states.
Subject Matter: Three categories-nature, people, and "open".
Submission Requirements: Send up to 4 color and/ or B&W prints. No size limit.
Entry Fee: $10 for 1st two entries; $7 for third entry; $7 for fourth entry.
Awards: A minimum of $500 in cash and purchase awards per category will be awarded at the juror's discretion.
The Hays Arts Council receives a 33% commission on all sales.
Entries are returned.
Write for entry.

GALLERY SEVEN: GLOUCESTER'S ANNUAL SILVER PRINT EXHIBITION
Sponsored by Gallery Seven: Gloucester
77 Rocky Neck Avenue
East Gloucester, MA 01930
(508) 281-6443
Contact: J.F. Weiler
Annual exhibition of gelatin silver prints and monochromatic prints (gum prints, platinum prints, etc.).
Eligibility: Open to amateurs and pros. Prints must be made by the photographer.
Subject Matter: Open.
Submission Requirements: Send up to 10 B&W work prints or slides for initial jurying. Prints will be required for exhibition. Maximum frame size of 17x21".
Entry Fee: $5.
Awards: Exhibition; possible sale.
Photographer retains all rights to photos.
Gallery charges a 35% commission on all sales.
Entries are returned (unless they are sold).
Write for prospectus.

GOLDEN ISLES ART FESTIVAL
Sponsored by the Coastal Alliance for the Arts
PO Box 673
2012 Demere Road
St. Simons Island, GA 31522
(912) 638-8770
Contact: Mittie Hendrix
Annual juried art festival.
Eligibility: Open to amateurs and pros.
Subject Matter: Open
Entry Fee: Not determined at press-time.
Awards: Not determined at press-time.
Photographer retains all rights to his or her work.
Write for more information/entry form.

GRAHAM HORSTMAN GALLERY
114 W. Congress
Denton, TX 76201
(817) 382-6558
Contact: Ken Horstman
The gallery sponsors several exhibitions each year. 1990 shows include "Primarily the Figure", "Rendered Realism", "Still Life" and "Current/Recurrent Trends".
Eligibility: Open to amateurs and pros.
Subject Matter: Varies.
Submission Requirements: Send up to three color and/or B&W photos. No size limit.
Entry Fee: $18 for three entries.
Awards: Purchase and cash awards. Exhibition.
All rights remain with the photographer.
Entries are returned.
Write for further information.

HARD KNOCKS
Sponsored by *Popular Photography* Magazine
1633 Broadway
New York, NY 10019
(212) 767-6000
Readers are invited to submit examples of their best work for analysis and critique in the magazine.
Eligibility: Open to all.
Subject Matter: Open.
Submission Requirements: Send up to 20 color and/ or B&W transparencies or prints. Prints no larger than 8x12".
Entry Fee: None.
Awards: $200; publication in the magazine.
Sponsor retains one-time editorial reproduction rights.
Entries are returned with SASE.

***HOOF BEATS* PHOTO CONTEST**
Sponsored by *Hoof Beats* Magazine and the U.S. Trotting Association
750 Michigan Ave.
Columbus, OH 43215
(614) 224-2291

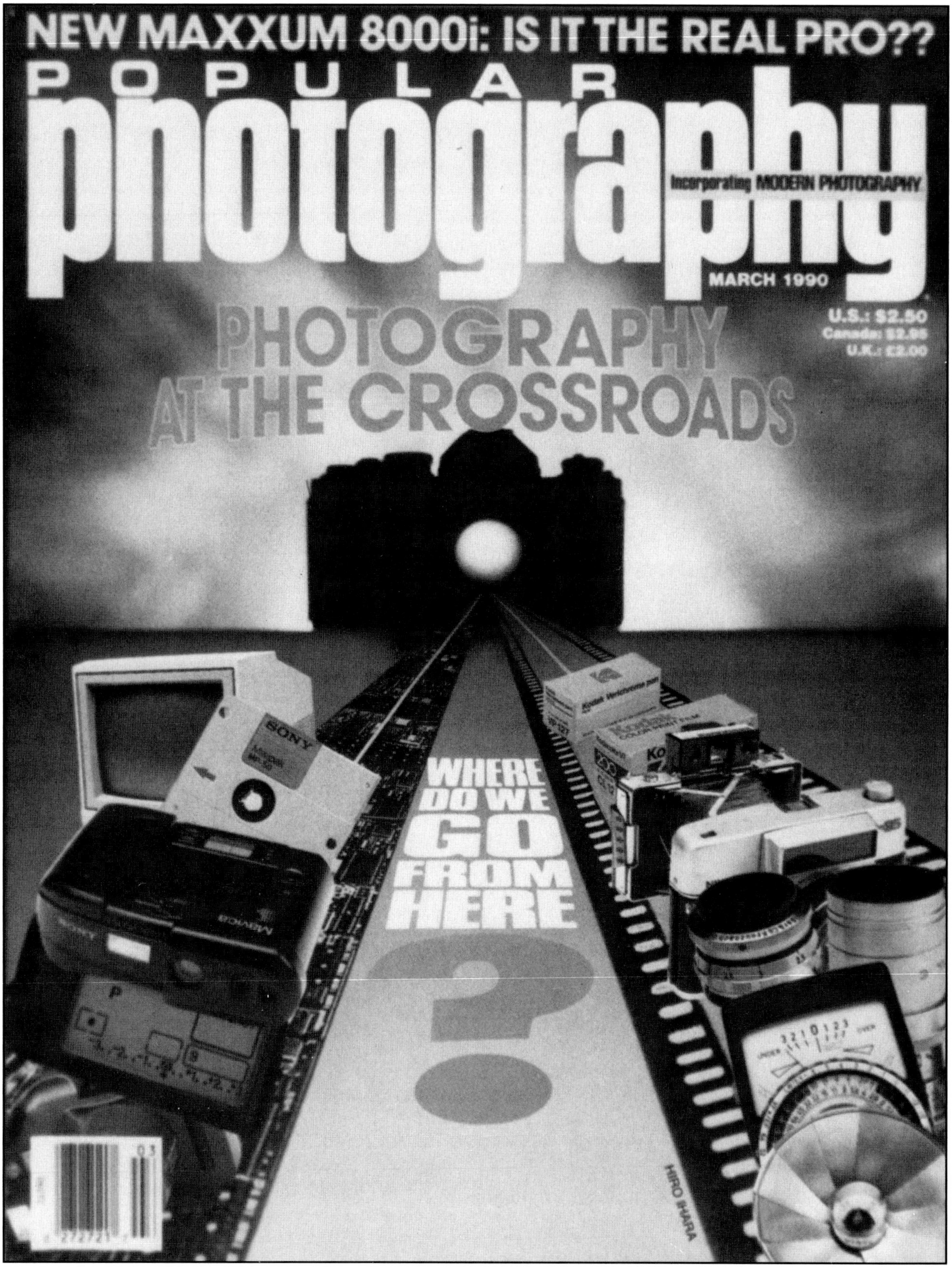

COURTESY OF *POPULAR PHOTOGRAPHY*

Popular Photography **sponsors two photo contests: "Your Best Shot" and "Hard Knocks".**

Contact: Dean A. Hoffman
Annual contest. World's largest harness racing magazine seeks best photos related to harness racing.
Eligibility: Open to amateurs and pros.
Subject Matter: Harness racing, farms, backstretch scenes.
Submission Requirements: Send up to 5 color and/or B&W prints and/or transparencies.
Entry Fee: $2 per photo.
Awards: $500-1st; $250-2nd; $100-3rd. Nine honorable mentions of $25 each.
Sponsor retains publication rights.
Entries are returned with SASE.
Write for information/entry form.

ILLUMINANCE
Sponsored by Lubbock Fine Arts Center
2600 Avenue P
Lubbock, TX 79405
(806) 767-2686
Contact: Connie Gibbons, Director
Annual national juried exhibition of works utilizing photographic processes. Sale of work is encouraged.
Eligibility: Open to amateurs and pros.
Subject Matter: Open
Submission Requirements: Color and/or B&W photo screenprints. No size limit.
Entry Fee: $15 for one to three works; $5 each additional work.
Awards: $1,000 to be distributed as juror sees fit.
Sponsor reserves right to publish photos for promotion.
Slides of accepted work are retained.
Entries are returned.
Write or call for prospectus.

INTERNATIONAL ART SHOW BY DISABLED ARTISTS
Sponsored by the Sister Kenney Institute
800 E. 28th St.
Minneapolis, MN 55407
(612) 863-4482
Contact: Nanette Boudreau
Annual art show provides forum for creative talents of people with disabilities and an outlet for disabled artists to sell their work.
Eligibility: Artist must have a disability that is a physical or mental impairment which substantially limits one or more major life activities (such as caring for oneself, performing manual tasks, walking, seeing, hearing, breathing, learning, and working). All work must be original.
Subject Matter: Open. Work will be judged in oils and acrylics, watercolor, graphics, three dimensional, drawing, and photography.
Submission Requirements: Send up to two color and/or B&W prints no larger than 36x36".
Entry Fee: None.
Awards: Cash and purchase awards ranging from $50-$400. First, second, and third place ribbons will be awarded in all categories, and first place winners will receive a prize. Honorable mention awards for all categories will be presented at the judges discretion.
Sponsor reserves the right to publish name, photo, biography, and artwork for publicity purposes.
Sponsor retains a 20% commission on all sales to defray expenses of the show.
Entries are returned.
Write for information/entry form.

INTERNATIONAL EXHIBITION OF PHOTOGRAPHY
Sponsored by the 22nd District Agricultural Association (Del Mar Fair).
2260 Jimmy Durante Blvd.
Del Mar, CA 92014
(619) 755-1161
Contact: Teresa Barth, Entry Supervisor
Annual exhibition photo contest for amateur and professional photographers.
Eligibility: Open to amateurs and pros.
Subject Matter: Must be suitable for family viewing.
Submission Requirements: Send up to 8 color and/or b&w prints. Each print must be mounted on 16x20" standard mounting board. No minimum print size; maximum print size is 16x20".
Entry Fee: $4 per print.
Awards: Best of Show-$275; 1st-$175; 2nd-$125; 3rd-$100; 4th-$75; 5th-$60; 6th-$50. Management's Choice-$75; San Diego Lifestyles-$100.
Sponsor reserves publication rights for exhibition promotion.
Entries are returned.
Write for brochure/entry form.

INTERNATIONAL MAIL ART SHOW
Sponsored by the City of Kent Arts Commission and Parks Department
220 4th Avenue South
Kent, WA 98032
(206) 859-3996

Contact: Liz Carpenter, Visual Arts Specialist
"Mail Art is a world-wide art movement—artists send their work to shows and each other, and receive documentation and/or artwork in exchange. Mail art is completely different from gallery/museum shows. We have all kinds of media represented including many photographers. Each year between 500 and 700 artists from approximately 30 countries send work."
Eligibility: Open to amateurs and pros.
Subject Matter: Depends on theme. 1990's theme was "goodwill".
Submission Requirements: Send color and/or B&W prints no larger than 5x8". No submission limit.
Entry Fee: None.
Awards: Each participant receives a show poster and mailing list of all participants.
Sponsor reserves right to use selected pieces on show poster.
Entries are not returned.
Art becomes part of the Kent City Art Collection.
All Kent Mail Art shows are available on loan for shows elsewhere.
Write for information/entry form.

THE INTERNATIONAL MARINE PHOTO AND VIDEO CONTEST
Sponsored by Ocean Expo International.
1141 NE 142nd St.
N. Miami, FL 33161
(305) 891-6095; Fax: 305-893-3486
Contact: Susan Payette
Annual marine-related contest for still photography and video. Winners' work is published in sponsoring magazine.
Eligibility: Amateurs only.
Subject Matter: Above-water sea related; underwater macro- close-up, and underwater wide-angle. Video entries must be 65% underwater.
Submission Requirements: Send videos, 35mm color slides, or color prints at least 7x10" but no larger than 11x14". No submission limit.
Entry Fee: Stills-$4 each; videos-$10 each; foreign entries- $6 each.
Awards: Over $5,000 in marine-related prizes, plaques, and certificates.
Sponsor reserves right to reproduce winning entries for promotion.
Entries are returned with SASE.
Send name/address to be placed on mailing list.

INTERNATIONAL SMALL WORLD COMPETITION
Sponsored by Nikon Inc., Instrument Group
1300 Walt Whitman Rd.
Mellville, NY 11746
(516) 222-0200
Contact: Barbara Loechner, Advertising Manager
Annual contest for photographs taken through a microscope.
Eligibility: Open to amateurs and pros. A description of the specimen, the microscope and camera equipment, technique used, and total magnification must accompany each transparency.
Subject Matter: All techniques are acceptable. Any type of specimen is acceptable.
Submission Requirements: Send up to three 35mm color transparencies.
Entry Fee: None.
Awards: Prizes for winning entries 1st through 10th; winning entries 11th through 20th receive 16x20" color print of entry; honorable mentions receive an award certificate. 1990 prizes included a vacation trip valued at $3,000, a Nikon F3HP, a Nikon N-8008, a Nikon N4004, various lenses, and compact binoculars. Twenty 1989 winners had their work published in a calendar.
All winning entries become the property of Nikon, Inc., and cannot be returned.
Non-winning entries will be returned with a SASE.
Write for information/entry form.

INTERNATIONAL WEDDING PHOTOGRAPHY AWARDS (IWPA)
Sponsored by Wedding Photographers International
1312 Lincoln Blvd., PO Box 2003
Santa Monica, CA 90406
Twice yearly contest for posed or candid wedding portraits.
"Entry photographs will be judged for photographic artistry and craftsmanship."
Eligibility: Open to Wedding Photographers International members only.
Subject Matter: Bride and groom together; bride or groom alone; bridal party; candids; engagement category; special effects. Model releases must be available. Negatives must be available.
Submission Requirements: Send 8x10" mounted or unmounted color prints. There is no submission limit, but an entry form must accompany each photograph.
Entry Fee: $5 per photo.

Awards: Award winners will be announced in "The Wedding Photographer" magazine.
"Any entered photograph may be used by Wedding Photographers International or the Rangefinder in any of their publications or printed materials."
Write for information/entry form.

JURIED PHOTOGRAPHY EXHIBITION

Sponsored by the Larson Gallery, Yakima Valley Community College
PO Box 1647
Yakima, WA 98907
(509) 575-2402
Contact: Carol Hassen, Gallery Director
Annual regional juried exhibition.
Eligibility: Open to amateurs and pros who live in Washington, Oregon, Idaho, Montana, and Wyoming.
Subject Matter: Open
Submission Requirements: Send up to 3 color and/or B&W prints larger than 5x7". Photographs must be framed and/or matted and ready for hanging.
Entry Fee: $15 with mailer, or $10 if hand-delivered.
Awards: Up to $750.
Sponsor reserves rights to use winning entries for limited publicity.
Entries are returned.
Call or write for information.

JURIED SHOW IN PAINTINGS, DRAWINGS, PRINTMAKING, AND PHOTOGRAPHY

Sponsored by the Anacortes Arts & Crafts Festival
PO Box 6
Anacortes, WA 98221
(206) 293-6211
Contact: Gail Weiss
Annual juried show for photography, painting, drawing, and printmaking.
Eligibility: Open to amateurs and pros.
Subject Matter: Open.
Submission Requirements: Send up to 5 color and/or B&W photos.
Entry Fee: $3.00 per piece.
Awards: $1,000 at the discretion of the jurors.
Sponsor retains sales rights and a 20% commission on all sales.
Entries are returned.
Write for information/entry form.

ROBERT F. KENNEDY JOURNALISM AWARDS FOR OUTSTANDING COVERAGE OF THE PROBLEMS OF THE DISADVANTAGED

Sponsored by the Robert F. Kennedy Memorial
1031 31st St., NW
Washington, DC 20007
(202) 333-1800
Contact: Linda K. Semans, RFK Journalism Awards Director
"As Robert Kennedy saw and listened to the poor, so did the journalists who traveled with him. The Robert F. Kennedy Journalism Awards program was founded by a group of these journalists in December, 1968, to encourage and recognize outstanding achievements in portraying those aspects of American life that occupied so much of his attention. It is the largest single program to honor outstanding reporting on the problems of the disadvantaged."
Eligibility: Open to professional and college undergraduate students (judged separately). Entries must have been published or broadcast in the U.S. for the first time in the appropriate calendar year.
Subject Matter: Entries may include accounts of the lifestyles, handicaps, and potentialities of the disadvantaged in the United States; insights into the causes, conditions, and remedies of their plight; and critical analyses of public policies, programs, attitudes, and private endeavors relevant to their lives. There are six categories for professionals: print, cartoons, television, radio, International, and photojournalism. Students may submit work in prints, broadcast, and photojournalism categories.
Submission Requirements: Photojournalism—Only one copy of each entry need be submitted. Prints should be mounted, and their mounted size may not exceed 11x14". Photo essays may be submitted in scrapbooks, whose pages may not exceed 14x17". Tear sheets of the published photo(s) must accompany each entry. An entry blank must be attached to every item.
Entry Fee: None.
Awards: A cash prize of $1,000 may be awarded to the entry judged most outstanding in each group. A grand prize of $2,000 may be awarded to the most outstanding of the six category winners. Honorable mention and citation certificates may also be awarded to both professional and student entries.
Only photo essays are returnable. Written request must be made at time or entry, and accompanied by

a check or money order to cover return postage. At the end of the contest all entries will be sent to the John F. Kennedy Library in Boston, to be placed in the Robert F. Kennedy Collection therein.
Write for information/entry form.

KODAK INTERNATIONAL NEWSPAPER SNAPSHOT AWARDS (KINSA)

Sponsored by Eastman Kodak and local newspapers. Since 1935, KINSA remains the world's largest annual amateur photo contest. Approximately 180 newspapers in the U.S., Canada, Mexico, and several other countries conduct a six-week photo contest for their readers. The newspapers then submit winning photos from the local level to an international jury of five non-Kodak individuals.
Eligibility: Open to amateurs only. An amateur photographer is anyone who derives less than 5% of their income from photography. Snapshots may be taken with any make of camera, but all entries must be taken on Kodak film. Photos previously entered in any KINSA contest are not eligible. Contestants are permitted to submit pictures to only one newspaper. Employees and their immediate family members of participating newspapers, of Eastman Kodak Company, and of its subsidiaries are not eligible to enter the contest.
Subject Matter: Local categories vary. There are 8 categories in the International Judging: Abstract & Still Life; Landscape & Scenic; Special Moments; People; Animals; Seniors -the over-60 club; Action; Environmental.
Submission Requirements: Contestant's name and address must be written clearly, in ink, on the back of each print or transparency mount. Mail entries to KINSA Contest Editor, care of the participating newspaper. Photographers should know the names and addresses of any recognizable persons appearing in the photograph.
Awards: Local winners receive merchandise. Cash prizes totalling $46,250 will be awarded in the International Judging as follows: $10,000 Grand Prize; $5,000 each First Place in each B&W and Color Category; $3,000 each Second Place in each B&W and Color Category; $2,000 each Third Place in each B&W and Color Category; $250 each 30 Honor Awards specific to the categories; $50 each Special Merit Awards. A five-day, four-night trip to Walt Disney World will be awarded to the Grand Prize winner and a guest, the First Prize B&W winner and a guest, and the First Place Color Winner and a guest. Winning photos will be exhibited at EPCOT Center, the National Geographic Society, and various trade shows, museums, newspapers, etc.
Newspapers reserve the right to publish pictures for local promotion of the contest. All photos submitted become the property of the sponsors and none will be returned. Local winners must sign a Prize Winner's Agreement that assigns to Eastman Kodak Company the original negative or transparency or their pictures and grants Eastman Kodak Company and others, with Kodak's consent, the right to reproduce and use the pictures for any business purpose, to use their names and likenesses in connection with the pictures, and with any exhibit or promotion of the contest.
Contact your local newspaper of KINSA for further information.

LASSEN COUNTY ARTS COUNCIL RAILS TO TRAILS PHOTO CONTEST

Sponsored by the Lassen County Arts Council
PO Box 91
Susanville, CA 96130
(916) 257-5222
Contact: Lori Collier
Annual photo contest for subject matter relating to railroad and trails. Work will be exhibited during Susanville's Founders Day Rails to Trails Annual Festival.
Eligibility: Open to amateurs and pros.
Subject Matter: Any subject matter relating to railroads and trails. May include people, animals, wildlife, nature, or any railroads—historical or New Age. Possible open category.
Submission Requirements: Send up to 3 color and/or B&W prints. Prints must be matted and no smaller than 8-1/2x11".
Entry Fee: $5 per photo.
Awards: 1st, 2nd, 3rd, and honorable mention in both amateur and pro categories. Cash and gifts.
Sponsor retains right to use winning work in press release for local publicity.
Entries are returned with SASE or resendable container with postage.
Write for information/entry form.

LIGHT WORK GRANTS IN PHOTOGRAPHY

Sponsored by Light Work
316 Waverly Avenue

Syracuse, NY 13244
(315) 443-1300
Contact: Jeffrey Hoone
The Light Work Grants are awarded each year to four Central New York photographers, critics, or photo historians to encourage the production of new work.
Eligibility: Open to amateurs and pros in Broome, Cayuga, Chemung, Chenango, Cortland, Herkimer, Jefferson, Lewis, Madison, Oneida, Onondaga, Oswego, Schuyler, Seneca, St. Lawrence, Tioga, and Tompkins Counties. Past Light Work Grant recipients and full-time students are ineligible.
Subject Matter: Open.
Submission Requirements: Send up to 10 color and/or B&W prints or transparencies. No size limit.
Entry Fee: None.
Awards: Four photographers will receive $500 each, their work will be exhibited in the Light Work Gallery and published in the *Contact Sheet.*
Sponsor asks that winners donate one print each to the gallery collection.
Entries are returned.
Write for information/entry form.

LOS ANGELES PHOTOGRAPHY CENTER ANNUAL PHOTOGRAPHY CONTEST
Sponsored by the Los Angeles Photography Center (part of the City of LA Cultural Affairs Dept.)
412 S. Park View St.
Los Angeles, CA 90057
(213) 383-7342
Contact: Willie R. Middlebrook.
This annual photography contest is held to seek out the best work of the year by new photographers who are members of the Photography Center. The winning photos are exhibited at the Center's gallery and listed in the bi-monthly newsletter Flashes.
Eligibility: Open to amateurs and pros.
Subject Matter: Categories include portraits, landscapes, journalism/documentary, and contemporary (alternative photography or new techniques).
Submission Requirements: Send up to 5 color and/or B&W prints. Overall mat size should be either 11x14" or 16x20".
Entry Fee: $5 per print, or $25 for yearly membership.
Awards: Photographic equipment, supplies, gift certificates, memberships, subscriptions, and/or cash prizes.
Sponsor reserves the right to exhibit the work and to reproduce it for exhibit announcement or publicity.
Entries are returned. Non-local entries should include packing and postage.
Write for information/entry form.

MATRIX INTERNATIONAL
Sponsored by the Matrix Gallery
1725 I Street
Sacramento, CA 95814
(916) 441-4818
Juried competition for all media presented by the Matrix Workshop of Women Artists.
Eligibility: Open to all artists.
Subject Matter: Open.
Submission Requirements: Send up to 3 color and/or B&W slides for jurying. Prints required for show.
Entry Fee: $8 per entry/maximum 3 entries.
Awards: Gallery exhibition of winning work. Substantial cash and merchandise awards.
Entries are returned. Slides of accepted works will be retained for Matrix files.
Sponsor reserves the right to photograph works for purposes of documentation, education, and publicity.
Matrix retains 40% commission on all sales of exhibition entries.
Write for prospectus.

MAYFAIR JURIED PHOTOGRAPHY EXHIBITION
Sponsored by Day-Timers, Inc. and Mayfair.
2020 Hamilton St.
Allentown, PA 18104
(215) 437-6900
Juried photography exhibition at Mayfair, a five-day community celebration in Allentown, PA.
Eligibility: Open to any photographer residing or maintaining a studio within a 60-mile radius of Allentown, PA.
Subject Matter: Open.
Submission Requirements: Photographers may submit no more than three original photographs—dry mounted/matted and framed. Photographs must be submitted for jurying in a manner suitable for hanging. Frames must be silvertone metal finish; all mats must be in tones of white.
Entry Fee: None.
Awards: Two first prize awards of $250; two second

prize awards of $150; two third prize awards of $100; and a People's Choice award of $75.
Entries will be returned with appropriate packaging and postage.
Write for information/entry form.

MINI PRINT INTERNACIONAL, CADAQUES
Organized by Taller Galeria Fort and sponsored by ADOGI
Apartado de Correos 9319
08080 Barcelona, Spain
Contact: Sr. Pascual Fort, President ADOGI
Annual travelling exhibition of graphic arts.
Eligibility: Open to all artists in all printing techniques and tendencies.
Subject Matter: Open.
Submission Requirements: Send up to 3 signed prints no larger than 10x10 c/m; mounted prints should be no larger than 18x18 c/m. Enclose a C.V. as well.
Entry Fee: $35 U.S.
Awards: Accepted works will be exhibited in Cadaques and will travel internationally. Six winning prints will be published in the catalog. Selected artists will be invited to have a one-person show.
ADOGI reserves the right to reproduce and exhibit any work accepted for publicity or cultural purposes.
33% commission will be charged on all sales.
Write for information/entry.

THE MOBIUS AWARDS
Sponsored by The United States Festivals Association
841 North Addison Ave.
Elmhurst, IL 60126-1291
(708) 834-7773
Contact: J.W. Anderson, Chairman; Patricia A. Meyer, Executive Director.
Annual, international competition to select and honor outstanding television and radio commercials. Entries in TV commercial area covers photography as one specific category.
Eligibility: Anyone involved in the making of a commercial is invited to submit entries. Open to pros only.
Subject Matter: Open.
Submission Requirements: Send in 16mm film or video tape on 3/4" U-Matic or 1/2" VHS formats in the NTSC, PAL, or SECAM standard. Color and/or b&w. All entries must be on tape or film; no slides or prints. No submission limit.
Entry Fee: $60-$80.
Awards: Mobius statuette, certificates.
Sponsor retains no rights to material.
Entries are returned.

MUSEUM OF ANTHROPOLOGY
California State University at Chico
Chico, CA 95929-400
(916) 895-5397
Contact: Linda Ragsdale.
Each year the Museum sponsors a juried competition. The theme varies from year to year, but relates to some aspect of American culture. 1990's contest was called "America's Pet Prints" the theme was the cultural significance of pets in America.
Eligibility: Open to amateurs and pros.
Subject Matter: People (but no portraits), places, objects.
Submission Requirements: Color and/or B&W prints. 8x10", 11x14", 8x12". Maximum of 3 in each category.
Entry Fee: $4 for first entry; $3.50 for each subsequent entry.
Awards: Art glass from Orient and Flume Glassworks. Prizes awarded in three categories; additional prize for Best of Show and People's Choice Award.
Entries are returned with postage and packing.
Call or write for information/entry form.

MYSTIC SEAPORT PHOTO DAY CONTEST
Sponsored by Mystic Seaport and Eastman Kodak Co.
Box 6000
50 Greenmanville Ave.
Mystic, CT 06355
(203) 572-0711
Contact: William C. North, Director of Marketing
Photo Day at Mystic Seaport is an annual all-day event in which costumed Seaport staff provide photo opportunities by posing on the ships and grounds of the Seaport.
Eligibility: Open to amateurs and pros. Photos must be taken on Photo Day.
Subject Matter: Mystic Seaport on Photo Day.
Submission Requirements: Color and/or B&W prints mounted on 8x10", 11x14", or 16x20" boards.
Entry Fee: none
Awards: Best in Show, 1st, 2nd, 3rd prizes and 3 runners up in color and black and white categories. Prize for 1989's Best in Show was a weekend for two in Mystic.

Sponsor retains right to use selected images for Photo Day publicity. Winners may or may not be exhibited in Photo Day show.
Entries are returned.
Write or call for information/entry form.

NATIONAL GEOGRAPHIC TRAVELER PHOTO CONTEST

Sponsored by *National Geographic Traveler* Magazine
PO Box 2523
Washington, DC 20013-2523

"The most precious things we bring home from our travels aren't objects we've collected but memories of places, events, people, and experiences—and photographs that crystallize those memories and make them visible for sharing. The editors of *National Geographic Traveler* invite our readers to send in their favorite travel images that capture such memories." Entries will be judged on the basis of creativity, photographic quality, and effectiveness in expressing the theme of "Travel Memories".

Eligibility: Open to all readers of *Traveler*, except professional photographers and employees of the National Geographic Society and their families.

Subject Matter: Travel images and memories.

Submission Requirements: Send up to four 35mm color transparencies and/or color prints only. For color prints, the original color negative (or transparency, if the print was made from a transparency) must be available for publication. Transparencies must be mounted on 2x2" cardboard or plastic slide mounts. Color prints no larger than 8x10". Photos must not have been previously published. Include a model release for any recognizable people, if feasible. An official entry blank must accompany each entry. Name and mailing address must be placed on the frame of each color slide and on the back of each color print.

Awards: First Prize-Holiday for two in Paris, including round-trip, first-class airline tickets, one week accommodations, and $2,500 in cash. Second Prize-Holiday for two in San Francisco, including round-trip, first-class airline tickets, three night's accommodations, and $1,500 in cash. Third Prize-$1,500 cash. Fourth Prize-$1,000 cash. Five Merit Awards-Olympus OM-88 35mm SLR camera with auto-focus 50mm f/2 lens. 25 Honorable Mentions of $100 and a copy of the *National Geographic Photographer's Field Guide*. All prize winners will also receive five rolls of Fujicolor film. Selected prize-winning photographs, and a complete list of winners' names will be published in *Traveler*.

Winners agree to allow the National Geographic Society to publish their photographs in a future issue or issues of Traveler and to use the pictures for advertising and promotional purposes without further payment.
Entries are returned with SASE.
See *National Geographic Traveler* for entry forms.

NATIONAL PRESS PHOTOGRAPHERS ASSOCIATION/NIKON DOCUMENTARY SABBATICAL AWARD

Sponsored by NPPA/Nikon
C. Thomas Hardin
1622 Forest Hill Drive
Louisville, KY 40205
(502) 582-4607

Annual competition awards a stipend of $15,000. NPPA/Nikon invite working photojournalists to create, research, and propose a documentary project illuminating the theme "The Changing Face of America".

Eligibility: Open to NPPA members.

Subject Matter: Open. Photographer must propose an extensive project depicting a significant change in the trends of our country—or a significant change in lifestyle, economic or other pressures.

Submission Requirements: Submit one portfolio of color and/or B&W prints or transparencies. No size limit.

Entry Fee: None.

Awards: $15,000 stipend enables the winner to undertake and complete the project during a three-month sabbatical.

Sponsor reserves the right to reproduce photographs for publicity and promotion.
Entries are returned.
Write to C. Thomas Hardin for information/entry form.

NATURAL WORLD PHOTOGRAPHIC COMPETITION AND EXHIBITION

Sponsored by The Carnegie Museum of Natural History
4400 Forbes Avenue
Pittsburgh, PA 15213
(412) 622-3375

Contact: Judi Bobenage

"For this annual competition, photographers submit

prints with accompanying caption information about how and why the photo was taken. All entries are juried by a panel of three judges, and 50-60 prints are selected for an exhibition at The Carnegie Museum of Natural History."
Eligibility: Open to amateurs and pros.
Subject Matter: Any interpretation of the natural world (e.g. plants, wildlife, landscapes, photo micrography).
Submission Requirements: Send up to 6 color and/or B&W prints. Prints must be mounted for exhibition and outside dimensions of photo plus board must be either 11x14" or 16x20".
Entry Fee: $5 per print.
Awards: 1st prize-$500; two 2nd prizes of $250 each; three 3rd prizes of $100 each; up to five honorable mentions. Prize winner and other selected photographs are exhibited. 1st and 2nd prize winners are published in *Carnegie* magazine.
Sponsor reserves the right to reproduce accepted work for publication, documentation, and promotion.
Entries are returned.
Entries are accepted during a two-week entry period. Call or write for information.

NATURE IMAGES PHOTO CONTEST
Sponsored by Nature Images, Inc.
PO Box 2037
West Palm Beach, FL 33402
(407) 586-7332
Contact: Helen Longest-Slaughter
Nature photography contest covering all aspects of nature. Winners have the opportunity to have their images exhibited at Nature Image Workshops and other locations around the country for one year after contest date.
Eligibility: Open to amateurs and pros.
Subject Matter: Nature, including wildlife, scenics, close- ups, flowers, plants, etc.
Submission Requirements: Color only. Transparencies and/or prints. Print size: 3-1/2x5", 4x6", 5x7", 8x10". No submission limit.
Entry Fee: $5 per slide or print.
Awards: 1st prize-$600; 2nd prize-$200; 3rd prize-$100; 4th prize-$50; plus ribbons for 1st, 2nd, 3rd, 4th, 5th, 6th, 7th, and honorable mentions.
Photographer retains all rights to entries.
Entries are returned.
Write for information/entry form.

NATURE PHOTOGRAPHY CONTEST FOR AMATEURS
Sponsored by the Tampa Audubon Society
PO Box 320025
Tampa, FL 33679
(813) 595-4831
Contact: Jeff Mitchell
Annual nature photography contest for amateurs.
Eligibility: Open to all amateur photographers who earn less than 50% of their annual income from photography, including teaching.
Subject Matter: Wild plants (trees, flowers, fungus, etc., or close-ups of their parts); wildlife (animals, birds, reptiles, fish, insects, etc. that are not captive); "scapes" (landscapes, seascapes, sunsets, etc.); miscellaneous (includes captive wildlife, domestic plants or animals, "set- ups" any nature photos not covered in categories 1, 2, or 3).
Submission Requirements: 35mm color slides in 2x2" mounts and/or color prints in 8x10" or 11x14" mounts. No submission limit.
Entry Fee: $2.50 per slide or print, or 5 entries for $10.
Awards: Slides and prints are judged separately. 1st place (in each category) 15% of the entry fees for category. 2nd place (in each category) 10% of entry fees for category. 3rd place (in each category) 5% of the entry fees for each category. There is a $25 additional prize for the top winner of each division.
Sponsor reserves right to use duplicates for educational purposes.
Entries are returned.
Write Jeff Mitchell at 9863 Portside Drive, Seminole, FL, 34646 for information/entry form.

NAVAL AND MARITIME PHOTO CONTEST
Sponsored by The U.S. Naval Institute and the Government Systems Division, Eastman Kodak.
U.S. Naval Institute
Preble Hall
Annapolis, MD 21402
(301) 268-6110, ext. 252
Contact: Patty M. Maddocks
Annual contest for photographs of military and maritime services.
Eligibility: Open to amateurs and pros.
Subject Matter: Each photograph must pertain to a naval or maritime subject.
Submission Requirements: Send up to five B&W prints, color prints, or color transparencies. Minimum print size is 5x7". Full captions and photographer's

name and address must be printed or typed on a separate sheet of paper and attached to the back of each print, or printed on the transparency mount.
Entry Fee: None.
Awards: 1st prize-$500; 2nd prize-$350; 3rd prize-$250; 15 $100-prizes for Honorable Mention.
Photographer retains all rights to photos.
Entries returned with SASE.
Photographs not awarded prizes may possibly be purchased by the U.S. Naval Institute.
Write for information/entry form.

NEVADA CITY FALL COLORS PHOTO CONTEST

Sponsored by the Nevada City Chamber of Commerce
132 Main Street
Nevada City, CA 95959
(916) 265-2692
Contact: Dave Carter (916) 265-NEWS
Annual contest to celebrate fall colors, Gold Rush history, and activities of the Nevada City area. Winning photos are displayed each December as part of Nevada City's Victorian Christmas celebration.
Eligibility: Open to amateurs and pros.
Subject Matter: Autumn in Nevada City; Nevada City history; fun in the Nevada City area.
Submission Requirements: Color and B&W transparencies or mounted prints. Prints should be 5x7" and larger. No submission limit.
Entry Fee: None
Awards: $750 in cash prizes was awarded in 1989. More is anticipated in the future.
Sponsor reserves the right to reproduce winning images for promotion. Credit will be given.
Entries are returned.
Write for information/entry form.

NEW AMERICAN TALENT

Sponsored by the Texas Fine Arts Association
3809-B West 35th St.
Austin, TX 78703
(512) 453-5312
Contact: Mary Kay Scott
Annual national exhibition open to all media including photography. Photography usually comprises a significant portion of the show.
Eligibility: Open to amateurs and pros.
Subject Matter: Open.
Submission Requirements: Send between 3 and 10 color and/or B&W transparencies for jurying.
Entry Fee: Members-$15 for 3 slides, $5 for each additional slide; Nonmembers-$22 for 3 slides, $5 for each additional slide.
Awards: Touring exhibition selected from show. Catalog published; Juror's Choice awards.
Photographer retains all rights to photos.
Entries are returned.
Write for information/entry form.

NEW YORK STATE FAIR PHOTOGRAPHY COMPETITION AND SHOW

Sponsored by the New York State Fair
Syracuse, NY 13209
(315) 487-7711
Contact: Janet J. Edison
Photography exhibition and sale held in the Harriet May Mills Art and Home Center at the New York State Fairgrounds.
Eligibility: Open to amateurs and pros. Work must be original and recent.
Subject Matter: Open
Submission Requirements: Send no more than two B&W or color prints. Prints must be unframed and mounted on a 16x20" mat board. No foamboard will be accepted. Actual photos may be 16x20" or smaller.
Entry Fee: $5.
Awards: A total of $1,000 in awards will be offered by New York State Fair; two Best of Show Awards in B&W and color sponsored by Eastman Kodak.
25% commission will be charged on all photos sold.
Entries do not have to be for sale.
Entries are returned.
Write or call New York State Fair for information.

NEW YORK STATE YOUTH MEDIA ARTS

Sponsored by the New York State
Education Department
Room 681
Albany, NY 12234
(518) 474-8773
Contact: Bob Reals, Administrator, Media Arts Summer School
Students exhibit works at any one of 12 shows. They are expected to answer questions about works' content, design, and techniques.
Eligibility: Open only to amateur students.
Subject Matter: Open.
Submission Requirements: Submit between 8 and

15 color and/or B&W prints and/or transparencies. No size limit.
Entry Fee: None
Awards: Opportunity to attend six-week summer school and work with professional photographer and other gifted students from New York State.
Photographer retains all rights to photos.
Entries are returned.
Write for information/entry form.

NIKON PHOTO CONTEST INTERNATIONAL (NPCI)

Sponsored by Nikon Corporation
1300 Walt Whitman Rd.
Melville, NY 11746
"This annual contest for photographers the world over offers you the opportunity to both match and share your skills with your fellow photographers across the seas, and win prizes, too."

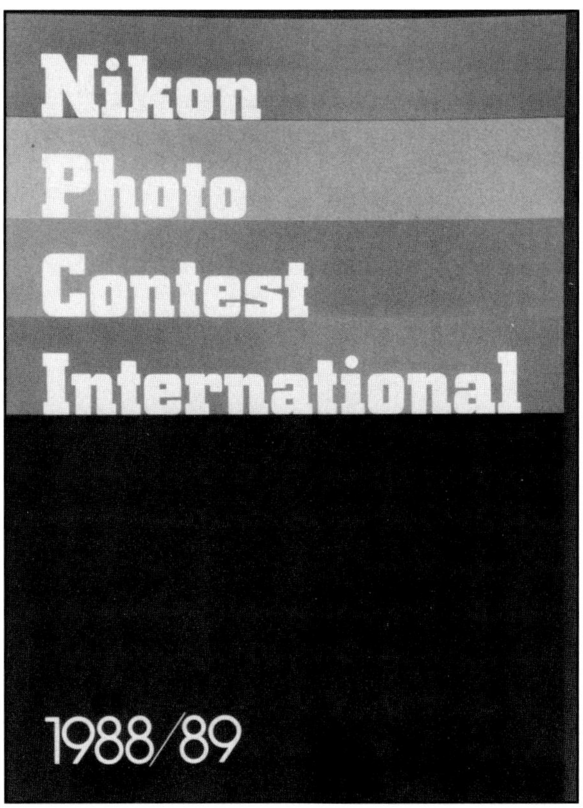

COURTESY OF NIKON PHOTO CONTEST INTERNATIONAL (NPCI)

Each year the Nikon Photo Contest International (NPCI) honors the winners of its contest by publishing their photos, names, and addresses in an annual.

Eligibility: Open to amateurs and pros. Residents of Japan are excluded. Photos must be taken with a 35mm camera. Previously published photographs are ineligible.
Subject Matter: Open. There is a separate category for underwater photos.
Submission Requirements: Send up to five photographs each for Categories A (Black and White), B (Color) and C (Underwater). Prints and slides are acceptable for Categories B & C; prints only for category A.
Awards: One Grand Prize winner overall; one 1st prize winner in each category; ten 2nd-prize winners each from Categories A and B; two 2nd-prize winner each from Category C; twenty 3rd-prize winners each from Categories A and B; three 3rd- prize winners from Category C; forty Honorable Mentions each from Categories A and B; five Honorable Mentions from Category C. 1989/90 prizes included a Nikon F4S, a Nikon N8008, Nikonos-V, and various lenses. All winning photos are published in the Nikon Photo Contest International Annual.
Entries are not returned. Do not send originals.
Write for information/entry form.

NON-MEMBERS ANNUAL SALMAGUNDI CLUB PHOTO AND SCULPTURE EXHIBITION

Sponsored by the Salmagundi Club
47 5th Ave.
New York, NY 10003-4396
(212) 255-7740
Contact: Scott Laperruque, Jack Kaminsky
An open non-member juried exhibition sponsored by America's oldest art club (est. 1871). The Salmagundi Club is looking for the beauty in all processes throughout the history of photography.
Eligibility: Open to amateurs and pros.
Subject Matter: Open.
Submission Requirements: Send color and/or B&W prints or slides for initial jurying. Matted and framed prints (no size limit) will be required for exhibition. No submission limit.
Entry Fee: $15 for 2 slides or prints.
Awards: Cash and merchandise.
Entries are returned.
All rights remain with the photographer. Sponsor reserves reproduction rights for show publicity.
Write for prospectus.

Nikon

NIKON PHOTO CONTEST INTERNATIONAL '89/'90

New Prize Added: F4s

NIKON CORPORATION invites you, through the Nikon distributor in your country, to participate in this year's Nikon Photo Contest International. This annual contest for photographers the world over offers you the opportunity to both match and share your skills with your fellow photographers across the seas, and win prizes, too.

Entry Categories

1. **Category A — Black-and-White (B&W)**
2. **Category B — Color**
3. **Category C — Color or B&W photos taken under water (subaqueous scenes)**

Awards & Prizes

GRAND PRIZE

(One overall winner of all three categories)

Gold medal with winner's name engraved, and following Nikon products.
(1) Set A + Nikkor lens(es) (maximum value US$1,000) or Set B + Nikkor lens(es) (maximum value US$2,000) or (2) Set C + Speedlight SB-102 + UW-Nikkor 20mm f/2.8 + Optical viewfinder DF-12

1st Prize

(One winner in each category)

Gold medal with winner's name engraved, and following Nikon products.
(1) Set A, or Set B + Nikkor lens(es) (maximum value US$1,000) or (2) Set C + Speedlight SB-102

2nd Prize

(10 winners each from Categories A and B, 2 winners from Category C)

Silver medal with winner's name engraved, and following Nikon products.
(1) Nikon N8008 camera body + AF Zoom-Nikkor 35-70mm f3.3-4.5 or (2) Nikonos-V camera body + UW-Nikkor 28mm f3.5 or (3) Nikon F3HP camera body

3rd Prize

(20 winners each from Categories A and B, 3 winners from Category C)

Bronze medal with winner's name engraved, and following Nikon products.
(1) Nikon N4004s camera body or (2) Nikon Zoom Touch 500 or (3) Nikonos-V camera body

Honorable Mention

(40 winners each from Categories A and B, 5 winners from Category C)

Bronze medal with winner's name engraved, and a special gift.

PRIZES

Set A
Nikon F4s camera body + AF-Zoom Nikkor 35-70mm f/2.8

Set B
Nikon N8008 camera body + AF-Zoom Nikkor 35-70mm f/3.3-4.5 + Speedlight SB-24

Set C
Nikonos-V camera body + UW-Nikkor 28mm f/3.5 + W-Nikkor 35mm f/2.5

Above items on Sets may be subject to change without notice.
*Grand Prize and 1st Prize winners can choose the Nikkor lens or lenses available at the time of awarding the prizes.

Nikon Photo Contest International entry form. (next 3 pages)

NPCI Entry Rules

1 The Nikon Photo Contest International (NPCI) is open to any photographer, professional or amateur, from any part of the world, except for residents of Japan.

2 Any subject matter is acceptable. Note, however, that generally nude photographs showing pubic hair, regardless of aesthetic qualities, are rejected by Japanese Customs to enter Japan. The rejected photographs will be disposed of through incineration by Japanese Customs officials.

3 Only photographs taken with a 35mm camera such as the Nikon may be accepted as entries, provided they conform to Rule 4.

4 Published photographs or those that have either been accepted or are presently submitted for publication are not eligible. A photograph selected from among those taken on the same scene with a limited time lag is also ineligible when any of these photographs has already been published or has been submitted to other contests. However, when submission was for other Nikon-related contests, the photograph is eligible provided that it has not yet been published. In the event an award-winning photograph is later found out to have violated this rule, NIKON CORPORATION reserves the right to take any action it may deem suitable, including the return of the prize or prizes awarded. Also, the winning position will be voided.

5 You may submit a maximum of **five photographs each** for Categories A, B, C. All entries should be accompanied by a properly completed Entry Form. **Please note that entry receipts will not be issued.**

6 **No entries, either prints or slides, will be returned to entrants.**
Please do not send your original slides; send only the high quality duplicates.

Category A–
Black-and-White (B/W)
Do not mount prints. Minimum print size 20×25cm (8″×10″), maximum 25×30cm (10″×12″). Indicate on the back of each print, in block letters, the following: (1)your entry number (2)your name (3)your address (4)the name of the country in which you enter the contest (5)the title of the photograph (6) picture number. (7) **"Top" mark on the back to indicate the top of the picture.**

Category B–Color
Photographs acceptable in this category can either be color slides or color prints. Do not mount prints and **do not send glass-mounted transparencies.** All slides must have the required indications (see illustration) on the judging side. **"Top" mark to indicate the top of the picture.** All unmounted color prints must be enlarged to the dimensions and have the indication specified for B&W prints.

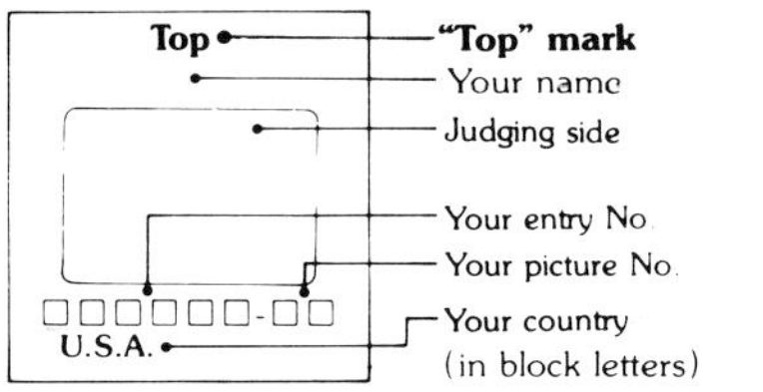

Category C-Underwater
The photographs acceptable in this category are only those taken under water **(Subaqueous scenes).** Either color or black-and-white photographs are acceptable. To indicate category, write in red an encircled C on the back of prints or on the mount of slides. All other entry procedures are similar to those prescribed for Categories A and B.

7 All entries must reach the NPCI, Nikon Inc., 623 Stewart Avenue, Garden City, N.Y. 11530 not later than **Octorber 31, 1989.** Entries sent directly to NIKON CORPORATION will be ruled ineligible for the contest.

8 All entries will be judged by a panel of judges appointed by NIKON CORPORATION the judges' decision will be final.

9 Only winners will be notified individually through Nikon Inc. by April 30, 1990.

10 All the winning photographs will be published in the Nikon Photo Contest International Annual 1989/90. You can get the Annual from Nikon Inc. at a price shown on the NPCI Annual Order Form that is attached to the Entry From. Only to the winners, complimentary copies will be sent. Payment for orders cannot be refunded.

11 Winners will be required to submit the original negatives or color slides—not duplicates—of the winning photographs to Nikon Inc. **within 10 days after notification.** These photos are used for printing in the NPCI Annual. Failure to comply with this rule may result in disqualification. The winners' original negatives and/or slides will be returned to the winners after completion of the NPCI Annual.

12 Prizes will be awarded to winning entries by NIKON CORPORATION through Nikon Inc.

13 NIKON CORPORATION will not be responsible for any claims or complaints from models used in winning photographs should these photographs be published or exhibited. Such responsibility will be deemed to be the entrant's. If necessary, NIKON CORPORATION may request the entrant concerned to submit a model-release statement before the prize is awarded.

14 NIKON CORPORATION reserves all rights to any NPCI-related reproduction, publication and exhibition of all winning photographs.

15 Failure to comply with and accept all the preceding rules and regulations may disqualify any entry and lead NIKON CORPORATION to take any action it deems fit.

16 There may be cases where several photographs are selected for insertion in Nikon calendars or other publicity media. NIKON CORPORATION will enter into separate contracts with entrants of such photographs.

17 Please do not enclose any materials other than Entries & Entry Form.

Judging

The panel of judges will be composed of the following:
Jun Miki, photographer
Yusaku Kamekura, art designer
Takamasa Inamura, photographer
Akira Sato, photographer
Ieyoshi Mihori, technical consultant
Jun Morinaga, photographer
Tsuneo Enari, photographer

Entry Form

Your Entry No.:

044793

This form must accompany your entry or entries. Note that the entry number shown at the left, printed in black, is your number. This number and each picture number (i.e. A1, B1, C1) must be written on the back of each print entry or on the mount of each color slide entry.

Please write by typewriter or in block letters.

Category A—Black-and-White (B&W)

PICTURE NO.	PICTURE TITLE	TECHNICAL DATA			
		Camera	Lens	Exposure	Film
A1			mm / f/	sec. / f/	
A2			mm / f/	sec. / f/	
A3			mm / f/	sec. / f/	
A4			mm / f/	sec. / f/	
A5			mm / f/	sec. / f/	

Do not cut here

Category B—Color Encircle P for color print or S for color slide.

PICTURE NO.	TYPE OF PHOTO	PICTURE TITLE	TECHNICAL DATA			
			Camera	Lens	Exposure	Film
B1	P S			mm / f/	sec. / f/	
B2	P S			mm / f/	sec. / f/	
B3	P S			mm / f/	sec. / f/	
B4	P S			mm / f/	sec. / f/	
B5	P S			mm / f/	sec. / f/	

Do not cut here

Category C—Underwater Special Category Encircle B for B&W print, P for color print or S for color slide.

PICTURE NO.	TYPE OF PHOTO	PICTURE TITLE	TECHNICAL DATA			
			Camera	Lens	Exposure	Film
C1	B P S			mm / f/	sec. / f/	
C2	B P S			mm / f/	sec. / f/	
C3	B P S			mm / f/	sec. / f/	
C4	B P S			mm / f/	sec. / f/	
C5	B P S			mm / f/	sec. / f/	

044793

Name **Sex**

Age Occupation

Address/Country

U.S.A.

Telephone

I hereby testify to the correctness of all the above information and agree to comply with all the rules and regulations of the Nikon Photo Contest International 1989/90.

Signature

Please note: When no signature is affixed, your entry may be determined ineligible.

Questionnaire

Names of cameras presently used

Types of lenses and accessories now being used

Items expected to purchase in the future

A brief note on the NPCI Annual: The NPCI Annual is a permanent record of all NPCI contest winners for a given year. In addition to handsome reproductions of all the winning photographs, it publishes the data relevant to these photographs—more than 80 color and B & W in all. The Annual consists of approximately 100 pages. Using high-quality art paper along with coated, reinforced paper cover binding, it should be a valuable addition to any library of books and publications on photography.

Size: 21cm × 29.5cm (approx. 8 in. × 11 in.)

Delivery: October 1990.

To order copies, fill in the NPCI Annual 1989/90 Order Form & Mailing Label and forward them both to:

N.P.C.I.
Nikon Inc.
623 Stewart Avenue
Garden City, NY 11530

PLEASE DO NOT INCLUDE ANNUAL ORDERS WITH ENTRIES. THEY MUST BE MAILED SEPARATELY. Note: you need not enter the contest to purchase the annual.

All orders must be accompanied by the required remittance in personal check or money order from, based on US $8.95 per copy which includes mailing and handling costs. They should reach Nikon Inc. not later than **October 31, 1989.** Do not order from other countries or from Nikon in Tokyo.

Distributor's Copy

NPCI ANNUAL 1989/90 ORDER FORM

Kindly fill in the blanks below in block letters.

I would like to order ______ copy/copies of the NPCI Annual at US$8.95 per copy, with a total price of ______. (I have included applicable sales tax for New York, Cal., Ill., Mass., Maryland, Conn., Georgia, Texas, Washington State.) I am enclosing a personal check/money order to cover this amount. I understand that this amount is not refundable. My check is made payable to Nikon Inc.

Order made by: Name

Address

City State Zip

Signature

NPCI ANNUAL 1989/90 Mailing Label

Kindly fill in the blanks below in block letters.

Name

Address

City State Zip

NORTHERN COUNTIES INTERNATIONAL SLIDE EXHIBITION

Sponsored by the Northern Counties Photographic Federation
c/o Mrs. Jane H. Black, LRPS, APAGB
15 Southlands
Tynemouth
Tyne and Wear
NE302QS England
(091) 259-2020

Contact: Mrs. Jane H. Black, LRPS, APAGB

Annual international exhibition of color slides.

Eligibility: Open to amateurs and pros.

Subject Matter: General Section-traditional and contemporary slides; Nature Section-nature and wildlife slides.

Submission Requirements: Send up to four 35mm color transparencies for each section (possible total of 8 per person).

Entry Fee: $50 per section.

Awards: General Section-8 medals, 4 blue ribbons, and 25 certificates of merit; Nature Section-8 medals, 2 blue ribbons, and 15 certificates of merit. Each entrant receives a color illustrated catalog and a "report card".

Sponsor reserves exhibition rights, and reproduction rights for illustrated catalog.

Entries are returned.

Write for information/entry form.

NORTHWEST INTERNATIONAL EXHIBITION OF PHOTOGRAPHY

Sponsored by the Western Washington Fair Association
PO Box 430
Puyallup, WA 98371
(206) 845-1771

Contact: Bonnie Nettnin, Superintendent

"One of the leading international exhibitions in the world...Entries are judged by a panel of three judges. The exhibition is viewed by an exceptionally large number of people."

Eligibility: Open to amateurs and pros.

Subject Matter: Open. There is a separate photo-journalism division.

Submission Requirements: Send color and/or B&W prints and/or transparencies. Prints should be 8x10" or 16x20". Prints for photojournalism section should be 8x10".

Entry Fee: $4 per section.

Awards: 5 gold medals by divisions of Photographic Society of America for Best of Show. 6 Fair Medals for originality; 1 Superintendent Award; 7 ribbon awards.

Sponsor reserves one-time reproduction rights for catalog.

Entries are returned (except to countries prohibiting transmission of funds).

Write for entry form.

OLYMPUS INTERNATIONAL PHOTO CONTEST

Sponsored by Olympus Optical Co., Ltd.
Poste Restante
Kyobashi Post Office
Tokyo 104
Japan

Annual photography contest that attracts entries from around the world.

Eligibility: Open to amateurs and pros. Pictures must have been taken with a 35mm SLR or 35mm lens shutter camera.

Subject Matter: Three categories- 1) General photo; 2) Nature photo; 3) My Best Shot.

Submission Requirements: Send 35mm color slides or 10x12" color and/or B&W prints. For category 3, send prints between 3.5x4.75" and 10x12". No submission limit.

Entry Fee: None.

Awards: Grand Prix awards, Semi-Grands Prix, Special Recognition Awards and Merit Awards in each category. Plus 70th Anniversary Special Awards, WWF Special Award, Quark Awards, and Merit Awards. 1989 Grand Prix winners received $4,000, an OM-4Ti Black camera, and 100mm f/2 and 28mm f/2 lenses. Other prizes include, cameras, magazine subscriptions, cash, and commemorative goods.

Photographers retain the copyright to their work. Olympus, reserves the right to publish and use any or all prize- winning entries for its advertising activities without payment. Olympus will contact each photographer before using his/her entries for promotional purposes.

Slides are returned with self-addressed envelope and 10 international reply coupons. Prints will not be returned.

NOTE: Rules and prizes for this contest vary from year to year. Write Olympus for information and entry form each year.

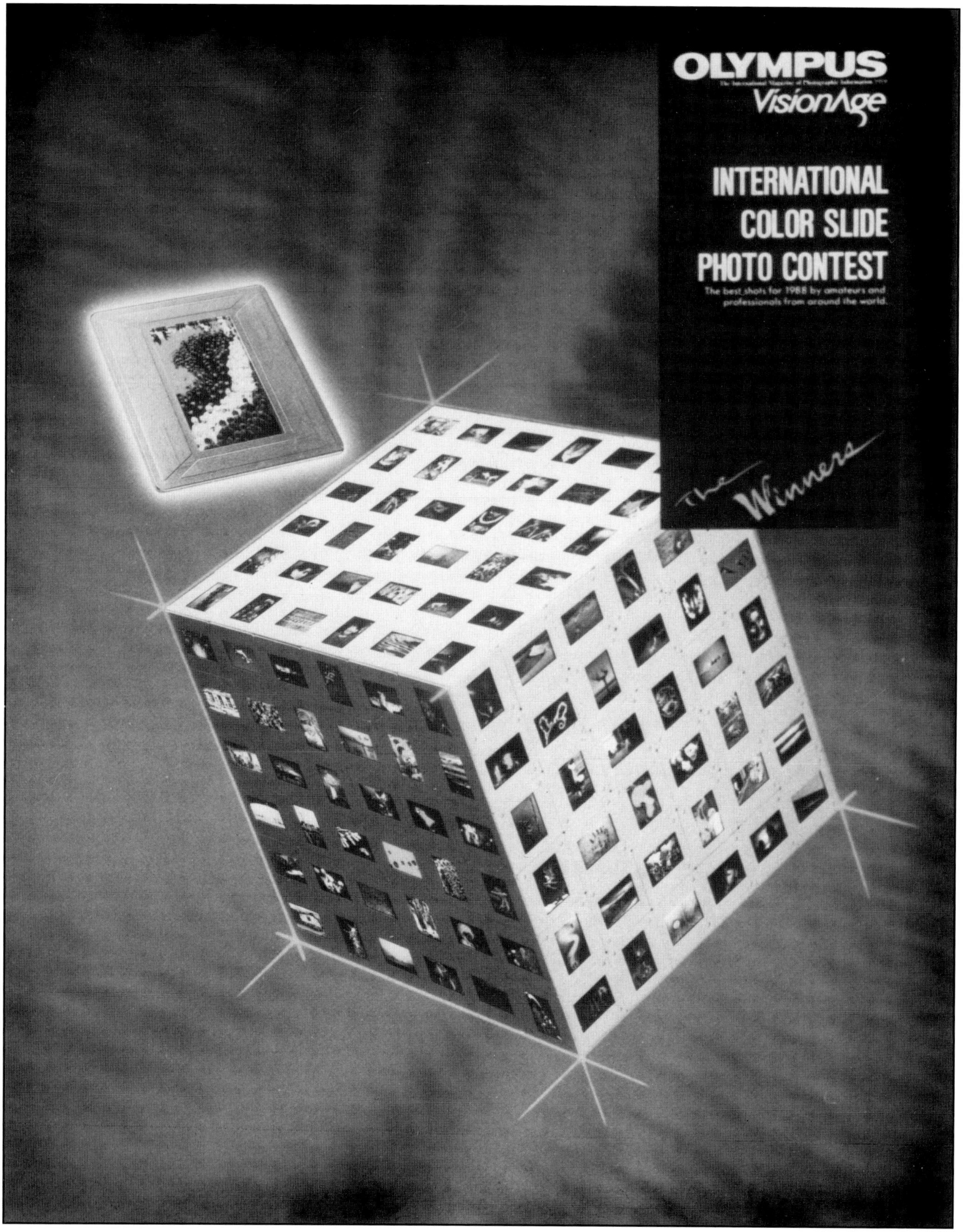

COURTESY OF OLYMPUS

Olympus publishes the winners of its annual photo contest in a special edition of *VisionAge* magazine.

ON CONSIGNMENT
Sponsored by On Consignment Gallery
222 Foothill Blvd., #224-E
La Canada, CA 91011-1456
(818) 569-3085
Contact: Christopher Morgan
On Consignment is an annual open gallery competition for artists working in any media including photography.
Eligibility: Open to amateurs and pros.
Subject Matter: Entries must deal with life or the celebration of life.
Submission Requirements: Send between 3 and 10 color and/or B&W transparencies for initial jurying. Actual work may be any size.
Entry Fee: $18 for 1-3 slides; $5 for each additional slide.
Awards: 1st prize-$1,000; 2nd prize-$500; 3rd prize-$250; two $100 Honorable Mentions.
Sponsor reserves the right to publish winning entries for promotion of the show.
Slides are not returned.
Write for information/entry form.

PCAA QUARTERLY CONTEST
Sponsored by the Photographic Competition Association of America
Box 53350
Philadelphia, PA 19405
(215) 279-2193
Contact: Director, Competition Committee
Quarterly contest (winter, spring, summer, and fall) for stills and prints that have won or have been selected in other contests. Themes vary from contest to contest.
Eligibility: Open to amateurs and pros.
Subject Matter: Open.
Submission Requirements: Send up to 5 color and/ or B&W prints. Maximum size 16x20".
Entry Fee: $5 per print, $15 minimum.
Awards: Cash awards; amounts vary from contest to contest.
Sponsor reservesone-timepublication/exhibition rights.
Entries are returned with SASE.
For information/entry write with SASE to:
PCAA Quarterly Contests, PO Box 53550-E, Philadelphia, PA 19105
NOTE: The Photographic Competition Association is an organization devoted exclusively to the promotion, development and support of the competition and exhibition of photography. PCAA acts as a support group for photographers, amateur or professional, who desire to participate in competitions and exhibitions. Some of the Association's activities include sponsoring photography competitions and publishing various newsletter-type publications devoted to current photo contest news and other photographic events throughout the year. Members are provided with helpful information such subjects as artistic evaluation, judging methods, technical advice, presentation standards and self promotion. Memberships are offered to photographers at any level from beginner through skilled professional. For more information write: PCAA, Box 53550, Philadelphia, PA 19105.

PDN/NIKON SELF-PROMOTION AWARDS COMPETITION
Sponsored by *Photo District News* and Nikon
PDN 49 East 21st Street
New York, NY 10010
Annual contest for photographers' self-promotion pieces. "It's your chance to show some of New York's best eyes your best work, and find out for certain how others truly see you. Win the satisfaction of knowing your promotion has impact and win some outstanding prizes, as well." Awards are based on "creativity, graphic excellence, professionalism and memorability—the basic ingredients necessary to any successful self-promotion."
Eligibility: Pros only.
Subject Matter: Self-promotion pieces. Three categories: Direct Mail includes cards, mailers and other printed pieces; Print Placements includes creative directories and annual, magazines; Best Ongoing Campaign includes divisions for established talent (any photographer who has been working as a professional for more than three years), and new talent (any photographer who has been working as a professional for three years or less).
Submission Requirements: Actual self-promotion pieces must be submitted (3 of each piece). Do not send original transparencies or other valuable artwork. Only one entry may be submitted in each category and you may enter no more than three categories. You must provide separate art and entry forms for each category entry.
Entry Fee: None.
Awards: (1990) First prize winners in each category will receive a Nikon N8008 camera body, 24-50mm

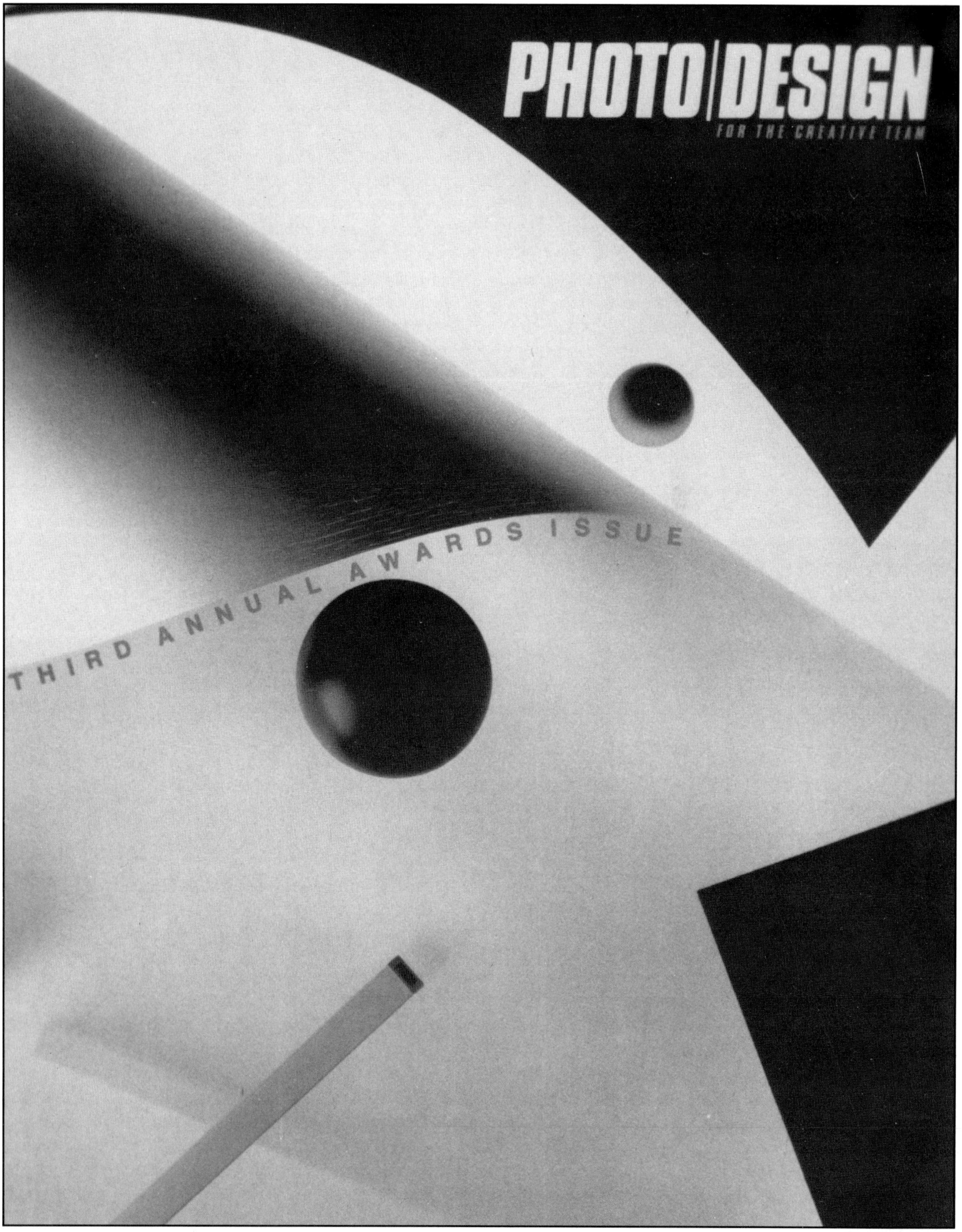

COURTESY OF *PHOTO/DESIGN*

Photo/Design **devotes an entire issue to winners of its annual contest.**

f/3.3.-4.5 AF Nikkor lens, SB-24 Speedlight and a regional two-page spread in the Adweek Portfolio of Photography. All winners in the category "Best Ongoing Campaign: New Talent" will receive a Nikon N8008 and coverage in the Awards Annual. All winning entries in each of the six categories will be featured in the PDN/Nikon Awards Annual and in the Awards Exhibit on display at Nikon House in Rockefeller Center.
Winning photographers consent to having their entries displayed at all Awards Exhibitions and reproduced in the awards brochure and any other promotional or editorial material related to the awards competitions. All other rights remain with the photographer.
Entries are not returned.
See *Photo District News* (or write) for information/entry form.

PARADE/KODAK PHOTOGRAPHY CONTEST
Sponsored by Parade Publications, Inc. and the Eastman Kodak Company
PO Box 3200
Grand Central Station
New York, NY 10163 (address changes each year)
(212) 573-7047
Contact: Catherine Braden Hemlepp
Annual contest sponsored by *Parade* magazine. Theme changes from year to year. 1990 theme was "Best Friends."
Eligibility: Open to amateurs and pros.
Subject Matter: Varies. 1990 entries must depict a special moment in a special relationship.
Submission Requirements: Send in color and/or B&W prints no larger than 8x10".
Entry Fee: None.
Awards: Exhibition. 100 winners receive $100 cash and an award certificate. Selected photographs will be published in Parade Magazine—photographers will receive a $200 publication fee.
Entries are not returned.
Write for information/entry form.

PATAGONIA FALL AND SPRING CATALOGS
Sponsored by Patagonia, Inc.
259 W. Santa Clara
Ventura, CA 93001
(805) 643-8616 x173
Contact: Jane Sievert
"We accept spirited submissions of Patagonia clothing in use for publication in our company's catalog."
Eligibility: Open to amateurs and pros.
Subject Matter: Shots of Patagonia clothing in use.
Submission Requirements: Color transparencies are preferred. No submission limit.
Entry Fee: None.
Awards: Payment and credit are given for anything published in the Patagonia catalog, ad, or hangtag.
Sponsor reserves the right to publish photos in catalog, ad, or hangtag.
Transparencies are returned; prints are not.
NOTE: This is not a contest per se, but it looks like a lot of fun. Write to Patagonia for guidelines.

PHOTO/DESIGN AWARDS COMPETITION
Sponsored by *Photo/Design* Magazine
1515 Broadway
New York, NY 10036
(212) 536-5325
Contact: Richard Reed
Annual contest for photographs as they are used in an actual project. Judging is on basis of quality of the photograph, quality of design, and the appropriateness of the entire project to its intended purpose.
Eligibility: Open to professional photographers.
Subject Matter: Categories: magazine advertising; newspaper advertising; magazine covers; book covers and jackets; magazine editorial; books; newspaper editorial; annual reports; brochures; calendars; catalogs; corporate and association publications; record jackets; posters; photographer's self-promotional materials.
Submission Requirements: Send in actual finished work. No submission limit.
Entry Fee: $20.
Awards: Gold, Silver, and Merit winners are published in special issue of the magazine. Plaques; certificates. Prizes aren't always awarded in every category. It depends on the quality of entries.
Entries are not returned.
All rights remain with photography.
Call or write for entry.

PHOTO METRO ANNUAL PHOTOGRAPHIC CONTEST
Sponsored by *Photo Metro* Magazine
6 Rodgers 207C
San Francisco, CA 94103
(415) 861-6453
Contact: Henry Brimmer

Annual contest. Guidelines and subject matter vary each year.
Eligibility: Open to amateurs and pros.
Subject Matter: All subject matters accepted; specific guidelines are announced in Call for Entry each year.
Submission Requirements: Send color, B&W, (or mixed-media) transparencies. No size limit.
Entry Fee: Varies; usually $10 - one slide, $20 - three.
Awards: Cash awards between $1,500 and $3,000. Winning entries are published in the magazine.
Sponsor reserves one-time reproduction rights.
Entries are returned.
Send SASE for entry.

THE PHOTO REVIEW NATIONAL PHOTOGRAPHY COMPETITION
Sponsored by *The Photo Review*
301 Hill Ave.
Langhorne, PA 19047
(215) 757-8921
Contact: Stephen Perloff
Annual contest. Accepted work is reproduced in the summer issue of *The Photo Review*, a widely acclaimed critical journal of photography with a national distribution. "536 photographers submitted over 2,100 prints in 1989. Past winners have been given one-person shows and have had their work bought by collectors because it was seen in *The Photo Review*."
Eligibility: Open to amateurs and pros. All photographic processes are accepted.
Subject Matter: Open
Submission Requirements: Send no more than 5 color and/or B&W prints, 16x20" or smaller (except for "unique" work).
Entry Fee: $16 for up to 3 prints; $4 for up to 2 more.
Awards: $1,000 in cash prizes. Winning photos are published in the magazine.
Sponsor reserves one-time reproduction rights.
Entries are returned.
Send SASE for prospectus.

PHOTOGRAPHIC EXHIBITION
Sponsored by the Phinney Center Gallery
6532 Phinney Ave. N.
Seattle, WA 98103
(206) 783-2244
Contact: Ed Medeiros
Annual open photographic exhibition.
Eligibility: Open to amateurs and pros. All photographic media works must have been completed in the past 18 months and must not have been selected for previous Phinney Center competitions.
Subject Matter: Open.
Submission Requirements: Send between 3 and 5 slides of color and/or B&W prints for jurying. Prints will be required for show. No size limit.
Entry Fee: $5 per slide.
Awards: Show award to jurors' choice.
Sponsor reserves right to reproduce work for publicity and promotion.
Entries are returned with SASE.
Write for information/entry form.

PHOTOGRAPHY ANNUAL
Sponsored by *Communication Arts* Magazine
410 Sherman Ave.
PO Box 10300
Palo Alto, CA 94303
(415) 326-6040
Contact: Patrick Coyne
Annual international competition in the area of photography for advertising, design, editorial and any other area of the communication arts. Work selected by jury will appear in the August issue of *Communication Arts*.
Eligibility: Open to amateurs and pros. Work must have been produced within the March to March calendar year.
Subject Matter: Open.
Submission Requirements: Send color and/or B&W transparencies or unmounted printed samples. No submission limit.
Entry Fee: $15 for single entry; $30 for a series (5 or less).
Awards: Award of Excellence certificates for the photographer, client, and art director of each accepted photograph. Winning work will be published in the *Photography Awards Annual*.
Sponsor reserves the right to reproduce the selected pieces in the August issue of *Communication Arts*.
Entries are not returned.
Write for information/entry form.

PHOTOGRAPHY 10
Sponsored by the Perkins Center for the Arts
Kings Highway and Camden Avenue
Moorestown, NJ 08057
(609) 235-6488

Contact: Sid Sachs
Largest annual juried photography competition in the metropolitan Philadelphia area.
Eligibility: Open to amateurs and pros.
Subject Matter: Open.
Submission Requirements: Send up to 5 color and/or B&W prints. Photographs must be suitably framed and ready to hang. Entries must be hand delivered and picked up.
Entry Fee: $4 per print.
Awards: $1,500 awards of merit, Smithsonian Institution and Philadelphia Museum of Art Prizes.

PHOTOGRAPHY '91
Sponsored by the Abington Art Center
515 Meetinghouse Road
Jenkintown, PA 19046
(215) 887-4882
Contact: Laura Burnham
Annual juried exhibition. Open to any photographic process.
Eligibility: Open to amateurs and pros.
Subject Matter: Open.
Submission Requirements: Send up to 3 color and/or B&W matted prints (unframed). Total height plus width of mat must not exceed 60".
Entry Fee: AAC members: $12; non-members: $15; mail-ins: $20.
Awards: $1,500 in cash prizes. $500 first prize; Philadelphia Museum of Art purchase award.
Sponsor reserves right to reproduce prints for publicity.
25% commission will be charged on sales.
Entries will be returned.
Write for information/entry form.

PHOTOSPIVA
Sponsored by the Spiva Art Center
Newman and Duquesne Roads
Joplin, MO 64801
(417) 623-0183
A national open fine art photography competition and exhibition.
Eligibility: Open to all photographers in the United States and its territories. Work must not have been previously exhibited at the Spiva Art Center.
Subject Matter: Open
Submission Requirements: Send up to four color and/or B&W matted prints. Window mats are preferred and should follow standard museum sizes: 8x10", 11x14", 14x17", 16x20", 20x24", 22x28". Sequences should be mounted together on one board; each board of sequences will be considered as one entry.
Entry Fee: $10.
Awards: The juror will bestow cash awards of $350, $250, and four $150, as well as six $50 honorable mentions. Award-winning images will be published in a catalog.
Sponsor reserves the right to reproduce any entry for catalog or publicity purposes related to the exhibition or future exhibitions.
Spiva Art Center will retain a 25% commission on all sales of work directly attributed to the exhibition.
Entries will be returned collect.
Send a SASE for entry.

PHOTOWORK
Sponsored by the Dutchess County Art Association at Barrett House
55 Noxon St.
Poughkeepsie, NY 12601
(914) 471-2550
Contact: Fran Smulcheski
National photography exhibition curated by museum/gallery staff member, usually from New York City. Show is judged from slide entries.
Eligibility: Open to amateurs and pros.
Subject Matter: Open. Art photography accepted. Traditional and experimental approaches encouraged. No commercial work, please.
Submission Requirements: Send at least three slides of color and/or B&W prints for initial jurying. No size limit for actual prints.
Entry Fee: $18 for three slides; $5 for each additional slide.
Awards: Cash prizes—amounts undetermined at presstime.
Entries returned with SASE.
Sponsor reserves the right to reject any work(s) which differ significantly from slides submitted.
Write for prospectus.

PHOTOWORK
Sponsored by Photogroup, The University of Miami Department of Art and Art History, Associated Photo, ISACO International, and Ryder System Incorporated.
The New Gallery
University of Miami
1300 Campo Sano Drive

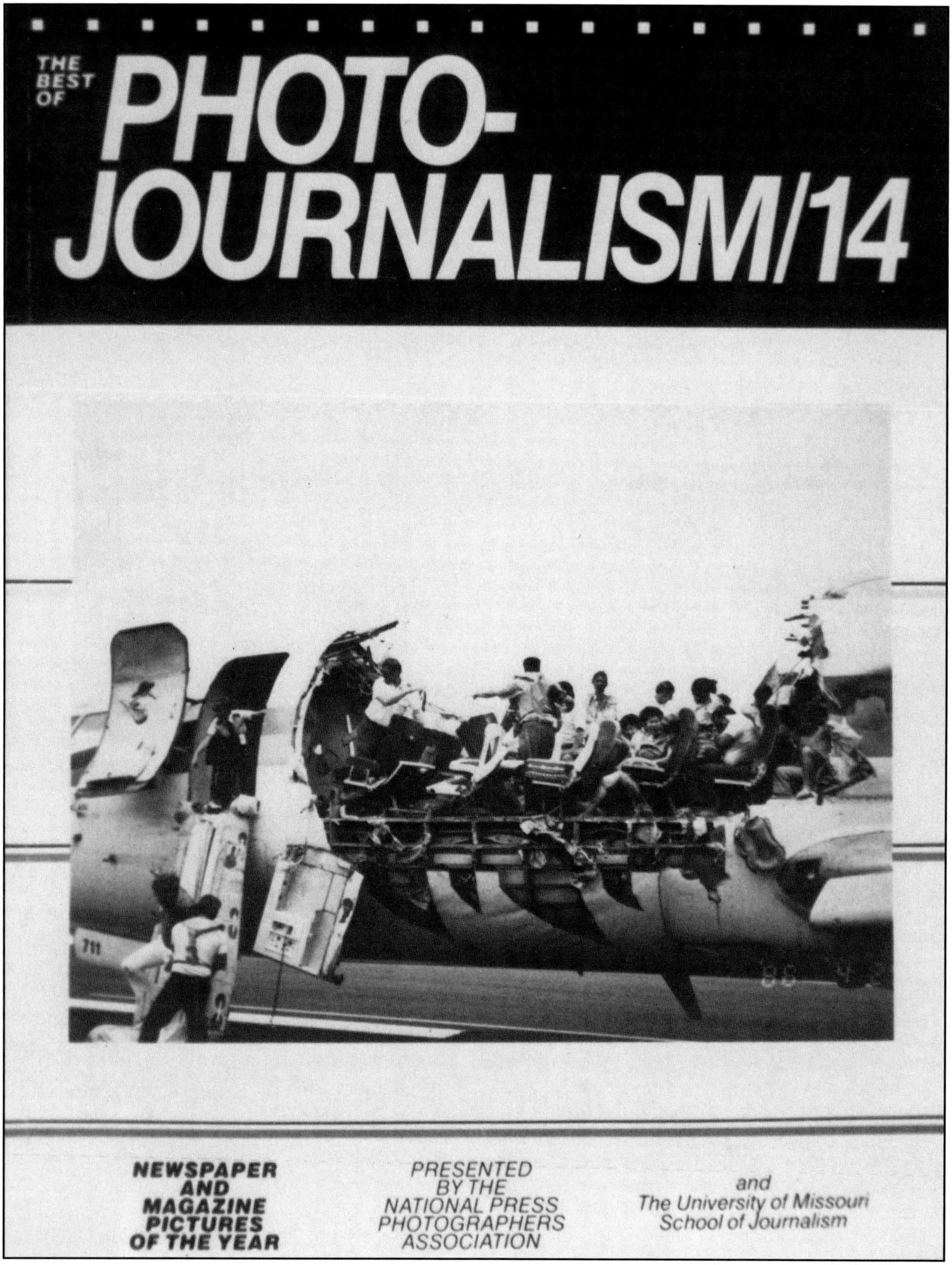

COURTESY OF NPPA/PICTURES OF THE YEAR

The Best of Photojournalism/14 features selected shots from the 1989 Pictures of the Year Contest.

Coral Gables, FL 33124
(305) 284-2542
Annual national competition and exhibition for photographers.
Eligibility: Open to all photographers, 18 years of age and older, currently residing in the U.S.
Subject Matter: Open.
Submission Requirements: Send up to two color and/or B&W prints. Prints may be any size but must be window matted with standard white mounting board and overall size must conform to either 16x20" or 20x24" format.
Entry Fee: $15.
Awards: Total of $1,500 cash to be divided equally among 3 winners.
Sponsor reserves the right to reproduce any entry for publicity purposes.
Entries will be returned.
Exhibited work will be for sale.
Write for information/entry form.

PICTURES OF THE YEAR
Sponsored by the University of Missouri School of Journalism; National Press Photographers Association; Canon USA, Inc; and Professional Photography Division, Eastman Kodak Company
University of Missouri School of Journalism
9th and Elm Streets
Columbia, MO 65201
(314) 882-4442
Contact: Julie Ostrem, Contest Coordinator.
POY is conducted annually to recognize excellence in photojournalism by honoring press photographers and editors and the institutions where they are employed. "POY is one of the largest contests of its kind; in 1989, 1,931 photographers and editors entered more than 36,000 photographs and tearsheets."
Eligibility: Open to amateurs and pros.
Subject Matter: Photographs are judged in 22 individual categories such as spot news, feature picture, sports action, and news picture story. Photographers may also enter portfolio, Canon Photo Essay, or Kodak Crystal Eagle Award competitions. In the editing division, publications may enter tear sheets in categories such as best feature page, best special section.
Submission Requirements: 35mm color and/or B&W duplicate slides. Entrants may submit up to 20 in individual categories, plus a portfolio, Canon Photo Essay and Kodak Crystal Eagle Award per entrant.
Entry Fee: $45; free to all members of the NPPA.
Awards: Trophies, Canon cameras, Kodak products, plaques, certificates, and cash prizes of more than $8,000 are given each year.
Photos may be used in the annual book, in exhibitions, and in promotion of the book and competition itself and for promotional, educational and historical record purposes. Winning photos and book selects become part of the permanent POY collection.
Only material entered in trays (portfolios, Canon Photo Essays, and Kodak Crystal Eagle Award submissions) are returned.
Write for information/entry form.

POSITIVE/NEGATIVE
Sponsored by the Slocumb Galleries
Dept. of Art
East Tennessee State University
Box 23740A
Johnson City, TN 37614-0002
(615) 929-4247
Contact: M. Wayne Dyer
Juried exhibition of drawings, fibers, graphics, painting, prints, mixed media, sculpture, ceramics and photography. The show is not judged by categories.
Eligibility: Open to all amateur artists residing in the U.S. with the exception of East Tennessee State University faculty and students. All work must be original and must have been completed after January 1, 1987.
Subject Matter: Open.
Submission Requirements: Send 35mm slides for jurying process. Prints smaller than 40" in any direction and weighing less than 50 lbs. will be required for exhibition.
Entry Fee: $15.
Awards: Up to $2,000 in purchase awards; place awards will be selected.
Sponsor reserves right to photograph or reproduce any and all works in the exhibit for the purposes of records and publicity.
No commission charged on sales.
Slides not accepted are returned.
Write for entry/information.

***PRINT'S* REGIONAL DESIGN ANNUAL**
Sponsored by *Print*
6400 Goldsboro Road
Bethesda, MD 20817
(212) 463-0600

Print's full-color Regional Design Annual provides a comprehensive design profile of the U.S.
Eligibility: Open to any art director, designer, illustrator, photographer, etc., working anywhere in the 50 states and the District of Columbia.
Subject Matter: Any printed communication that was published during the previous January 1-December 31 calendar year. Includes advertising, promotion, annual reports and other corporate publications, posters, magazines, newspapers, book and record album covers, logos and symbols, letterheads, menus, calendars, packaging, billboards, etc.
Submission Requirements: Send the actual printed piece, unmounted. Do not send slides except in the case of packaging and billboard entries.
Entry Fee: $15-$100.
Awards: All accepted entries receive Certificates of Distinction and are published in the *Print Regional Design Annual.*
Entries will not be returned.
Write or call for entry.

PRO FOOTBALL HALL OF FAME PHOTO CONTEST

Sponsored by Canon, the Official Camera of the Pro Football Hall of Fame
Pro Football Hall of Fame
2121 George Halas Drive NW
Canton, OH 44708
(216) 465-8207
Contact: Don Smith
Annual contest for photographers on assignment to NFL pre-season, regular season, or post-season games.
Eligibility: Open to pro photographers who meet the above requirements.
Subject Matter: Action or feature of NFL football games.
Submission Requirements: Send up to 12 B&W prints at least 10x14" mounted on 16x20" boards, or up to 12 35mm duplicate color transparencies. (24 image total submission limit.)
Entry Fee: None.
Awards: Total of $4,200 in cash. Winning photos will be displayed at the Hall of Fame as space permits.
Hall of Fame reserves the right to use entries for publicity of contest or for displays.
Entries are not returned, but all copyrights remain with photographer.
Write for information/entry form.

PULITZER PRIZES

Sponsored by Columbia University
702 Journalism
Columbia University
NY, NY 10027
(212) 854-3841
Contact: Robert C. Christopher
Endowed by the will of Joseph Pulitzer and administered under the trusteeship of Columbia University, each year the Pulitzer Prize is awarded to two photographers for outstanding work in the spot news and feature photography categories.
Eligibility: Open to amateur and pro photographers. Photo(s) must have been published in an American daily or weekly newspaper. Generally the newspaper that published the photo(s) enters it in the contest.
Subject Matter: Open. Spot news and feature photography categories.
Submission Requirements: Send up to 20 color and/or B&W prints or tear sheets. Maximum size-11"x14".
Entry Fee: $20.
Awards: $3,000 for each category.
Prints and tear sheets become Pulitzer Prize property.
Photographers retain copyright.
Write for information/entry form.

PURE-BRED DOGS/ AMERICAN KENNEL GAZETTE ANNUAL PHOTO CONTEST

Sponsored by the American Kennel Club
51 Madison Ave.
New York, N.Y. 10010
(212) 696-8332
Contact: Jeff Dorl, Photo Editor
Annual photo contest. Theme varies from year to year.
Eligibility: Open to amateurs and pros.
Subject Matter: AKC-recognized pure-bred dogs. Candids only; no show poses or dogs in costumes.
Submission requirements: Send one color and/or one B&W print; 5 x 7" or 8 x 10".
Entry Fee: None.
Awards: $500 - first place color and B&W; $250 - second place color and B&W; $150 - third place color and B&W; Honorable Mentions certificates.
Sponsor reserves first time publication rights.
Entries are not returned.
Contact Pure-Bred Dogs/American Kennel Gazette for contest theme.
Send SASE for contest theme, rules and regulations.

RATED X
Sponsored by Neikrug Photographica Ltd.
224 East 68th St.
New York, NY 10021
(212) 288-7741
Contact: Marge Neikrug
Annual exhibition of erotic photography.
Eligibility: Open to amateurs and pros.
Subject Matter: Only nudes or erotic photos. Can be humorous, serious, landscape, cityscape, S&M.
Submission Requirements: Send up to eight 11x14" or 16x20" color and/or B&W prints.
Entry Fee: $25 if accepted in exhibit.
Awards: Exhibition.
50% commission will be charged on all sales.
Entries are returned.
Write for information/entry form.

***READER'S DIGEST* ARTISTS AT GIVERNY**
Sponsored by *Reader's Digest* and the College Art Association
275 Seventh Ave.
New York, NY 10001
(212) 691-3893
Contact: Elizabeth Nesbitt
Reader's Digest invites artists who are citizens of the United States to apply for one of the three six-month artist residencies to live and work in Giverny, France—home of Impressionist painter Claude Monet for the last forty years of his life.
Eligibility: Open to artists with a minimum of the Bachelor's degree, or equivalent. Recipients of the *Reader's Digest* Artists at Giverny program may not hold other fellowships concurrently. Participants may not hold a regular job in France during their residency. Accomodations at Giverny are not suitable for children. Artists with children must make separate living and child-care arrangements at their own expense. (Artists employed by *Reader's Digest* or any of its subsidiaries are not eligible to participate.)
Subject Matter: Open.
Submission Requirements: Submit at least ten, but no more than 18, slides of your work in a clear acetate 8-1/2x11" slide sheet. Finalists will be asked to submit no more than three original works of art. A proposal summary/career plan and references are also required.
Entry Fee: None.
Awards: Three artists will each receive round-trip transportation to Giverny for the artist, a furnished studio apartment at Giverny, a working studio to be shared by the three resident artists, $2,000 before departure to France, $1,600 payable in French Francs, on the first day of each month at Giverny, $1,000 upon return to the United States, and use of a car while in residence in Giverny. *Reader's Digest* will arrange for an exhibition in Paris and/or New York of selected works inspired by the artist's residency at Giverny.
Entries returned with SASE.
Write for application.

READER'S PORTFOLIO
Sponsored by *Outdoor & Travel Photography* Magazine
1115 Broadway, 8th Floor
New York, NY 10010
Contact: Portfolio Editor
"Each issue we choose 10-15 photos sent in by readers and display them in a 6-page article. The winner's autobiography accompanies the photos. This feature is designed to showcase our readers' work, and help them gain national recognition. Submissions must be addressed to Portfolio Editor'. If the images are used in a different part of the magazine, to illustrate a feature story, for example, a separate payment will be negotiated. Our advice: Be patient. If you don't win the first time you enter, continue shooting and send us a new set for the next issue. Although entries are often returned within four weeks, it can sometimes take up to four months. This is because we are a quarterly magazine, and finalists' are held onto until the last possible moment. Our final suggestion is to study the magazine. It will give you a good idea of what we're looking for."
Eligibility: Open to amateurs and pros. Include a caption for each photo, information on how each shot was taken (camera, lens, film, exposure, and technique) if known; and a 1/2 page autobiography.
Subject Matter: Scenic, nature, wildlife, travel, action sports—anything Outdoor & Travel Photography readers are interested in photographing.
Submission Requirements: Send an unlimited number of color and/or B&W prints or transparencies. Slides or 8x10" prints are preferred.
Entry Fee: None.
Awards: $25 and 3 copies of the magazine that contains your photos. Occasionally, winners also receive photographic equipment prizes, which are announced ahead of time in the magazine.

COURTESY OF SCHOLASTIC ART™ AWARDS

The Scholastic Art Awards list the names and schools of all of its winners in booklets like this one.

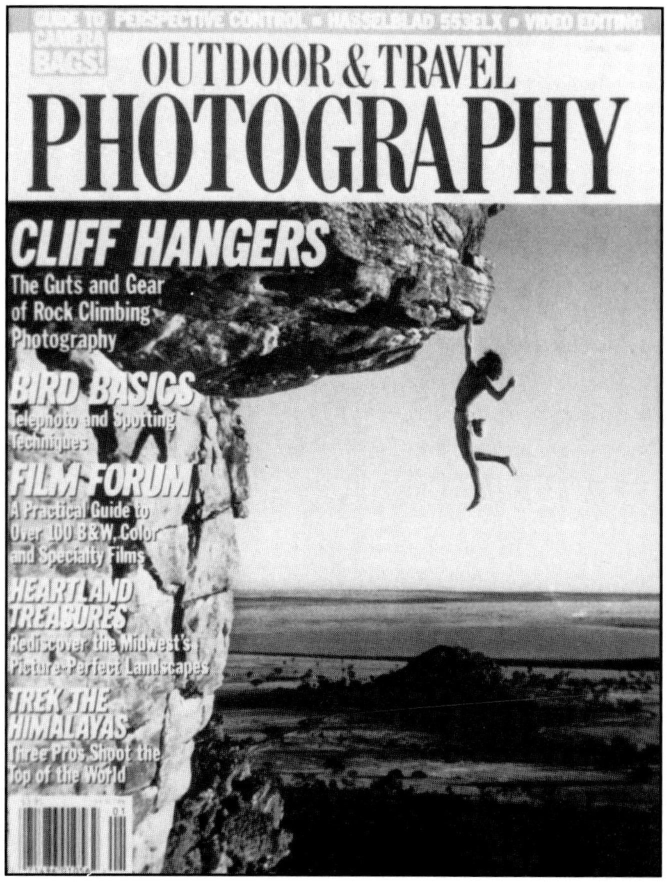

COURTESY OF *OUTDOOR & TRAVEL PHOTOGRAPHY*/HARRIS PUBLICATIONS

Outdoor & Travel Photography **magazine publishes readers' photos in each issue in a section appropriately titled *"Reader's Portfolio"*.**

Sponsor reserves rights for one-time usage.
Entries are returned with SASE or International Reply Coupons.

SALON INTERNACIONAL DE ARTE FOTOGRAFICO
Sponsored by Foto Club Buenos Aires
Casilla Postal 5377
1000 Buenos Aires
Argentina
Contact: Mirta Cavallero
Annual international exhibition since 1946; conducted according to PSA and FIAP regulations.
Eligibility: Open to amateurs only.
Subject Matter: Pictorial, free subject, photojournalism, nature, wildlife.
Submission Requirements: Send color and/or B&W prints or transparancies depending on subject category. Prints should be unmounted.
Entry Fee: $6 per section.
Awards: PSA, FIAP, and sponsors' medals and diploma.
Sponsor retains the right to reproduce entries for publicity/promotion.
Entries are returned.
Write for more information/entry form.

SCHOLASTIC ART AWARDS
Sponsored by Scholastic Inc., and Ricoh Cameras and Video
Scholastic Inc.
730 Broadway
New York, NY 10003
(212) 505-3566
Contact: Chuck Wentzel
Annual awards program open to high school students in grades 7-12. National awards for individual photographs; scholarships for high school seniors submitting outstanding portfolios. This is the oldest high school competition in the United States.
Eligibility: Open to amateurs in grades 7-12 only. Entries must be submitted through entrant's school with teacher approval.
Subject Matter: Open. Experimental photographs accepted.
Submission Requirements: Color and/or B&W prints or transparencies. Prints must be at least 24 square inches and matted to at least 11x14". Photographs, including mat, may not exceed 20x26".
Entry Fee: Varies.
Awards: Plaques and scholarships; some equipment awards.
Sponsor retains two-year reproduction rights.
Entries are returned.
Write for details.

SEEING DOUBLE
Sponsored by Hill Coutry Arts Foundation
P.O. Box 176
Ingram, TX 78025
(512) 367-5121
Contact: Betty Vernon
Annual national juried exhibition of photography, graphics, and fine crafts.
Eligibility: Open to amateurs and pros.
Subject Matter: Open.
Submission Requirements: Send slides for initial jurying and color and/or B&W prints 8 x 10" and larger for show.
Entry Fee: $22 non-members; $15 members.
Awards: $2,200 in awards.
Slides are kept; prints are returned.
Sponsor reserves the right to use images to publicize show.

SELECTIONS BEST SERIES
Sponsored by the Eye Gallery
1151 Mission Street
San Francisco, CA 94117
(415) 567-6153
Contact: Tom Ferentz
Two winning series will be chosen by a juror to be exhibited at the Eye Gallery.
Eligibility: Open to amateurs and pros.
Subject Matter: Open.
Submission Requirements: Submit 15-20 slides, a resume, and a one-page statement of intent.
Entry Fee: $25
Awards: Two photographers will be awarded exhibitions at the Eye Gallery.
Entries are returned with SASE.
Write for information/entry form.

SELECTIONS PRINT COMPETITION
Sponsored by the Eye Gallery
1151 Mission Street
San Francisco, CA 94117
(415) 567-6153
Contact: Tom Ferentz

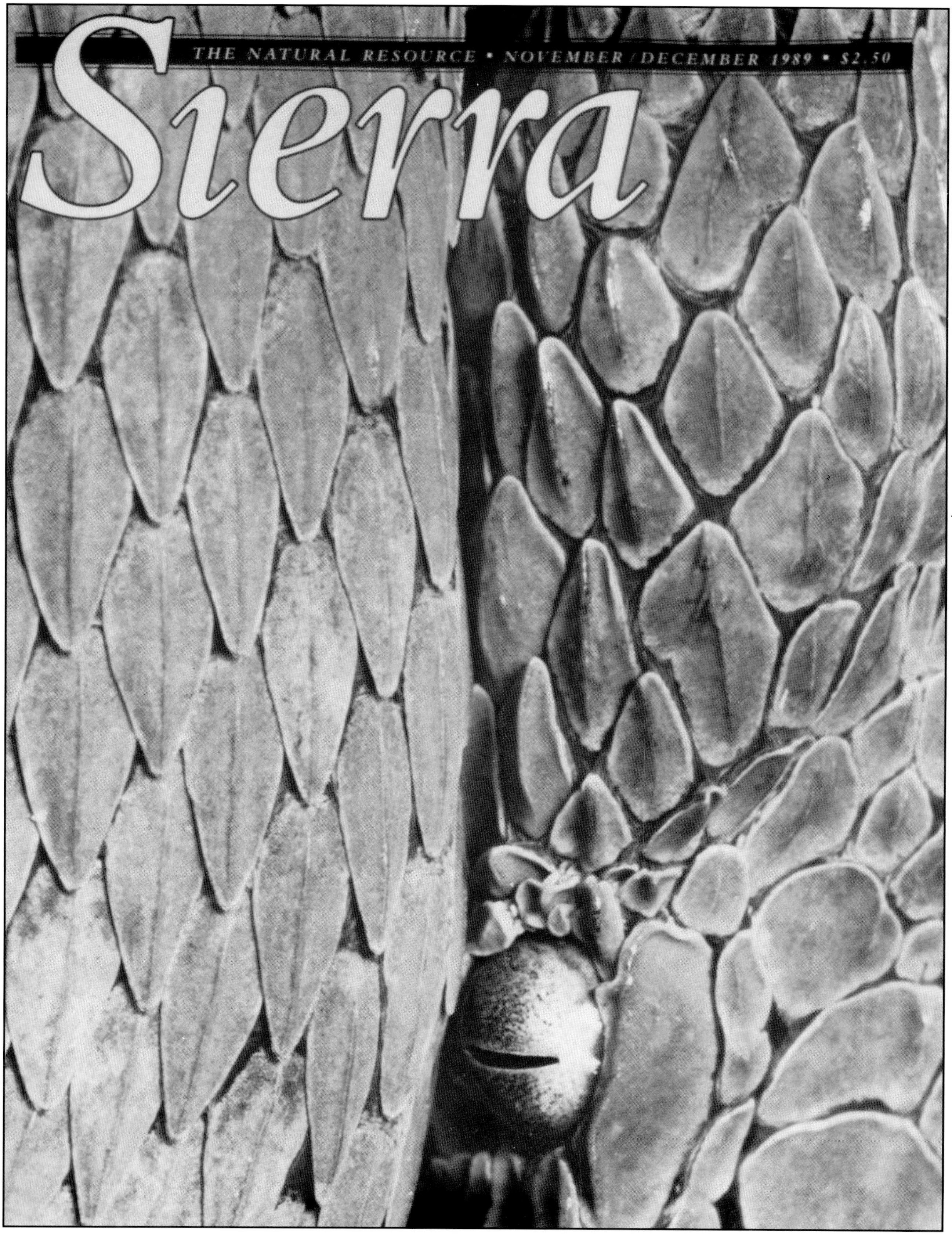

COURTESY OF *SIERRA*/COVER PHOTO BY DAVID BARKER

Sierra magazine publishes the winners of its annual photo contest in the magazine each year. Grand Prize winner David Barker, whose shot of a pit viper graces this cover, won a Nikon N4004, an AF Zoom Nikkor 35-70mm f/3.3-4.5 lens, and an all-terrain bicycle.

Annual juried photography exhibition.
Eligibility: Open to amateurs and pros.
Subject Matter: Open
Submission Requirements: Submit color and/or B&W prints. Matted prints preferred. No submission limit.
Entry Fee: $7 each print; $5 each print for Friends of the Eye.
Awards: Cash prizes, gift certificates, and photo materials.
Entries are returned with SASE.
Write for information/entry form.

SEPTEMBER COMPETITION
Sponsored by the Alexandria Museum of Art
PO Box 1028
Alexandria, LA 71309-1028
(318) 443-3458
Contact: Marguerite McCarthy
Annual competition open to all media including photography.
Eligibility: Open to amateurs and pros over the age of 18 working in all media. Work must have been completed in the last two years.
Subject Matter: Open.
Submission Requirements: Entries will be juried by 35mm slides. Submit no more than two slides of color and/or B&W prints that do not exceed 6 feet in any dimension.
Entry Fee: $15.
Awards: $2,000 in purchase and cash awards.
Accepted slides remain property of the museum.
Entries are returned COD.
Write or call for prospectus.

***SIERRA* MAGAZINE PHOTO CONTEST**
Sponsored by *Sierra* Magazine
(publication of Sierra Club).
730 Polk Street
San Francisco, CA 94109
(415) 923-5656
Contact: Silvana Nova
Annual photography contest; some rules vary from year to year. Winners' work is published in magazine and displayed at Sierra Club headquarters in San Francisco.
Eligibility: Open to amateurs and pros who are not Sierra suppliers. Previously published work, photos pending publication, or photos that have won other contests are not eligible.
Subject Matter: Categories vary from year to year; 1989 categories were: Abstracts in Nature; The Meeting of Land and Water; Wildlife; and Our Troubled Earth.
Submission Requirements: Send 35mm, 4x5", or 2 1/4" color transparencies, or black-and-white prints up to 11x14". Two image per category submission limit.
Entry Fee: $5 (paid when requesting submission forms).
Awards: Publication, merchandise. 1989 prizes included a Nikon N4004, and all-terrain bicycle, and Vivitar binoculars.
Sponsor retains one-time reproduction rights. Black-and-white winners are retained for matting for the lobby. Color entries are returned.
Entry rules and information are published in full-page notice in the March/April and May/June issues.

SPRING PHOTOGRAPHY CONTEST
Sponsored by *Photographer's Forum* Magazine
511 Olive Street, Dept. 7
Santa Barbara, CA 93101
(805) 963-0439
Annual photography contest sponsored by photography magazine dedicated to the "emerging" professional photographer. Winning photos are published in the magazine. All contest finalists (8% of all entries) will be published in *The Best of Photography Annual.* All entrants who are new subscribers receive a free six-month subscription to the magazine.
Eligibility: Open to amateurs and pros.
Subject Matter: Open.
Submission Requirements: Send B&W prints, color prints, or color slides. Entries must be unmounted 8x10" or smaller. No submission limit.
Entry Fee: $2.75-$3.75 per photo.
Awards: Two grand prizes of $1,000 each for Best Color and Best B&W; two second prizes of $500 each for Best Color and Best B&W; two third prizes of $350 each for Best Color and Best B&W; ten fourth prizes of $25 each for top five color prints or slides and top five B&W prints; 100 Honorable Mentions. All Honorable Mentions will be listed in the magazine and will receive a certificate of outstanding merit from Photographer's Forum. Winning photos will be published in the magazine. All contest finalists (top 8% of entries) will be published in *The Best of Photography Annual.*
Photographers retain all rights to photos. *Photographer's Forum* reserves the right to publish all contest winners and finalists.

Entries returned with SASE.
Write for information/entry form.

TAYLOR COUNTY FAIR PHOTO CONTEST
Sponsored by the Taylor County Photo Club and the Taylor County Fair
c/o Taylor Co. Photo Club
PO Box 613
Grafton, WV 26354-0613
(304) 265-1895
Contact: J.P. Isner
Eligibility: Amateurs only.
Subject Matter: Open.
Submission Requirements: Send up to ten color and/or B&W prints between 8x10" and 16x20". Prints must be mounted. Color and B&W are judged together.
Entry Fee: $5 for first print; $3 each additional print.
Awards: Best of Show-$75; First-$60; Second-$35; Third-$20.
Entries returned with SASE or return postage.
Write Taylor County Photo Club for information.

TEN BEST OF THE WEST
Sponsorship rotates among the six Movie Club Associations located in the Western half of the United States and Canada.
Contact: George W. Cushman, Executive Secretary
Box 4034
Long Beach, CA 90804
(213) 498-1634
Annual motion picture festival for non-professional motion picture makers (film or video). Held each fall in conjunction with a 3-day seminar on subjects related to all forms of picture making.
Eligibility: Open to amateurs only.
Subject Matter: Open, but X-rated efforts may not be included in the public screenings.
Submission Requirements: Send color or B&W 16mm, 8mm, Super 8mm (film) and 1/2" video. No submission limit.
Entry Fee: An entry fee of $5 allows the entry of 2 films by the same producer.
Awards: Certificates, trophies in certain categories (humor and sound).
All rights remain with the producer.
Entries are returned.
Requests for 1990 entry forms (available in June '90) to: Harold Stern, Competition Chairman, 33 Miramonte Court, San Carlos, CA 94070. Contact Ten Best of the West for other years.

THREE RIVERS ART FESTIVAL
Sponsored by the Carnegie Museum of Art
207 Sweetbriar St.
Pittsburgh, PA 15211
(412) 824-2041
Contact: Harriett Mendelowitz
Annual juried exhibition, which is part of visual and performing arts festival. Includes photography as well as major curated exhibitions, and commissioned works by major artists.
Eligibility: Open to amateurs and pros.
Subject Matter: Open.
Submission Requirements: Send 1 to 3 color and/or B&W prints. No size limit.
Entry Fee: $15.
Awards: Cash awards of $1,000, $500, $300, $250; and purchase awards.
Sponsor reserves reproduction rights for festival PR usage and receives 25% commission on any sales.
Entries are returned.
Write for information/entry form.

TOLEDO FRIENDS OF PHOTOGRAPHY REGIONAL JURIED PHOTOGRAPHY EXHIBITION
Sponsored by the Toledo Friends of Photography
3154 Makkway Road
Toledo, OH
(419) 535-1528
Contact: Mary Field
Competitive exhibition open to persons currently living in the Midwest region. All forms of photographic media are accepted.
Eligibility: Open to amateurs and pros.
Subject Matter: Open
Submission Requirements: Send up to 4 transparencies of color and/or B&W prints for first jurying. Prints required for second jurying of accepted work. No size limit on prints.
Entry Fee: $17 for non-members; $10 for members of the Toledo Friends of Photography.
Awards: Cash awards.
Sponsor reserves right to photograph accepted work for publicity purposes.
Sponsor receives 50% commission on sales.
Entries returned with SASE.

For information/entry form write: Regional Exhibit, TFP, Box 8408, Toledo, OH 43623.

U.S. INDUSTRIAL FILM AND VIDEO FESTIVAL
Sponsored by the United States Festivals Association
841 North Addison Ave.
Elmhurst, IL 60126-1291
(708) 834-7773
Contact: J.W. Anderson, Chairman; Patricia A. Meyer, Executive Director.
Annual international awards competition to select and honor the world's most outstanding sponsored, business and industrial audiovisual productions. Competition includes categories for photography.
Eligibility: Pros only.
Subject Matter: Business and industrial a/v productions.
Submission Requirements: Send in 16mm film or video tape on 3/4" U-Matic or 1/2" VHS formats in the NTSC, PAL or SECAM standard. No submission limit.
Entry Fee: $130.
Awards: Gold Camera and Silver Screen Award plaques, certificates and special industry sponsored awards.
All rights remain with producer/photographer.
Entries are returned.
Write for entry/info.

WELSH INTERNATIONAL COLOUR SLIDE SALON
Sponsored by The Welsh Photographic Federation
c/o 43, Heol-Y-Drudwen
Morriston
Swansea, W. Glam.
SA6 6TA, United Kingdom
(+44) 792-701535
Contact: Gary and Jennifer Thomas
Annual International color slide salon/exhibition run in accordance with the rules for special recognition of the P.S.A. and with F.I.A.P. recognition.
Eligibility: Open to amateurs and pros.
Subject Matter: Two categories: 1) General-any topic, 2) Natural history.
Submission Requirements: Send up to four color transparencies in 2"x2" mounts.
Entry Fee: $5 (U.S.) per category; $7 (U.S.) if airmail return required. Only checks drawn on a U.K. bank and made payable to the Welsh Photographic Federation in U.K. funds will be accepted. U.S. bank notes (i.e. dollar bills) or bank notes of country of origin are acceptable.
Awards: 2 PSA Gold Medals, 2 PSA Silver Medals, 1 each of FIAP Gold, Silver, and Bronze Medals; 6 FIAP "Mention D'Honneur" Ribbons; 6 WPF Special Awards.
Sponsor reserves right to publish award-winning photographs in exhibition catalog.
Entries are returned.
Write for information/entry form.

WESTCHESTER INTERNATIONAL SALON
Sponsored by the Color Camera
Club of Westchester, Inc.
PO Box 248
Larchmont, NY 10538
(914) 834-1555
Contact: Mrs. Finkelstein, Dr. Bruce.
Annual color slide competition. More than 40 countries represented.
Eligibility: Open to amateurs and pros.
Subject Matter: 4 divisions-nature, pictorial, phototravel, photojournalism. Nature requires "no hand of man."
Submission Requirements: Send color slides in 2x2" mounts. 4 slide per division limit.
Entry Fee: $5 domestic, $6 foreign.
Awards: PSA- and FIAP-sponsored medals.
All rights remain with photographer.
Entries are returned.
Write for entry form.

WESTMORELAND ART NATIONALS
Sponsored by the Westmoreland Arts
and Heritage Festival
Box 203, RD#12
Greensburg, PA 15601
(412) 830-3950
Contact: Olga Gera
Annual juried show.
Eligibility: Open to amateurs and professionals.
Subject Matter: Open.
Submission Requirements: Send up to 4 color and/or black and white transparencies or prints. Minimum print size-11x14" mounted.
Entry Fee: $25.
Awards: $5,000 in cash and purchase awards.
Best photo-$500.
Entries are returned.
Write for information/entry form.

WILDBIRD PHOTO CONTEST

Sponsored by *Wildbird* Magazine.
PO Box 6050
Mission Viejo, CA 92690
Annual contest for birdwatchers.
Eligibility: Open to pros and amateurs. Unpublished photos only.
Subject Matter: Five categories: open, flight, backyard, hard-to-get, and humor. All photos must be of bird species found in North America. Birds must be alive and living in the wild.
Submission Requirements: Send up to three original color transparencies or prints per category (slides only for "open" category). Each photo must be accompanied by a separate entry form. Each photo must be accompanied by a SASE. No multiple entries (several photos in a single package) will be accepted for judging.
Entry Fee: None.
Awards: Prizes will be awarded to the top three entries in each of five categories. First prize: $100; second prize: $50; third prize: $25. Winners' photos will be published in magazine. Winner of "open" category will be featured on the cover. If entry is used in *Wildbird* magazine subsequent to the publication of contest winners, photographer will be paid in accordance with then-prevailing contributor rates.
Entries are returned with SASE.
Write for entry forms.

WILDLIFE PHOTO CONTEST

Sponsored by the International Wildlife Film Festival
IWFF
Environmental Studies
University of Montana
Missoula, MT 59812
(406) 243-2477
Contact: Michael Bashkin
Annual international photo contest is part of the International Wildlife Film Festival to encourage excellence in wildlife filmmaking and photography and to focus public attention on wildlife issues. A juried selection of the best entries will be displayed at the University of Montana during the festival. Winners and runners-up will be displayed in a Winner's Tour following the festival.
Eligibility: Open to amateurs and pros.
Subject Matter: Photographs must contain some aspect of wildlife: wildlife species, habitat, or wildlife and humans.
Submission Requirements: Send color and/or B&W prints, mounted and matted. Dimension of photo (not including mat) should be between 8x10" and 16x20". (Slides are acceptable for judging, but a print must be available for hanging.) Photos must be shrink-wrapped or framed, ready for hanging. No submission limit.
Entry Fee: $5 per photo.
Awards: Gift certificates and merchandise donated by sponsors. Exhibition of winners and runners-up.
Photographers retain all rights to photos.
Entries are returned.
Write for entry.

WOMEN IN PHOTOGRAPHY

Sponsored by Women in Photography
419 No. Larchmont Blvd., Suite 246
Los Angeles, CA 90004
(213) 913-7570
Contact: Nancy Clendaniel, Executive Director
Bi-annual juried competition and exhibition with various themes. 1991 theme is "Women Photographers Celebrate Freedom."
Eligibility: Open to amateurs and pros.
Subject Matter: Photography by women photographers— international and national.
Submission Requirements: Send color and/or B&W 35mm transparencies for initial jurying. No submission limit.
Entry Fee: Members-$10 per slide; non-members-$25 per entry.
Awards: Work is printed in catalog and shown in exhibit.
Sponsor reserves the right to use winning photos for publicity and promotion.
Entries are returned with SASE.

WOMEN IN THE ARTS

Sponsored by Erector Square Gallery
315 Peck St., Bldg. #20
New Haven, CT 06513
(203) 865-1273
Contact: Jane Miller, Director
Annual exhibition juried by nationally known juror. Exhibition is in conjunction with the City of New Haven's celebration of International Women's Day.
Eligibility: Open to all women artists over the age of 18 working in any medium including photography. Work must be original and completed within the past two years.

Subject Matter: Open.
Submission Requirements: Send up to three 35mm slides for judging. If work is accepted, print will be required. No size limit.
Entry Fee: TBA.
Awards: Best in Show; Merit Awards.
Sponsor reserves right to reproduce accepted works for publicity.
A 30% commission will be charged on any sales.
Entries are returned with SASE.
Write for entry.

WORLD PRESS PHOTO
Sponsored by the World Press Photo Foundation, Eastman Kodak, KLM/Royal Dutch Airlines.
World Press Photo Foundation
Van Baerlestraat 146
1071 BE Amsterdam
the Netherlands
Phone: +31 (20) 766-096
Fax: +31 (20) 764-471
Telex: 10611 aoc nl att WPPh
Contact: Ben Ten Berge, Manager contest and exhibitions
Annual international competition and exhibition for professional press photographers. "For the 1989 contest 10,197 pictures were submitted by 1,294 photographers from 62 countries. Apart from the prize-winning pictures 150 others were selected for the exhibition and the yearbook."
Eligibility: Open to professional photojournalists. Publishers and organizations may enter on behalf of the photographer.
Subject Matter: Single pictures and picture stories can be entered in the following categories: Spot News, News Features, People in the News, Sports, Humor, Arts, Science and Technology, Nature, Daily Life.
Submission Requirements: Send B&W or color prints and 35mm slides. Enclose one duplicate print (8x10") or all B&W and color prints for possible publication. Enclose one duplicate of each slide (reproduction quality) or one 8x10" print. No submission limit. However, picture stories must be limited to 10 photos or they will not be accepted.
Entry Fee: None.
Awards: Golden Eye trophies and Grand Diplomas in each category for the best single picture and best picture story. Numbers 2 and 3 will receive the

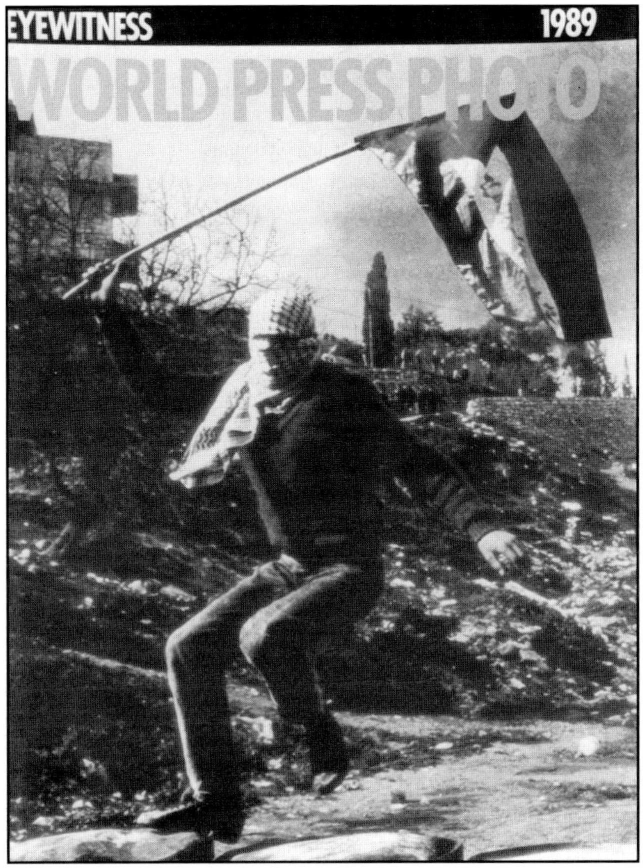

© ALLAN TANNENBAUM/SYGMA, USA; COURTESY OF WORLD PRESS PHOTO FOUNDATION.

Winners of the World Press Photo Contest have their work published in an annual each year.

Foundation's Golden Eye medal and a Diploma. Premier Award to the Press Photo of the Year. Includes a cash prize of Dfl. 15,000, the Diploma of Excellence, and a return flight to Amsterdam by KLM Royal Dutch Airlines. The Canon Image Centre in Amsterdam offers the Premier Award winner a exhibition of his or her work. Oskar Barnack Award (sponsored by Leica) of Dfl. 10,000 and a return flight to Amsterdam to attend the awards ceremony to the photographer of the picture story which expresses in the most positive, perceptive and illustrative way the relationship between man and his environment. Budapest Award (sponsored by the Hungarian Tourist Board) of Dfl. 2,500 and a return flight to Budapest and expenses to cover the Budapest Spring Festival to the picture or picture story which best expresses the idea and the importance of human relations. World Press Photo Children's Award (sponsored by KLM Royal Dutch Airlines and the Dutch daily newspaper De Volkskrant) of Dfl. 2,500 and return flight to Amsterdam for

best press photo as selected by an international children's jury. All prize-winning pictures and a selection of runners-up will be published in the World Press Photo yearbook. All prize-winning pictures and selected runners-up will be displayed in a travelling exhibition. Photographers whose work has been selected for the yearbook and/or exhibition will receive a certificate and a copy of the yearbook.
Prints and slides will not be returned. The Foundation can dispose of them and use them at exhibitions or other displays and in publications under its own auspices. In such cases full credit will be given to the photographer.
Write for information/entry form.

WORLD OF WEDDING PHOTOGRAPHY AWARDS OF EXCELLENCE PRINT COMPETITION
Sponsored by Wedding Photographers International
1312 Lincoln Blvd.
Santa Monica, CA 90401
(213) 451-0090
International competition honors outstanding portraiture in every segment of the wedding photography field.
Eligibility: Pros only.
Subject Matter: Bride and groom together, bride or groom alone, bridal party, engagement, special effects, studio bridal formals.
Submission Requirements: Send 16x20" mounted color prints. 6 print maximum. Entry form must be attached to back of each print. Model releases must be available for all recognizable individuals.
Entry Fee: WPI members-$26 per initial entry; $20 thereafter. Non-members-$33 per initial entry: $28 thereafter.
Awards: Award of Excellence. Winners displayed at The World of Wedding Photography Convention/ Workshop and Trade Show.
Applicants agree that any entered photograph may be used by Wedding Photographers International or The Rangefinder in any of their publications or printed materials.
Entries returned with $20 postage and handling fee.
Write for entry.

YOSEMITE RENAISSANCE
Sponsored by Yosemite Renaissance, Inc.
P.O. Box 313
Yosemite, CA. 95389
(209) 372-4775
Contact: Kay Pitts
Annual contest to encourage diverse interpretations of Yosemite. Three categories: Photography; Painting; All other media.
Eligibility: Open to amateurs and pros.
Subject Matter: Recent works limited to Yosemite.
Submission Requirements: Submit color and/or B&W slides. No submission limit.
Entry Fee: $15 per slide.
Awards: $1,500 - best of show; $1,000 - photography division.
Entries are returned.
Sponsor reserves the right to use selected works in catalog and for publicity.
Call or write for prospectus.

YOUR BEST SHOT
Sponsored by *Popular Photography* Magazine
1633 Broadway
New York, NY 10019
(212) 767-6000
Contact: Bob Lazaroff
Monthly, on-going open photo contest.
Eligibility: Open to amateurs and pros.
Subject Matter: Open.
Submission Requirements: Send up to 20 color and/ or B&W prints and transparencies. Prints no larger than 8x12", please. Include information about camera, lens, film, and exposure used, as well as Social Security number and daytime phone.
Entry Fee: None.
Awards: $300-1st prize, $200-2nd prize, $100-3rd prize, two $50 honorable mentions each month; publication.
Sponsor reserves one-time editorial reproduction rights.
Entries are returned with SASE. Allow up to 12 weeks for return.

While extensive, the above listings are by no means exhaustive. We have made every effort to include as many details as possible, however the individual listings are not comprehensive. Contact the individual contests for complete entry rules and entry forms. Because entry rules may be subject to change at any time, Winning Photo Contests and Images Press assume no responsibility for any of the contests listed here.

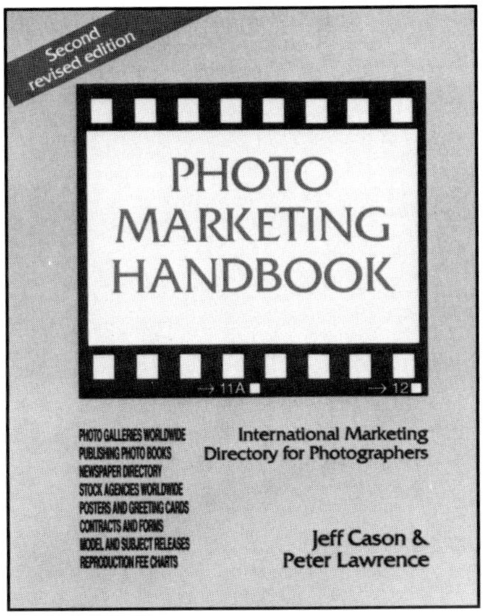

What does it take to successfully sell your stock photos?

The PHOTO MARKETING HANDBOOK tells you how.

What are the biggest money-making markets for your photos? How do you meet the top picture editors? What is the most important picture in your portfolio? How do you protect your rights to your photos? Should you self-market or use an agency? How do you start your own self-publishing postcard business? How do you get a photo book published? What should you do if a picture editor loses one of your photos?

The Photo Marketing Handbook answers these questions and more. Written by experienced picture agents and editors, The Photo Marketing Handbook is the most up-to-date book of its kind. The serious amateur and the professional photographer will find loads of essential information about successfully selling stock photos, including:

- Detailed market listings, publishers, paper product companies, domestic and foreign agencies, telling you exactly what editors and agents are looking for.
- In depth profiles with professional photographers, editors and agents, telling you what it takes to succeed.
- Sample business forms, photographer-agency agreement, and book publishing contracts.
- A chapter on how to publish a photo book detailing the process of both commercial and self-publishing.
- New gallery listings worldwide.
- New newspaper listings.

$19.95

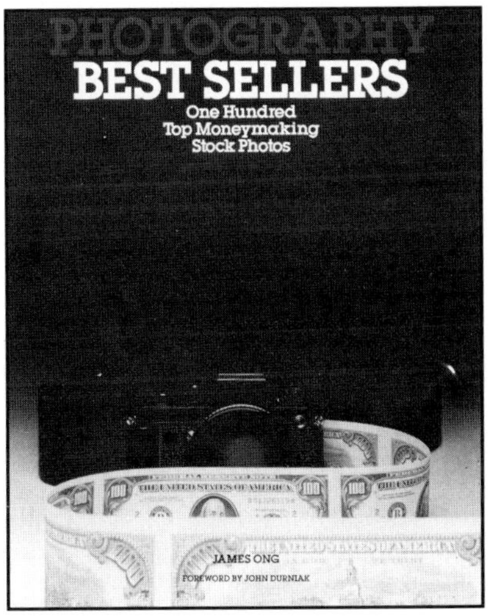

R A V E S !

"...Photography Best Sellers is an excellent thesis on how to make a bundle selling stock photos." **Photo District News**

"The book is an invaluable tool and lesson to the serious pro..." **Outdoor Photography**

"...presents sales and usage figures for the 100 best sellers and includes a section on some of the many varied ways in which they've been used." **The Adcrafter**

PHOTOGRAPHY BEST SELLERS

By Ong. One Hundred of the top money making stock photos from a leading stock agency... each photo is presented with complete reports of sales volumes, background, times sold, etc. A real eye-opener, this book is a fascinating look into the stock photo business. 9 x 11. 120 photos.

Originally H $29.95 **SPECIAL H $18.95**

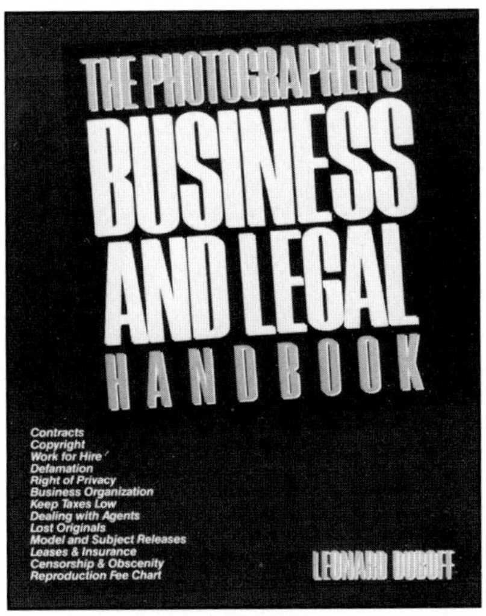

What do you need to know to protect yourself legally as a photographer?

What you don't know can hurt you.

The PHOTOGRAPHER'S BUSINESS AND LEGAL HANDBOOK can help you!

- How do you obtain copyright protection for your work?
- What release do you need?
- How do you avoid invading someone's privacy rights?
- What are your rights when your film, negatives, or photographs are lost, stolen or destroyed?
- What contracts do you need with publishers, agents, etc.
- What is the safest business form?
- How do you go about selecting an attorney?

The Photographer's Business and Legal Handbook answers these questions and more. Written by Leonard D. Duboff, a professor of law and practicing attorney who represents numerous photographers and publishers.

The Photographer's Business and Legal Handbook will be of use to any amateur or professional photographer. The book is full of the most up-to-date information available, including:

- Sample contracts and business forms such as photo releases and agent contracts.
- Tax tips
- An in-depth discussion of copyright, including international protection and the Berne Convention, which the U.S. recently joined.
- A chapter on the expansion of privacy and publicity rights in the U.S.

$18.95

Ask for these Images books at your local camera shop, bookstore, or order directly from:
Images Press ▪ 22 East 17th Street, New York, NY 10013 ▪ 800-367-4854 or 212-243-2306